Ephemeral Bibelots

Hopkins Studies in Modernism
Douglas Mao, *Series Editor*

Ephemeral Bibelots

How an International Fad Buried American Modernism

Brad Evans

Johns Hopkins University Press
Baltimore

This book was brought to publication with the generous assistance of the Rutgers University Research Council.

Printed in the United States of America on acid-free paper
9 8 7 6 5 4 3 2 1

Johns Hopkins University Press
2715 North Charles Street
Baltimore, Maryland 21218-4363
www.press.jhu.edu

Library of Congress Cataloging-in-Publication Data

Names: Evans, Brad, 1968- author.
Title: Ephemeral bibelots : how an international fad buried American modernism / Brad Evans.
Description: Baltimore : Johns Hopkins University Press, 2019. | Series: Hopkins studies in modernism | Includes bibliographical references and index.
Identifiers: LCCN 2018055789 | ISBN 9781421431550 (hardcover : alk. paper) | ISBN 9781421432694 (pbk : alk. paper) ISBN 9781421431567 (electronic) | ISBN 1421431556 (hardcover : alk. paper) | ISBN 1421432692 (pbk : alk. paper) | ISBN 1421431564 (electronic)
Subjects: LCSH: Little magazines—United States—History—19th century. | Little magazines—United States—History—20th century. | Little magazines—Social aspects—United States—History—19th century. | Little magazines—Social aspects—United States—History—20th century. | Literature and society—United States—History—19th century. | Literature and society—United States—History—20th century. | Modernism (Literature)—United States.
Classification: LCC PN4878.3 E93 2019 | DDC 051—dc23
LC record available at https://lccn.loc.gov/2018055789

A catalog record for this book is available from the British Library.

Special discounts are available for bulk purchases of this book. For more information, please contact Special Sales at 410-516-6936 or specialsales@press.jhu.edu.

Johns Hopkins University Press uses environmentally friendly book materials, including recycled text paper that is composed of at least 30 percent post-consumer waste, whenever possible.

Contents

Illustrations

Color Plates

Color illustrations appear following p. 96

Black-and-White Illustrations

Acknowledgments

This project took shape in the basement of the Zimmerli Art Museum at Rutgers University, where Mary Shaw and Dennis Cate introduced me to the turn-of-the-century print ephemera associated with Le Chat Noir cabaret and Montmartre. I thought, at the time, that tracing the travels of the black cat might take me to France, and it did motivate a memorable afternoon stroll up the hill of the 18th arrondissement in Paris; as it turns out, however, the Rutgers collection is almost too complete, and I'd encourage other scholars to come take a look. My sincere thanks to the outstanding team of curators and librarians here at Rutgers who have helped me navigate the piles of magazines and prints: Marilyn Symmes, Megan Lotts, Francesca Gianneti, Nicole Simpson, Kevin Mulcahy, and Christine Giviskos.

Recovering the black cat's movement around the United States has taken me farther afield in the United States than I would have guessed, and I'd like to express my gratitude to the archivists at Conde Naste in Times Square, the Bancroft (UC Berkeley), Beinecke (Yale), Houghton (Harvard) Libraries, and the University of Wisconsin Library in Madison, which, oddly, was the only one able to put their hands on a full run of the Russian skinny magazine *Oskolki*. My home base for studying the American ephemeral bibelots has been at Rare Books and Special Collections at Princeton University, where Stephen Ferguson and AnnaLee Pauls proved exceptionally accommodating with my many requests for information and reproductions.

It has been my privilege to have exceptional colleagues and graduate students at Rutgers with whom to share material and ideas over the course of writing this book. I would like to thank Edyta Bojanowska, Ann Coiro, Elin Diamond, Richard Dienst, Ann Fabian, Paul Gilmore, Neha Gondal, Chris Iannini, Greg Jackson, Colin Jager, Myra Jehlen, Stacy Klein, Jeff Lawrence, Jackson Lears, Alex Leslie, Jim Livingston, Meredith McGill, Jonah Siegel,

Kurt Spellmeyer, Henry Turner, Michael Warner, and Carolyn Williams. In particular, I would like to thank Mukti Mangharam, who helped me track down the nineteenth-century magazine work of Rabindranath Tagore; Susan Sidlauskas for talks on Sargent and James; Paul McLean for his help understanding the intricacies of network visualizations and great conversation on long bike rides; and to the many exchanges over the years with Nicholas Gaskill about all things modern and American at the turn of the century. Both graduate and undergraduate students have shared my enthusiasm for these materials. In the early stages of research, Ariane Mühlethaler scoured archives up and down the east coast for various rare examples of ephemeral bibelots. My thanks to Julian Castronovo for his work photographing black cats on the pages of magazines on the stacks at the UW Library. Jess Cain spent a summer as an undergraduate research assistant creating an index for me of almost twenty-five ephemeral bibelots held in the archives at Princeton. More recently, Rebecca Lipperini and Elizabeth Dean helped organize my notes on the various bibelots and prepare the final manuscript.

Initial stages of this research began with the support of a year-long fellowship from the American Council of Learned Societies. My thanks for the opportunity to share this work at numerous university venues and conferences, and, especially in the early stages, for talks at Johns Hopkins University and the University of Chicago. My thanks to James Connolly and Patrick Collier for the invitation to participate in the conference at Ball State, "Print Culture beyond the Metropolis" (and especially to Patrick for sharing his astonishing expertise in Modernist magazines). Similarly, my thanks for the invitation from Nathaniel Cadle to Florida International University and the Wolfsonian, where Liesl Olson and I had the chance to peruse their extensive Modernist print collection. It has been a pleasure to become more entwined in the expanding network of scholars working in and around Modernist little magazines, especially with those instrumental in promoting the Modernist Journals Project, first among them the late Robert Scholes. My thanks to Ann Ardis, Peter Brooker, Mary Chapman, Suzanne Churchill, Maria DiBattista, Jeffrey Drouin, David Earle, Mark Gaipa, Barbara Green, Catherine Keyser, Sean Latham, Adam McKible, Andrew Thacker, and Clifford Wulfman. Most significant in this regard is surely Kirsten MacLeod, who has long shared my fascination with the little magazines of the fin de siècle. Kirsten was kind enough to invite me to participate in a symposium she arranged at the Grolier Club, and it is there that I met and began to exchange ideas about purple cows with Johanna Drucker, whose enthusiasm for this material I wholeheartedly share.

I want to extend my appreciation to all of those who have listened to me carry on about black cats, and to others who read and provided feedback on parts of the manuscript. These include Dorri Beam, Nancy Bentley, María Bianco, Michael Collins, Merve Emre, Jennifer Fleissner, Nancy Glazener, Christopher Looby, Michael Moon, Ross Posnock, John Rowe, and Jane Thrailkill. My ongoing appreciation goes to Bill Brown for his advice and inspiration. Since graduate school, Leigh Anne Duck and Sabine Haenni have been my surest readers and most cherished academic friends.

I have been lucky to have such an exceptional editorial team working on the project at Johns Hopkins University Press. My sincere thanks to Douglas Mao for the enthusiasm with which he took up the project and to Catherine Goldstead for shepherding it to its conclusion. My deep thanks to the anonymous readers for the press, who not only were in sympathy with the aims of the project but offered exceptionally precise suggestions for improvement and nuance.

As always, my most valued feedback has come from those who have had to hear me enthuse about black cats the most. Sophie, Simon, and Théo, this one is for you.

Ephemeral Bibelots

Prologue
The Black Cat Goes Walking

The cover of *Vogue* on January 31, 1895, featured a tightly corseted young woman, presumably a debutante, with an opera mask in one hand and a scruffy black cat with an erect tail and white saucer eyes on her head (see plate 1). A monocled suitor, rather too old and too attentive, stands behind to help her with her cloak. The cat looks at us, while the woman looks up and to the left, with a smile expressing pleasure, contentment, daring, or maybe even a challenge. "Can't grab this," she seems to say, shielding herself from the old man.[1]

This appears to be some kind of joke, but are we actually expected to catch the meaning?

Our debutante is a modern figure, hardly the reclining subject of a classical European painting. We're let in on her modernity by the wry regard, and also by the bow delicately overflowing from the inset, dropping strategically below the waist, that points to a caption reading, in French, LE CHAT NOIR, a reference to the fin-de-siècle bohemian cabaret in Paris. In the 1880s and 1890s, Le Chat Noir was at the international heart of bohemian counterculture, host to artists known as the Hydropathes and expositions of Les Arts Incohèrents, a gathering place for specialists in offbeat parodies and puns now understood to anticipate the early twentieth-century avant-garde. It was there that exotic shadow theater adaptations of Flaubert's *La Tentation de St. Antoine* were staged using zinc cutouts and elaborate smoke and light effects, and that some of Mallarmé's circle of Symbolist poets collaborated with musicians, Post-Impressionist graphic artists, actors, and actresses to create an art that they all understood to be edgy and unpredictable.

The cabaret's iconic black cat had been made famous by a sign painted by Adolphe Léon Willette featuring the same black cat from the *Vogue* cover perched on a crescent moon. If you have ever been to Montmartre, or to a college poster sale at the beginning of the fall semester, you'll be entirely familiar with reproductions of Théophile Steinlen's famous poster for the cabaret, this time with the black cat wearing a halo on an orange background, "Prochainement—Tournée du Chat Noir." Willette had also done a painting, notable in reference to our *Vogue* cover, which hung inside the cabaret of a woman holding a black cat on her head, an image known today as *La Vierge Verte*. (To see this and many other images mentioned but not pictured in this book, readers are invited to visit a companion website, https://sites.rutgers.edu/bibelots.)[2]

I first came across the image in *Vogue* in the microfilm room at the Firestone Library in Princeton, where I was trying to discover why a fashion magazine like *Vogue* would have published the American writer Kate Chopin, best known for her novel about the dawning of female sexual desire, *The Awakening*, and for regional stories about racism in the Deep South. *Vogue* published some of the latter but seemed more interested in another genre, devilishly humorous short stories about love and disappointment. The picture of the black cat on the head of a debutante seemed to offer a clue to *Vogue*'s interest in these tales, since I also knew that Chopin was an enthusiast of French literature, especially of Guy de Maupassant. In my mind, they both could be loosely associated with the cabaret, which suggested that *Vogue* may have had a better sense that Chopin was "*chic*" in the late nineteenth-century sense of the term than do many of us today, who tend to think of her first as an American regionalist and feminist, and only then as a bohemian in the aesthetic arts tradition.[3]

What I didn't know then was that the cabaret played a seminal role in accelerating the vogue for proto-Modernist little magazines known as "ephemeral bibelots." Of course, then, I didn't know about the bibelots at all. You might not either: their brief éclat is the main subject of this book, but the lines connecting bibelots to literary and cultural history are exceptionally obscure. Suffice it to say, for now, that the cabaret published a little magazine—an ephemeral bibelot—called *Le Chat Noir* (1882–1895), and it featured a cover design by Henri Pille of another version of the same black cat, this time standing in front of Montmartre's iconographic windmill. Composed mostly of information about what was happening around Montmartre, the cabaret's magazine was notable both for its illustrations and doggerel, and also for exuding the sense of being very much of the moment. Any number of young bohemians from around the world who made the pilgrimage to the cabaret appear to have been inspired to start their own little magazines once

PREMIÈRE ANNÉE. — N° 1. LE NUMÉRO 15 CENTIMES SAMEDI 14 JANVIER 1882

LE

CHAT NOIR

RÉDACTEUR EN CHEF : ÉMILE GOUDEAU

Rédaction et Administration : 84, Boulevard Rochechouart.

DIRECTEUR : RODOLPHE SALIS

ADMINISTRATEUR : VICTOR REY

ABONNEMENTS

PARIS

1 An . . . . 10 »
6 Mois . . . . . 7 »

DÉPARTEMENTS

1 An . . . . 12 »
6 Mois . . . . . 8 »

Les manuscrits non insérés, ne sont pas rendus.

(Paraissant le Samedi)

Organe des intérêts de Montmartre

SOMMAIRE

Montmartre.	JACQUES LEHARDY.
Les Polonais (poésie).	EMILE GOUDEAU.
Voyages de découvertes.	A'KEMPIS.
Le Chat de la tante Agathe.	RODOLPHE SALIS.
De ci, de ça.	ODIO.
Ballade du Chat Noir.	FLORENT FULBERT.
Théâtres.	ODIO.
Annonces.	
SUPPLÉMENT : *Le Chat Noir* (Gravure).	
Ballade de joyeuse Bohême.	EUGÈNE TORQUET.

MONTMARTRE

Il est grand temps de rectifier une erreur qui a pesé sur plus de soixante générations complètes.

L'Écriture que l'on dit sainte — je ne sais trop pourquoi, — n'a fait pour parler poliment, que se moquer du peuple.

La version des Septante est une bêtise.

Nous lisons dans la Genèse que l'arche de Noé a jeté l'ancre au mont Ararat.

Qu'est-ce que cela peut signifier, le mont Ararat?

Lisez : Montmartre!

En effet, ce vieux pochard de Noé, lorsque les eaux diluviennes commencèrent à se retirer, aperçut le sommet d'un mont, et dit : « Je m'arrête. »

Il faudrait être aveugle comme Homère ou borgne comme Gambetta — que certains loustics appellent Péricoclès — pour ne pas voir que ces deux mots : « Montm'arrête, » sont les radicaux inéluctables de Montmartre.

Donc, Montmartre est le berceau de l'humanité.

Je dirai plus : Montmartre est une mamelle, et je l'explique.

Deux grandes rivières prennent leur source dans les flancs de cette montagne sacrée et vont former un grand fleuve que l'on nomme la Seine.

Seulement, ces rivières coulent sous terre. Autrefois elles roulaient leurs flots à ciel ouvert, témoin la rue Grange-Batelière.

Donc, Montmartre est le centre du monde.

Ces considérations ethnographiques et philologiques le prouvent surabondamment, cependant, nous ne devons pas négliger la question archéologique dont la solution accablera mes contradicteurs, s'il était quelqu'un assez osé pour me contredire.

C'est à Montmartre que fut construite la première ville de l'humanité.

D'abord les descendants de Noé logèrent dans les cavernes qui sont encore visibles aujourd'hui.

Puis ils construisirent une citadelle sur le sommet de la montagne : *Oppidum*. On retrouve encore les vestiges de la muraille.

Puis ils bâtirent un moulin et firent de la galette.

Ensuite ils se répandirent par le monde.

Je suis plein d'une pitié miséricordieuse et sardonique, quand je vois des archivistes pâles écrire des volumes indigestes sur Thèbes, Ninive, Babylone et Carcassonne, afin de prouver que ces bourgades ruinées sont les plus anciennes villes de toutes les antiquités.

Toutes les élucubrations ne tiennent pas debout devant les arguments irréfutables que je viens de produire. Du reste, ils trouveront dans la bibliothèque du *Chat Noir*, tous les documents qui m'ont servi pour établir mes preuves d'une façon victorieuse.

Montmartre est isolé, parce qu'il se suffit à lui seul. Ce centre est absolument autonome. Dans une petite ville située à une grande distance de Montmartre et que les voyageurs nomment Paris, une académie locale discute, dit-on, les conditions de l'autonomie municipale. Il y a longtemps que cette question est résolue à Montmartre. Les peuples qui pullulent à la surface du globe n'ont qu'à venir s'en assurer.

Le *Chat Noir*, moniteur de Montmartre, a été créé dans le seul but de raconter à tout l'univers habité, comme quoi cette ville, la plus ancienne du monde, ainsi que je l'ai dit plus haut, est encore la plus belle, la plus riche et la plus florissante de notre époque. Le *Chat Noir* en décrira toutes les ressources, tous les agréments, toutes les somptuosités. Et, pour ne pas pratiquer un exclusivisme de mauvaise compagnie, pour ne pas avoir l'air de mépriser les petites cités qui se sont édifiées bien longtemps après Montmartre, le *Chat Noir*, qui ne recule devant aucune dépense, a déjà organisé une légion de hardis explorateurs qui n'hésiteront pas à risquer leurs jours pour aller, au loin, recueillir des documents qui enrichiront les connaissances scientifiques des habitants de la Montagne où l'on s'arrête.

Les uns iront aux Batignolles, d'autres à Bercy ; des hommes dévoués et capables de tous les sacrifices, pousseront jusqu'à Paris, et, par leurs correspondances ruisselantes d'intérêt, permettront au *Chat Noir* d'apprendre aux Montmartrois les mœurs, les coutumes, la civilisation des peuples les plus lointains.

Par conséquent, notre journal sera la feuille la plus intéressante qui soit jamais sortie des presses « gémissantes, » et celui qui ne le lira pas, ne pourra être — je n'hésite à l'affirmer, — qu'un simple lecteur du *Mercure Galant* ou de la *Gazette de Hollande*.

JACQUES LEHARDY

Voir à la 3e page notre dessin de la semaine, et surtout réclamer le supplément encarté dans ce numéro, représentant le CHAT NOIR, *dans toute sa splendeur, photographiant l'Univers jusqu'à ce jour connu.*

Henri Pille, cover illustration for *Le Chat Noir*, the magazine started in 1882 by Rodolphe Salis for his cabaret of the same name

they got back home—home to England, Germany, Russia, South America, South Asia, and all across the United States. And as we will see in later chapters, the sign of their belonging to the group often involved punning on the icon of modern Montmartre, *le chat noir*. *Vogue* seemed to be chasing this same effect.

The newly founded American magazine of society and fashion must have known that the black cat, that particular one, represented something like a bohemian version of locker-room talk. Pussy, of course, is one of those very old slang words. The *Oxford English Dictionary* cites a number of examples of the pun, starting in the seventeenth century, including one by "Philocomus" in an 1865 book called *The Love Feast; or, A Bride's Experience*, which reads "My poor *pussy*, rent and sore, Dreaded yet longed for one fuck more." And it meant the same in French as in English. The story told about the cabaret at the time was that a young bohemian could earn himself a slap in the face from a newsstand *vendeuse* by asking for the magazine by name, "avez-vous la chatte noir?"[4]

If *Vogue* was enough in the know to make a connection between an American debutante and the underworld of Parisian nightlife represented by Le Chat Noir, then it seems altogether likely that it would have been meaning to make a pun of just this sort. But it also seems clear that in its new situation, on the cover of an American women's magazine, *Vogue*'s *chat noir* connoted something more than simple bohemian bonhomie.

By the 1890s, the black cat had been caught up for decades at the symbolic nexus of art, fashion, and the woman question. Consider, for instance, Poe's story "The Black Cat" (1843), which finishes with a mania-inducing black cat meowing hideously from behind a brick wall, where it sits perched—on the head, nonetheless—of the narrator's murdered wife. The story was celebrated in France by Baudelaire, who translated it, and whose own poems on cats in *Les Fleurs du Mal* (1857) take up the theme. He published three "pussy poems" there, like the one in which his hand becomes drunk with pleasure from caressing a cat's electric corpse and elastic back, encouraging him to dream of a woman, cold, deep, and with a subtle air of dangerous perfume swimming over her dark body.[5]

Was this the pussycat we see on *Vogue*'s hat cover in 1895? Or perhaps it was the black cat crouched at the foot of the divan in Manet's *Olympia*, from 1863—the one that replaces the little, white dog in Titian's *Venus of Urbino*, from 1538, thus shifting the meaning from canine fidelity to feline promiscuity, an effect probably heightened by indexing race as well.

Black cats were being relayed back and forth across the Atlantic during this period. On the French side of the ocean, materials from the cabaret, and especially from the seminal little magazine *Le Chat Noir* show the cat appearing repeatedly in unexpected places. It turns up in Japanese lanterns inside the cabaret, on a zinc cutout hanging over the piano player inside the hall, and, most tellingly, on the heads of artists' models as they join a "solemn march" down Montmartre hill with Chat Noir notables like Paul Verlaine (angel with harp), George Auriol (in plaid), Henri Rivière (with dog

The devil and his lover perched on the black cat's tail, *M'lle New York* 1:10 (January 1896)

and whips), and Pierre Loti (with a sailor's hat and below the Moulin de la Galette).[6]

In 1894, the American *Chap-Book*'s editor, Herbert Stone, commissioned Aubrey Beardsley to illustrate some of Poe's stories, one of the most well-known of which, "The Black Cat," gives us another opportunity to see the black cat on a woman's head.[7] In a bibelot called the *Lotus*, Wilbur Macey Stone chronicled the appearance of cats on fifteen advertising posters, such as one for *Poster-Lore* showing "a very much startled cat with her back up and looking altogether as though she wished she hadn't come."[8] Images of the black cat make over eighteen more appearances in the bibelot *M'lle New York* over the short run of its publication in 1895 and 1896, including one accompanying an appreciation of the vaudevillian actress Maggie Cline that describes her as "the perfect flowering of the Walt Whitman ideal of womanhood," and another above a poem by the French Symbolist Jules Laforgue where the devil and his lover sit perched on the cat's tail.[9] A painting from the American-born, Paris-trained artist, Cecilia Beaux, *Sita and Sarita* (1893-1894), featured very much this same cat on the shoulder of her dark-haired sitter. That same year, Rubén Darío, the Nicaraguan poet generally credited with the development of *Modernismo* in Spanish American poetry, published *Los Raros*, a volume of essays on contemporary influences, including Poe among a number of the French Symbolists, and it had the black cat on the cover. An art poster from the 1890s, *Le Chat Domestique et Son Caractère*, shows the black cat in a dozen emotional states—the one from the *Vogue* cover, with tail straight up, being clearly an example of *la franchise*, frankness.

Frank, but not entirely so. Much of what is implied remains to be read between the lines to an extent less suited for our literal-minded times. No talk of actual bodies (or body parts), here, or even of suffrage, which wouldn't get its own costume until the next decade, or of the fact that this pussy was black, which, racially speaking, would have been the most suggestive color for representing women and sexuality together in the eyes of many of the period's artists and painters.

And yet, apparently cognizant of the implications, the woman on *Vogue*'s cover is there to remake the joke. She could be taken for an artist or an actress, a celebrity at a ball, a gilded-age sex kitten, a platinum blonde flagrantly sincere in her performance of sexuality. She is most certainly not the *Venus of Urbino*, directly inviting viewers with her puppylike eyes and languid pose to take visual pleasure in her form; more likely, she is the Countess Olenska, whom Edith Wharton describes decades later in *The Age of Innocence*, a woman of style whose bohemian free-spiritedness was taken as lewd when transplanted to New York.

The relays multiply the harder you look. In addition to everything else, the *Vogue* model is wearing a most unusually low-cut gown that is missing the late Victorian "gigot de mouton" sleeves puffed high above the shoulders, a Romantic-era touch which had come back into fashion in the 1880s and 1890s; instead, her gown has thin straps the likes of which you are unlikely to find in fashion plates from the period but which do match those that caused a scandal in 1884, when John Singer Sargent first displayed *Madame X*, his painting of the wife of Pierre Gautreau.

When it got its start in 1892, *Vogue* was more than just a magazine of fashion for society elites. Although it was that, it also published editorials advocating for freedom in marriage and flexibility in religion, suggesting that adultery not be condemned out of hand, and arguing for women to have careers. It was a magazine for the New Woman, edited by and featuring cutting-edge fiction by women. Its editorial pages were given over to denouncing the moral hypocrisy of relations between the sexes, and especially of societal expectations for women with regard to marriage and careers. It makes perfect sense that its featured fiction writer was Chopin, whose short pieces for the magazine offered sharp commentary on the reality of women's sexual desire and the stultifying effects of marriage on it. *Vogue*'s editor was Josephine Redding, a strong advocate for feminist causes who has been suggested as the model for Mademoiselle Reisz, the angular piano teacher in Chopin's *The Awakening* who schools the novel's heroine in the senses and the need for female self-sufficiency.[10]

So *Vogue*'s chat noir seems meant as a provocation. If still in doubt, another cover is even more explicit. Running a few months later, in an Easter number published on April 18, 1895, the young woman appears wearing a bunny hat, an image that was equally strange and laced with an even more extreme sexual joke. Over a caption about the "natural history . . . of head adornment," the model places her hands across her mouth in a fur muff—another old slang word—as if *Vogue* means to suggest that her speech is hidden or restrained behind the public display of her sexual wares, and that it ought not be.

The *Vogue* cover is provocative for linking fashion to sex, art to commodities, public to private, courtship to consumption, and beauty to humor and scandal. But the remarkable thing is that there's nothing in the black cat, as such, to give it a political valence, an aesthetic charge, or even a personal meaning. Its provocation only takes shape by the way the image evokes the black cat made famous in Montmartre, keying a very particular set of relays, assembling a highly reflexive network of associations. What meaning is to be found in the *Vogue* cover, that is to say, comes from the social effect of circulation: it comes from ties and connections as loose as these to the history of Le Chat Noir, writers like Chopin, the brief fad for ephemeral bibelots, and the reflexive sense of being part of a community that actually gets the joke.

American literary and artistic culture of the late nineteenth century is not remembered for this kind of joking, and the reason has everything to do with what we know about the period's print culture, and what we don't. Largely because of the dominance of the elite literary monthlies, like the *Century Illustrated*, *Harper's Monthly*, the *Atlantic*, and *Scribner's*, the period is remembered as the age of American Realism and Naturalism.[11] The aesthetic and moral proclivities of that genre, associated with its main protag-

Cover of *Vogue*, April 18, 1895, "NATURAL HISTORY SERIES OF HEAD ADORNMENT PROPHESY FOR AUTUMN OF 1895"

onist, the editor and novelist William Dean Howells, would seem almost diametrically opposed to the wispy internationalism, aesthetic provocation, and sexual free play represented by the circulation of the black cat. Whereas Realism devoted itself to "the light of the common day," the unmediated representation of democratic life, and the steady negotiation of the social upheavals of the late nineteenth century, the spirit of Montmartre extended an invitation to upset the cart.[12] The black cat became the iconographic aesthetic index of the celebration of the unreal, the hothouse flower version of aesthetic experimentation, a reanimation of European Decadence, a smoky countercultural alternative to Realism, and her walkabout leads us to an alternative sphere of print culture.

This book is largely devoted to an excavation of that aesthetic arts public sphere, especially as it is decipherable by way of the short-lived fad for the class of proto-Modernist little magazines known as ephemeral bibelots. By tracking their circulation in the mid-1890s, we can gain access to what was understood to be "modern" and "new" in a period not generally remembered by historians of American art and literature for much of anything of the kind. We can also begin to understand how knowledge about the existence of such things in America came to be buried, in the early twentieth century, alongside the bibelots themselves. This book takes us out walking with the black cat.

Introduction
The Ephemeral Bibelots

> Why should an etiolated Lark alone be naif? Let us all be naif. Let us be Humperdincked and rejoice with childish laughter at Purple Cows and Chortling Turtles.
>
> *M'lle New York*, November 1895

> *The Lark* is so good that it ought to die, in order to make its life perfect. . . . Looking back on a year of *The Lark* is delightful; looking forward to half-a-dozen years of it is intolerable, unless, indeed, it deteriorates and we cease to read it. And that would be pathetic, which again is impossible, pathos not being in *The Lark*'s line of flight.
>
> The *Chap-Book*, July 15, 1896

Between 1894 and 1903, more than three hundred eclectic little magazines appeared in the United States, many of which, in retrospect, can be seen to have had distinctly proto-Modernist aesthetic tendencies. Known variously as "freak magazines," "chapbooks," "fadzines," "brownie books," "toy magazines," and "ephemeral bibelots," most of them did not last more than a year.[1] To judge by their titles, their ephemerality seems built in, as if a part of their aesthetic makeup: *Moods* (1894–1895), *Chips* (1895–1896), the *Echo* (1895–1897), the *Fad* (1896–1897), the *Fly Leaf* (1895–1896), *Impressions* (1900–1903), *Jabs* (1901–1903), *A Little Spasm* (1901), the *Pebble* (1900–1901), the *Shadow* (1896), *Snap Shots* (1901), and *Whims* (1896). These were volumes beautifully illustrated in the devilishly colorful style of Aubrey Beardsley and Art Nouveau, with writing that was generally light and witty, at times bitingly parodic, and almost uniformly opposed to the prevailing schools of Realism and Naturalism that, even today, define the period's literary establishment.

They appear to have been in some vague way the forerunners of the more famous little magazines of the next decade but without the latter's bluster, artistic manifestoes, or oversized personalities—and also without, or so it would seem from the critical record, noteworthy or lasting contributions to art and literature. Their editors never made a name for themselves. They published very few things that were remembered and almost none that have made it into the canon. They did not spawn a lasting movement. They did not fully engage in the period's tumultuous social politics. Although frequently noted by the daily press, they were not commented upon or reviewed by the major literary monthlies, like the *Century Illustrated*, *Harper's*, or the *Atlantic Monthly*, which, at the time, were determinative in establishing norms for the reception of art and literature. They were only rarely collected. They have been largely overlooked even by the major academic chroniclers of the periodicals, scoring scant mention in Frank Luther Mott's magisterial history of American magazines and being dismissed outright in the classic work on Modernist little magazines by Hoffman, Allen, and Ulrich, who simply wrote that they "were not very inspiring."[2] The most recent book on early twentieth-century avant-garde magazines, which like this one recognizes them to be essential to the world-literary form of Modernism, has not a single word about any of the ephemeral bibelots—not one of them cited, nor even mentioned in passing.[3]

And yet the numbers are quite astounding, especially when considering that in addition to over two hundred titles in the United States, there were many hundreds more worldwide. Taken together, they feel something like a movement, and at the very least an international aesthetic vogue. The wave seems to have originated in the 1870s in Paris, where they were first published by the cabarets of Montmartre, most notably at Le Chat Noir, which published a journal of the same name. They soon spread throughout Europe, Asia, and South America. Magazines like Henry Harland and Aubrey Beardsley's the *Yellow Book* and its American counterpart the *Chap-Book* became the movement's models, but most of them had far less serious pretensions to establishing a lasting market presence. Longevity and a large subscription base, the generally accepted way of judging a periodical's success, are inapplicable here. More like to them was the publication fad in Japan. An article in the *Dial* in 1896 commented on the popularity of magazines and newspapers in Japan, where an average of nearly eight hundred such publications were being published, noting that "the most surprising thing about these statistics is the revelation they afford of the brevity of life . . . the ephemeral life."[4] And similarly ephemeral magazines were being published elsewhere. Anton Chekhov published his first stories in three magazines whose titles would have sounded immediately familiar to their American counterparts: *Dragonfly*, *Fragments*, and *Alarm Clock*.[5] In Latin America, *fin de siglo* periodicals also began to play a pivotal role in developing Modernist literary discourse.[6] The Nobel Prize-winning Bengali writer Rabindranath Tagore brought out a little magazine called *Sadhana* from 1891 to 1895, in which he published a number of important short stories.[7]

It may well be that little has changed about what motivates authors and artists to start independent little magazines since book production became part of the entertainment industry—since, that is to say, the beginnings of the modern print genres, and especially so in America. As Jonathan Baumbach wrote in the 1970s, recalling his involvement with the Fiction Collective, an experimental, author-run group dedicated to bringing new work to press, "The publication of fiction in America, with fewer and fewer exceptions . . . is a desperate transaction with the devils of greed. Something ought to be done, everyone said."[8] The writers propelling the bibelot craze in the 1890s would have agreed, as, too, would have the editors of the Transcendentalist *Dial* in America or the Pre-Raphaelite *Germ* in England in the 1850s; of *Blast* and *Poetry* and the *Blind Man* during the height of the Modernist little magazine movement in the 1910s and '20s; of the academic press art magazines of the 1930s and '40s, like the *Southern Review* and *Kenyon Review*, known for avant-garde poetry; of the black literary magazines of the 1960s and 1970s, like *Free Lance*, *Dassein*, *Umbra*, and *Yard Bird*; and of *McSweeney's Quarterly Concern*, David Eggers's publishing project which started in 1998 by featuring only works that had been rejected by other magazines. These are imprints of the counterculture, or more precisely what Michael Warner would call "counterpublics," their sociality being organized through networks of print circulation, some obviously more so than others, all united by their resistance to the dictates of popular taste and commercial success.[9] As Gelett Burgess, the most prolific of the American bibelot editors, wrote when he was winding down publication of his pathbreaking bibelot, the *Lark*, in 1897, "[T]he movement asserted itself as a revolt against the commonplace, it aimed to overthrow the staid respectability of the larger magazines and to open to younger writers opportunities to be heard before they had obtained recognition from the autocratic editors."[10]

We have come to know the commonplace Burgess referred to in late nineteenth-century America as that belonging primarily to the bourgeois institution of genteel literary monthlies, which exerted an outsized influence on determining upper- and middle-class cultural competence and status in the second half of the nineteenth century. Referred to by Mott as the "quality group" of magazines and by Nancy Glazener as "the *Atlantic* group," these included the *Atlantic*, *Harper's Monthly*, *Lippincott's*, the *North American Review*, *Scribner's Magazine*, and the *Century Illustrated*. They constituted a distinguished class of monthly magazines selling for twenty-five to thirty-five cents in which the "war for Realism" was waged by the likes of William Dean Howells and Richard Watson Gilder, and which ushered in a golden age of illustration. It is largely because of the cultural place held by these magazines, both at the time and in the eyes of later critics, that we remember the period for its Realism and Naturalism, for a literary style offering itself as a sober and democratic representation of social life and the local forces from which it took shape.[11] As we will see, nothing could be further from the wispy and stylish internationalism of the American ephemeral bibelots.

Then, too, especially as the century came to a close, there was the increasing significance of the mass-market monthlies, ten-cent magazines with sprawling advertising sections whose circulations by the end of the century had far eclipsed those of the *Atlantic* group, including *Ladies' Home Journal*, *Munsey's*, and *McClure's*. There was increasing competition from the Saturday-evening and Sunday editions of the daily newspapers, especially after 1897 by the reconceived *Saturday Evening Post*, which were near equivalents in size and circulation to the monthlies. Of these newspapers, hundreds were directed toward black readers, and by 1900 the *Colored American Magazine* would join late nineteenth-century African American newspapers like the *New York Age*, the *Freeman*, and the *Christian Recorder*.[12] Other magazines, described encyclopedically in Mott's history of American magazines, were devoted to specialized readerships and abounded in fields as wide-ranging as education, religion, medicine, engineering, horticulture, law, banking, insurance, women's activities, sports and recreation, humor, and hobbies.

There was, in short, a heavily saturated marketplace for serials, which reached something of an apex in terms of its institutional ability to exert an influence on the whole of the reading public at precisely the time the ephemeral bibelots had their vogue. In 1890 there were about 4,400 periodicals published in the United States; in 1895 that number was around 5,100; in 1900 it was around 5,500.[13] The vogue for ephemeral bibelots took up but an exceedingly small bit of space in this serial print marketplace. At its height, there may have been somewhere around three hundred bibelots; this book deals in some detail with only a few dozen of those. It may seem like a misuse of time to try to dust them off, here, were it not for the little scene of revolt that they staged against the print marketplace as a whole. The bibelot craze of the 1890s can serve as a fulcrum for leveraging the modern free from what, for far too long, has been understood to be an age of American gentility and restraint, national reconciliation and consolidation.

Any number of characteristics might be suggested as identifying qualities of the ephemeral bibelots, for example, their Decadence, their campy queerness, their coy sexual libertinage, their juvenility, their unusual shapes, their astounding Art Nouveau covers, their brevity, their distinctly fin-de-siècle line and color schemes, their practiced bohemianism, their deckled edges and innovative types, their cosmopolitanism, their Paris-centrism, and their ephemerality.[14] On the whole, they offered a vehement argument against the dominant narrative of Realism in art, as well as a forum for aestheticism and internationalism in American art, but the character of that argument varied greatly. The most interesting of the bibelots featured stunning Post-Impressionist graphic arts, experimental short stories and prose poems, and acerbic commentary on topics ranging from aesthetic fashions to politics and social mores. They varied widely in size and shape but were generally short, rarely more than thirty-two pages in length. Many were associated with printing companies, not publishing houses. Quite a few got their start with young men in or just out of college. They published well-known authors and many who were less so. They dallied in fin-de-siècle Decadence but were at the same time comfortable in the increasingly consumer-driven commodity culture of the day. They were compellingly and uniformly devoted to "the new." In this regard, what Paula Bennett has said of the poetry of the 1890s is also true of the bibelots: they were devoted to *an idea of the new* that "knew itself to be 'new' but at the same time did not know what that 'new' was. Not with any security at any rate."[15]

What I have come to think of as the ephemeral bibelots' most significant and defining quality is their cultivation of a "relational aesthetics," an aesthetics in which the work of art locates not in images or texts but rather in the communal sense taking shape among readers that there might be some kind of fleeting, parodic, foreign, flirtatious relation taking shape between them. The sense of relation might be nothing more than an inkling, it is almost never definite, and it leaves readers grasping after the possibility that there might be something more if they could just get to it.

The idea is quite similar, in many respects, to how relational aesthetics is used in contemporary art circles, where the term was coined by the French curator Nicolas Bourriaud to describe what he took to be a new turn in art exhibits of the 1990s, "the community effect in contemporary art." As Bourriaud explains, relational aesthetics describes "an art taking as its theoretical horizon the realm of human interactions and its social context, rather than the assertion of an independent and private symbolic space."[16] A famous example is González-Torres's *Untitled (Portrait of Ross in L.A.)* (1991), which consisted of a pile of hard candies in colorful wrappers that viewers were invited to share, a pile that was perpetually replenished to an ideal weight of 175 pounds, the same as the artist's lover before he contracted AIDS. Viewers were thus brought into ephemeral and ever-changing relations with the artist, the artist's lover, the candy, and each other—all in the communal, temporary space of the museum exhibit room. Art associated with relational aesthetics has been said to be collective not private; contingent not portable; intersubjective not object-oriented; ephemeral not permanent; politically provisional and pragmatic not utopian; collaborative not confrontational; millennial not Postmodern; and open-ended not whole or complete.

Of course, a significant difference with the bibelots comes from the fact that Bourriaud's relational aesthetics described public exhibitions, with shared communal spaces typical of late twentieth-century urban life, whereas what I will be discussing was almost entirely a print phenomenon taking shape in internationally distant locales. There is, nonetheless, a striking resonance between relational aesthetics and the community dynamic of the ephemeral bibelots. Art in the bibelots took shape *between* the pages as much as *on* them, as much in the open-ended reception of the bibelots en masse as in any single one of them.[17] A highly self-reflexive movement, the international fad for ephemeral bibelots depended for its aesthetic charge upon the redistribution and cross-referencing of particular optic and linguistic cues to produce coterie publics. As suggested by the ribald joke of *le chat noir* (see the prologue), the story here is not about originality but about how innovation comes to be attributed to artistic work that engages readers directly with the dynamics of circulation and recognition. The aesthetic sense flits on gossamer wings between the situational specificities of a black cat hissing from a crescent moon in Steinlen's illustrations for *Le Chat Noir*, to the head of a debutante in *Vogue*, and to the cover of an issue of the bibelot *M'lle New York*.

The idea is neatly illustrated by an alphabetical acrostic that Burgess published in 1896 in the most outrageous of the American bibelots, *Le Petit Journal des Refusées*, which collects and pulls into relation an entire "clubbing list" of "freak magazines" (see plate 2). *Le Petit Journal* makes an art, here, out of pointed allusions to an ongoing list of fellow *refusés*. For instance:

C is for *Chap-Book*, the pater familias
Of magazines started by many a silly ass.

D is for Darn it—it's awfully shocking
Your Dekel-edge Hosiery, Mistress Blue Stocking.

E is for Editor; what does it mean?
Everyone now runs his own magazine.

F is for Freak: see the great exposition
Of freak magazines—5 and 10 cents admission

G is for Goup; I would much rather be
A nice Purple Cow than a G-O-U-P.

H is for Humbug attempts to be Horrid!
(See *Mlle. New York*, she's decidedly torrid.)

I am an Idiot, awful result
Of reading the rot of the *Yellow Book* cult.

J is for JENSON the TYPE of the day,
Some people can't read any other, they say.

K is for Kimball, assistant of Stone;
I wonder how he will get on all alone.

L is for *Lark* and the fellows who planned it
Say even they cannot but half understand it!

M is for Magazines recklessly recent
I know of but one that is anyway decent.

N stands for Nothing; I wish it had stood for
A little bit more than the *Fly-Leaf* was good for.

O's for Oblivion—ultimate fate
Of most of the magazines published of late.

The relational aesthetic, suggested in these examples by the witty citation of fellow travelers, cultivates an art of movement not stasis, flights not conclusions, analogies not definitions, conjunctions not nouns, and edges not nodes. Even the margin illustration of "Our Clubbing List" emphasizes the maniacally interwoven limbs and tentacles of make-believe figures. Everything is connected to everything else, but it is far from clear as to how. The excitement comes from trying to figure it out, but the quest for a solution has the tendency to come off feeling ridiculous, borderline absurd, because sure knowledge about the nature and extent of relations is always just out of reach.

If the primary characteristic of the bibelots is this relational aesthetic, then their secondary trait is the coincident feeling of obscurity and breathless incompleteness that defines the community taking shape around them. We have, with the bibelots, American art at its flightiest, a craze for connections pushing well past the constraints of the commonplace normally associated with American art and culture of the period. The bibelots were given over to the new and the modern in art and life, and what most characterizes that modernity is their cultivation of an impressively difficult to follow field of allusions and references. As the craze hit its stride around 1896, a multiplier effect seems to have taken over. As relation relates to relation relates to relation, the whole field of reference becomes ever more obscure. Those trying to track it down become more intense in their efforts. One bibelot, the *Bauble*, devotes itself to little more than an ongoing rant about the shortcomings of its contemporaries: "IT SEEMS as though *The Bauble*, like a certain soothing syrup, fills a real want. There are so many good subjects for ridicule, that the Fool is kept busy directing his bauble against them."[18]

This obscurity could become, in itself, the thing around which the counterpublic took shape. It seems likely that the bibelot vogue became aware of itself by way of what Daniel Tiffany describes as the "poetics of obscurity" that, at the same moment, was linking the lyric genre to the nightlife of the fin-de-siècle cabaret. Tiffany argues that obscurity allows for "the possibility of communities that defy the seemingly inexorable logic of transparency and continuity implicit in the social imaginary of the Internet"; the poetics of obscurity becomes "the very ground, or medium, of negative sociability," leading him to think about lyric poets and their readers in terms of fragmented "sleeper cells" and "underworlds."[19] These are communities that know themselves for knowing what others do not. I have little doubt that Burgess would have taken delight in such a description, fond as he was of describing his corner of San Francisco, where he published several of his bibelots, in terms of a remarkably heterogeneous "Bayside Bohemia," a "little cosmos, bizarre, isolate, remote, all things to all men, wrapped in a variegated mantle of chance and change, where Tuesday becomes Thursday with scarcely time for a Wednesday between."[20] And the situation seems unlikely to change given that the bibelots are now so rare as to fall largely outside the purview of digitization projects.[21]

Again, this characteristic is not necessarily unique to the bibelots but is shared by any number of other countercultural movements. The bibelot craze is very like the social formation that Roland Barthes described in terms of the pleasure of reading Sade, a way modern texts have of "perforating discourse *without rendering it meaningless*," of emphasizing gaps, tears, and intermittences in ways that flame desire. Fabio Cleto has described something similar as "camp," arising from "a discursive resistance, a semiotic excess." And Alan Liu calls it "cool," "the proscriptive ellipsis . . . the rhetoric of unproducible knowledge."[22] We might without much trouble see them as queer little things; they called themselves "freakish," which in the parlance of the day came to something close to the same.[23] They played upon the prospect of what Rita Felski once described as an aesthetic of "surface, style, and parody" in which artists tentatively feminized masculinity and sexualized feminism, "an aestheticized and feminized modernity."[24] The bibelots did not fall into obscurity; they reveled in it. The relational aesthetic sent them chasing after a horizon that was forever vanishing in plain sight.

Much of this book is given over to finding the best way to describe the group dynamics of this little explosion in print culture. How were the relations engendered by the circulatory networks of the bibelots reflected in the poetry, fiction, criticism, and illustration of the time? What distinguishes the bibelots as an interactional medium not only from more personable forms of social communication in the cabarets, music halls, and stages but also from other serial formats? How does reading for the group dynamics of the international craze for these magazines change our understanding of their meteoric rise, and, perhaps, even explain why they were so utterly forgotten? The relational aesthetic of the bibelots gives them their visual and literary interest, but its obscurity also renders them particularly vulnerable to being dropped from the stories we tell about the cultural past. Or as Burgess put it in "Our Clubbing List," "O's for Oblivion—ultimate fate/Of most of the magazines published of late." Might that, perhaps, give us the link we need to see once again how to dance within the marginalia of this fin-de-siècle print culture?

Vogue and Ephemera

The story of the bibelots is that of vogue and ephemera—of the rapid, international expansion of a little magazine counterpublic and its equally abrupt slide into "oblivion." A remarkable aspect of this fad aesthetic is that those most responsible for it, "the little wasp-like privateers that have swarmed the seas of Journalism," in Burgess's phrase, failed to establish a story for the work they had done that would have tied it to the evolving scene of art's evolution and revolution—and this despite the fact that, in retrospect, so much of it would now be familiar under the rubrics developed to discuss Modernism.[25] It is a problem characteristic of the 1890s, when, as Glazener has pointed out, critics pursued a proliferation of classifications for new fiction. These included such varied options as the "philosophical romance," the "book of everyday life," the "problem novel," the "animal story," the "romance of power of money," and even, whimsically, the "Vegetable school of fiction," which was so intensely regionalist that its characters grow right out of the soil.[26] Jennifer Fleissner has described the decade as a "seething cauldron of faddishness."[27] Fitting in neatly with Fleissner's description, the bibelots were the decade's faddish fanzines.

The craze for ephemeral bibelots is frequently described as a "little storm" that gathered and burst. But how, exactly, does a vogue like this one gather momentum and *not* become a movement, the movement known as Modernism? How might we best explain not only the volatility within the movement but also its failure to circulate out of the 1890s?

The answer is tied directly to the dynamics of group movements, and in this respect the localized problem of the ephemeral bibelots opens out more broadly onto a matter of some concern in the humanities today, that of understanding the fad aesthetics of networked associations—how things go viral. Since they were such marginal things, most of the hundreds of ephemeral bibelots are currently, and likely will continue to be, largely outside the purview of Google acquisitions and other database projects, and yet they register a dynamic that a Google search depends upon, namely, the peculiar thrill of discovering unexpected links in an ever-expanding network of associations. The frisson of discovering such relations rose, in the case of the ephemeral bibelots, to the level of an aesthetic style, an intellectual and visceral excitation of mood that was anticipatory and insatiable, leaving readers with a feeling of having been caught up and swirled around. The bibelots tried to cultivate the feeling, but, almost by definition, it couldn't last.

The ephemeral bibelots became one of the key media in the late nineteenth century for the circulation of avant-garde ideas about art, a networked realm for the discussion and production of new modes of relating to culture that ran counter to and largely free of engagement from the dominant print culture of the illustrated literary monthlies. They clearly anticipated the role that the Modernist little magazines would come to play in the 1910s and 1920s; as Bulson has argued, convincingly, "No little magazines, no Modernism: it's as simple as that."[28] Taking in the bibelot craze as a whole reveals a coterie public of insiders who could follow the expansive international circulation of stylistic allusions and inside jokes emanating out of Europe. This group much preferred the artful derivative to the real thing, understanding that the new was never new, the one was always the many, and the lines of transition were more interesting than the endpoints.

Interestingly, the aesthetic frisson of the bibelots derived from a perpetual sense of perceptual inadequacy. The thrill of playing in this aesthetic public sphere came not only from recognizing some of the connections but from sensing that there must be more of them flitting around on the periphery of vision, just out of sight but maybe still within reach. It depended on the sense of being inadequate to the task of completing the circuit, of befuddlement at the apparent incompleteness and ultimate inconsequence of the presumed relations, which contributed to making it a momentary affair. And it depended on the sense that others shared this same hopeful and hopeless belief in a set of connections that would add up to nothing at all. Once missed, a line of reference was gone forever; and for the fad to work, as such, that ephemerality has to be taken as a positive.

The bibelots were in the moment, compulsively so. But they were also out of history, prone to oblivion both by definition and by the structure of their relational field. As will be suggested (see chapter 2), the relational network spurring their aesthetic also made them vulnerable to extinction; this we know from sociological and mathematical studies of the function of networks.[29] But for now, it is important to see that the whole ethos of the bibelots was defined by their commitment to ephemerality. Their revolt against the commonplace of the literary establishment not only absolved them of the need to pass the test of time, the traditional prerequisite of all great art, but seemed even to demand something like their programmatic evanescence. If the bibelots did not fold on their own, their editors would simply decide to stop publishing them after a year or two. The movement was declared over almost before it began.

Walter Blackburn Harte provides a remarkable example of bibelotic ephemerality. He had founded the *Fly Leaf* in 1895, a "Pamphlet Periodical of the New—the new man, new woman, new ideas, whimsies and things," in which he published the first short story by his sister-in-law, Edith Maude Eaton, also known as Sui Sin Far.[30] He made a quick stop with the *Philistine* and then served as editor of the *Lotus*. But by 1897, he was done with what he demeaned as the "queer little epoch of the revolt in American Literature," proclaiming on October 30 of that year in the *Criterion*, which itself was arguably a little magazine representative of the revolt in print, that "this remarkable literary revolution, which broke in the winter of 1895-6, is now, in 1897, about played out—dying." Harte described the movement as "a little black thunder cloud" and "a little hurricane," and he lamented the passing of the "poor little whirlwind!—it did not last long." And yet he had been in the thick of it, behind it and on its leading edge. It is counterintuitive to think that he would be the one setting the terms for its premature dismissal unless the rupture, the moment, the flash, was the point.

Frederick Faxon, the movement's first bibliographer, struck the same time-shortening note just six years later. He explained the urgency of his work by pointing out that "hardly any one now collects these publications, and unless the names, and the dates of their births and deaths are somewhere recorded, no future collector will ever be able to obtain accurate information concerning this large, somewhat useless, but very interesting class of periodicals."[31]

The most astonishing of the eulogies came from Burgess, who in the first half of the 1890s, had gone from being an MIT-trained draftsman for the Southern Pacific Railroad and instructor of topographical drawing at Berkeley to one of the leading bohemian artists working on the edge of San Francisco's notorious Barbary Coast. Burgess was thirty-one years old in 1897. He had grown up in Boston, the fourth of five children in a family with eight generations of New Englanders behind it, and as he wrote in the draft of an unpublished autobiography, "I was the first generation of my family . . . to effect a complete break with puritanical thought and contact."[32] He had done the European tour, familiarized himself with the cabarets of Montmartre and the aesthetic and moral contours of the continent. He had surveyed the west for the expanding railroad networks. He had famously gotten himself relieved of his teaching position at the University of California after toppling a statue of the temperance advocate and San Francisco benefactor Henry Cogswell. And shortly after that, in the frenzy of the Camp Ha-Ha studios, he and a group of artist friends started the *Lark*—as a lark—in the spring of 1895. Among his main collaborators were the artist Bruce Porter, printer Porter Garnett, and illustrator Ernest C. Peixotto. Every three months, a beautiful, Art Nouveau poster for the *Lark* by one of California's first female designers, Florence Lundborg, was issued. The magazine was printed on the cheapest paper to be found in Chinatown. Visually distinct, it featured loosely drawn illustrations and an unusual header running across the top of all its pages on which Burgess, in the role of editor and jester, offered both summary and snide commentary on the contents of each page.

The *Lark* was in revolt against cultural pretension, Paris-inspired and yet unusual for its optimism and imperviousness to fin-de-siècle malaise—"a small, thin creature, but incredibly, even impossibly, 1895," according to the *New York Times*.[33] For Burgess, it would lead to other bibelot ventures, including *Phyllida: or, the Milkmaid*, *L'Enfant Terrible*, and the extraordinary *Le Petit Journal des Refusées*, a sixteen-page trapezoidal affair that appeared in the summer of 1896 and featured absurd illustrations of Corinthian columns wearing sunglasses and circuitous prose worthy of Gertrude Stein. The journal's ruse was that everything it published had been submitted from thrice-rejected female authoresses, although it was actually all written by Burgess himself. Just as *Le Petit Journal des Refusées* gathered something of its aesthetic charge from having only one number, so too, from the first, was the *Lark* conceived as a bird of passage. Bruce Porter's "invitation," printed on the first pages of the first issue of the *Lark* in May 1895, had made the point that the magazine proceeded "[w]ith no more serious intention than to be gay—to sing a song, to tell a story;—and when this is no longer to our liking,—when the spring calls, or the road invites,—then this little house of pleasure will close its doors; and if you have cared for our singing, and would have more of it, then you must follow us a-field." A few months later, the *New York Times* would have a laugh at the eccentricity of readers who had actually sent in for an annual subscription, which the *Lark*'s editors had promised not to refund in the case of nonfulfillment.[34]

Why did Burgess and his cohort shut down the *Lark* after exactly two years? Was it, in the manner of Baudelaire's take on Poe's "Ligeia," too miraculously beautiful to live?[35] In May 1897, as if on schedule, they brought out what would have been the *Lark*'s twenty-fifth issue—only, instead, they named this one the *Epi-Lark*. Anticipating Harte by several months, and incognizant of the fact that he would go on to bring out a New York-based bibelot, *L'Enfant Terrible*, the very next year, Burgess officially declared "the freak fleet" of which he was the commodore disarmed:

> Suddenly, without warning, the storm broke, and a flood of miniature periodicals began to pour over the land. The success of the "Chap Book" incited the little riot of Decadence, and there was a craze for odd sizes and shapes, freak illustrations, wide margins, uncut pages, Jenson types, scurrilous abuse and petty jealousies, impossible prose and doggerel rhyme. . . . It was a wild, hap-hazard exploration in search of a short cut to Fame; it proposed to carry Prestige by storm.
>
> But the war is almost over now, and the little wasp-like privateers that have swarmed the seas of Journalism are nearly all silenced; the freak fleet has disarmed, but who knows how many are missing?[36]

After the *Lark*, Burgess made his way to New York, and then on to London for a year, and then back to Boston, and later again to San Francisco; with each move, he left the bibelots further behind. In New York, he wrote for the *Criterion* alongside Harte and other former bibelotists. In London he dined at Lamb House with Henry James, and he met the young American Henry Harland, editor of the *Yellow Book*, Barrie Fawcett, Harold Frederic, Herbert Stone, and Edmund Gosse. Back in Boston, his funds declined, but he went on to publish the famous children's book series, *Goops*, an important introduction to European Modernist painters in 1910, and dozens of other exceedingly clever but largely forgotten novels featuring cerebral and erotically ambiguous heroines, as well as collections of essays and short stories.

Burgess never went back to magazine editing after 1900, even though the one thing he would be remembered for upon his death in 1951 was a four-line nonsense poem that had baptized the first number of the *Lark*, his infamous "The Purple Cow": "I never saw a Purple Cow / I never hope to see one / But I can tell you anyhow / I'd rather see than be one." (For the accompanying image, see chapter 1.) These four lines on the purple cow are the exceptions that prove the rule that the ephemeral bibelots were just what Harte and Burgess said: they were ephemeral, and quite often programmatically so. The purple cow had legs—becoming the mascot of Williams College in 1907 and being remembered by Franklin Delano Roosevelt in 1938, when he concluded birthday greetings to Burgess, "Long live the purple cow!"—but the bibelot vogue did not.[37]

The bibelot fad was not, obviously, the only modern art movement to be so short-lived, but it was one of the most quickly forgotten. Part of the reason was structural, having to do with the dynamics of viral networks. Another part was programmatic, with editors, authors, and artists choosing to leave their recently old work behind. A third part was that the aesthetic of the fad depended on the temporariness of its existence to generate the intensity of its reception, and, circling back, this intensity led to the temporariness of its existence. Such is the nature of the relational aesthetic, full of gaps and missed connections. What I hope to convince you of in this book is that the forgetting was not only unjustified but also that the story of how an art movement like this one is forgotten is almost as fascinating as how it is produced. In a sense, this is a story not only about the anonymity of a proto-Modernist American art movement but about the curiously beautiful dynamic of cultural evanescence.

Relational Obscurity as a Historical Problem

The emphasis on ephemerality has had a negative influence on what critics have generally thought about the movement, which is not much. These are objects that do not fit our received narrative about how to judge the significance either of magazines or art more generally, for which success means survival. It is easier to call them proto something—proto *anything*—proto-Dadaist, say, or proto-Futurist, proto-Imagist, or simply proto-Modernist; and some of them are, the best example coming with *Le Petit Journal des Refusées*. There are very few degrees of separation, as we will see in more detail (chapter 1), between *Le Petit Journal des Refusées* and a full-fledged Dadaist effort like Marcel Duchamp's little magazine, the *Blind Man*, which appeared out of New York in 1917. Why is it that we know about the *Fountain* but not about Burgess's "proto-Dadaist" work from the mid-1890s, his "*reductio ad absurdum* of the 'freak' journal"?[38]

Even from the rather dry perspective of print runs, we can see that the fad aesthetic made the ephemeral bibelots quite different from the more well-known Modernist little magazines of the 1910s and '20s. First, the movement as a whole was much more volatile, with more new publications appearing each year than in the later movement, and with fewer bibelots making it past their first year. Bibliographies of the bibelots typically run to two or three hundred titles; those of the Modernist little magazines, when limited to a comparable period of time, typically run to seventy or eighty titles. The average run of an ephemeral bibelot started between 1894 and

1904 was just over a year; by contrast, the later Modernist little magazines started between 1912 and 1922 frequently lasted longer, sometimes much longer.[39] Second, the perceived success of the ephemeral bibelots had nothing to do with their survival. Many of the Modernist little magazines of the later period paralleled mainstream journals to the extent that, while some of their titles were exceptionally short-lived, a significant number had, and continue to have, remarkably long runs. Most notably, these include the *Little Review* (1914–1929), the *Criterion* (1922–1939), and, of course, *Poetry* (1912–present)—now not merely a magazine but the lifeblood of the Poetry Foundation. The status attached to the longevity of these magazines has absolutely no corollary among the bibelots, which were, most often, short-lived by design. Even for those with more robust expectations for sticking around than others, the sensation of ephemerality proved a significant aspect of their appeal, generating much of the buzz about them and, in some cases, constituting the sum of the aesthetic intervention they meant to make.

What we can gather about the general contours of the fad must be deduced from the slenderest of historical sources. H. L. Mencken was one of the only early twentieth-century critics to recall the chapbook movement in America with anything like enthusiasm, and even he did so only just barely. He mentions them in passing in the first series of his *Prejudices*, published in 1919, during a discussion of the almost entirely forgotten American critic, Percival Pollard, who had been a regular contributor to short-lived efforts like the *Lotus*, the *Echo*, the *Fly Leaf*, *Whims*, the *Clack Book*, the *Anti-Philistine*, the *Chap-Book*, the *Criterion*, and the *Goose-Quill*. If Pollard is remembered today, it is mostly for having penned one of the few early appreciations of Kate Chopin's 1899 novel, *The Awakening*. This makes sense because Chopin was also a bibelot writer of the first order (see chapter 4). Writing against the prevailing tide of censure, Pollard suggested that Chopin was one among an underappreciated cadre of women writers of erotic literature; the only thing wrong with her novel was the absurdity of its asking us to believe that its heroine, Edna Pontellier, "had been several years married, and had borne children, [but] had never, in all that time, been properly 'awake.'"[40] Pollard's request for more frank explorations of sexual desire, which was a regular theme in many of the bibelots, seems to have tinged Mencken's recall of them. The resounding note of his brief mention is that of youthful excitement and second thoughts, as if in coming upon Pollard and the ephemeral bibelots he had cleverly stumbled upon material that sent his mind racing but needed reconsideration in his maturity. "How, as a youngster, I used to lie in wait for the *Criterion* every week," he wrote, "and devour Pollard, Huneker, Meltzer and Vance Thompson! That was in the glorious middle nineties and savory pots were brewing. Scarcely a week went by without a new magazine of some unearthly *Tendenz* or other appearing on the stands; scarcely a month failed to bring forth its new genius."[41]

An interesting clue to the historical fate of the *Tendenz* can be found in the magazine Mencken cites, the *Criterion*, which had been the venue for Harte's aforementioned obituary for "The Chap Book Movement in America" in 1897. Although seemingly on very solid footing, the *Criterion* did not manage to clear the imaginative hurdle of the turn of the century. It was both genetically related to the first wave of bibelots, having recuperated many of the movements of main players like Harte and Burgess, but also a successor to them.[42] It was a weekly, not a monthly, and it was exceptionally substantive for a bibelot in terms of number of issues and length. Mencken would have read the *Criterion* as it appeared under the editorship of the French-born Henri Dumay, who recruited a large number of the most important authors and editors of the bibelots to write for it, including Chopin. Those cited by Mencken had all been involved with bibelots; in addition to Pollard, Vance Thompson was coeditor with James Huneker of *M'lle New York*, and Charles Meltzer was a contributor to the same and also to a smaller bibelot, the *Philosopher*, published out of Wausau, Wisconsin, from 1897 to 1906. Among other notables, the *Criterion* also carried Bliss Carman, a former editor of the *Chap-Book*, and featured two-color political cartoons on most of its covers by Rob Wagner, who had also been a contributor to the *Chap-Book*. With the help of Mrs. Grace L. Davidson, a wealthy female backer in St. Louis, the magazine made a go at becoming what Dumay described as "a sort of literary free lance," a counter to the mainstream periodical press: "[W]e believe that much young talent and not a little talent no longer young is now wasting in obscurity for lack of friendly help. To speak of literature only, it is well known that all originality is being persistently kept down, warped or destroyed by the snobbish and musty conservatism of the coteries that reign."[43]

The *Criterion*'s bohemian, modern, internationalist field of relation was fully fin de siècle. William Marion Reedy noted in his *St. Louis Mirror* on February 22, 1900, that the magazine was given over to "Ibsenism, Hauptmannism, Husmanism, Verlaineism, George Bernard Shawism, and George Mooreism." At the end of October 1897, Pollard announced the formation of "the Criterion Independent Theatre," whose first production was to be Ibsen's 1896 drama, *Johann Gabriel Borkman*. Their goal, as Pollard described it, was "to give plays by men who, the world over, are original forces, not bound by any ever so ancient or plausible conventions; observant of every new tendency changing to-day's life from yesterday's, and yet to please both the people who wish to be amused and the people who wish the thrill of an earnest intention."[44] The effort was noted approvingly by the *Philosopher*, which highlighted the seriousness of an effort "controlled by men who are qualified by education, special training and natural inclinations to decide what is good and to point the way for others."[45] In the *Criterion* three issues later, Pollard contributed a review article in which he lauded a literary group in Hartford, Connecticut, calling itself the Black Cats, after the Montmartre cabaret, which had arranged a program of reading for the coming season including, among others, Du Maurier, Whitman, Hauptman, James Lane Allen, Anthony Hope, Frank Stockton, H. G. Wells, Ambrose Bierce, Ibsen, Bjornstjerne Bjornsen, and Pollard himself.[46] A *Criterion* essay from May 1902 described James Huneker, a music critic and former associate editor of *M'lle New York*, in representative terms: like the journals he wrote for, Huneker was an adept in "exposing the freakish whims, the egoistic loves, the morbid joys, the theories upon theories, the contempt of common sense, the unwholesome methods of thought, sympathy and life, of a large class" of fin-de-siècle musicians, writers, and artists.[47]

While "new" in the nineteenth-century sense of the term, it seems likely that such a lineup would also have left the magazine feeling dated in the early twentieth century. Mencken clearly looked back on the magazine as a harbinger of the Modernism of his own time, as too, perhaps, did T. S. Eliot when he chose in 1922 to call his own little magazine the *Criterion*. The writers of the magazine provided the young Mencken a slender line into a world of music, illustration, and writing quite unlike that which we have come to expect in the American periodicals of the day. The *Criterion* had assembled the best of *les jeunes* from around the country, the young drivers of the bibelot vogue in the United States, and gathered them in New York for a more cerebral, internationally focused, cutting edge artistic affair. But instead of giving new momentum to the movement, the *Criterion* ended by being even less well known than many of the bibelots it drew upon.

When Harte's eulogy for the chapbook movement was published, the *Criterion* found itself not so much moving past them as mired in their wake. When he described the movement as "a little thundercloud . . . that made the shop-keepers gasp for a moment—and then they collected themselves, and looked up and saw their old green cheese in the sky, and they were happy again," it seems unlikely that he also meant to wrap up the *Criterion*, but later historians did. Mott gave the *Criterion* only two paragraphs, suggesting that it was "over the heads of many readers" and that Dumay ended up shocking his St. Louis benefactor with some of the journal's more "mauve" stories, and he was discharged in 1898.[48] In his colorful history of the 1890s, *The Mauve Decade* (1926), Thomas Beer linked the *Criterion* to *M'lle New York*, with which it is said to have shared "a devilish legend" and "vanished into the leaden haze of the Decade of Muck."[49] By April 1900, two and a half years after moving to New York, the *Criterion* had changed from a weekly to a monthly, aiming to provide a more finished product with which to offer to "that large, cultivated audience of what is new in literature and the arts" a "criterion" by which to assess and debate the "field of belles-lettres and art." Although some of the bibelot writers continued to publish in it, the journal had clearly lost its edge, taking up instead the innocuous and, for the period, mundane header "A Family Magazine of Literature, Drama, Music and Art." Mencken's *Tendenz* was of an earlier moment that, by 1900, had already passed.

What follows from the dismissal of the *Criterion* and the rest of the bibelot craze is that Modernism in America is generally thought to have started only sometime after the Armory Show in 1913. That is clearly a mistake, one with a fuller explanation having to do with the marketing of American Modernism and the American novel in the 1910s and 1920s.[50]

And yet, it is not altogether an exaggeration to say that the failure of the bibelots to take hold buried Modernism in America for decades. In them, one can discover not only *proto*-Modernist material but work long recognized to be *quintessentially* Modernist. For example, in 1895, *M'lle New York* reproduces Edward Munch's *The Scream*, just two years after its initial appearance, alongside a Pierrot poem by the French Symbolist Jules Laforgue. At the same time, the *Chap-Book* is publishing original poetry by Mallarmé in French. Literary and visual abstraction, outrageous artistic parody, music reviews attending to the new atonality in music, automatic writing, Symbolism and Decadence, Beardsleyesque line drawings and aesthetic arts decoration, something akin to Imagist poetry, stream of consciousness fiction, and a worldly sense of being part of something new: all this is to be found in the bibelots in the 1890s. Had anyone remembered them, the story of T. S. Eliot discovering the French Symbolists when stumbling upon a copy of Arthur Symons's volume in the Harvard Library in 1908 could never have achieved the status it currently has as a turning point in American Modernism. Symons was published in or cited by a half-dozen bibelots between 1894 and 1896 (see chapter 5). Nor would we be able to countenance Amy Lowell's claim in the 1920s that Stephen Crane's poetry "sprang from practically nowhere."[51] A point I make later in this book is that Crane's poetry was entirely recognizable in the American 1890s context of the *Philistine*, which published much of it. The notion of the late arrival of Modernist aesthetics to the United States is simply wrong as a historical fact.

But by the same token, because so much of the bibelots' practice depended upon an intense relational aesthetic, a constant unfolding like that suggested by *Vogue*'s black cat and *Le Petit Journal des Refusées*' "Our Clubbing List," it would also be wrong to simply say they were like what comes later with Pound, Eliot, Moore, H. D., Williams, and Stevens in the 1910s and '20s. In one sense, the relays I mean to describe give a concrete example of the most familiar story we tell about modernity, namely, that it is recognizable by its radical dissociative impulses, by the sentiment of fragmentation and dispersal that it left in its wake. Indeed, what one sees most fundamentally acknowledged in the more radical exemplars of the bibelot vogue—acknowledged as pleasure more often than pain, as surprise more often than disbelief—is a consciousness of the dissociative affects of modern circulation. And yet, as we will see, this recognition of the fragmentation of experience associated with modernity was different in the 1890s. In the bibelots, dissociation made tracing relations exhilarating, whereas later on dissociation became the story's end. Formally, the bibelots encouraged an art that emphasized reiteration and transition, which made it qualitatively distinct from the professed singularity and autonomy of form in much of the Modernism of the early twentieth century. And being vehicles of redistribution, the bibelots developed an aesthetic that felt different too, which, prejudicially, I would describe as being like a gleeful grasp after allusions blown by the wind, whereas later, after the breeze died down, only the scattered wreckage remained. It would be some time before Eliot's *The Waste Land* would set about "shoring up their ruins," and his allusions would be ancient and footnoted. The associative art of the bibelots was thus "new" but not "Modernist" in the way made famous by, say, Pound, who quipped that "[l]iterature is news that STAYS news."[52] The bibelots' news did not.

The Breathlessness of Aesthetic Expectation

If pressed, then, how best would we describe the éclat made by these fugitive publications? Writing only about Gelett Burgess, Johanna Drucker has noted that his "circle of references is always closed, and closing in, with a claustrophobic sense that the literary universe is a sort of no exit, in which one recycles one's reputation and pieces endlessly."[53] This *huis clos* also characterizes Mencken's appreciation of the early numbers of the *Criterion* and, as I will argue, sets the essential tonal quality of the aesthetic public sphere that developed in America in the 1890s around the bibelot fad. It is a tone of breathlessness, the gasp of finding oneself on unsure footing, on a precipice but delighting in the danger.

There is no better example of this breathlessness than Mencken himself, describing his reception of the *Criterion* and its writers, whom he took to be models for his own style of aggressively polyglot and impressionistic criticism. It spins on high and is obsessively conjunctive. In one characteristically hallucinatory passage recounting a conversation with the *Criterion*'s Huneker over an hours-long luncheon, Mencken pens a one-sentence description worthy of a cocaine-fueled ride with the Beats of a later generation:

> What a stew, indeed! Berlioz and the question of the clang-tint of the viola, the psychopathological causes of the suicide of Tchaikovsky, why Nietzsche had to leave Sils Maria between days in 1887, the echoes of Flaubert in Joseph Conrad (then but newly dawned), the precise topography of the warts of Liszt, George Bernard Shaw's heroic but vain struggles to throw off Presbyterianism, how Frau Cosima saved Wagner from the libidinous Swedish baroness, what to drink when playing Chopin, what Cézanne thought of his disciples, the defects in the structure of "Sister Carrie," Anton Seidl and the musical union, the complex love affairs of Gounod, the varying talents and idiosyncrasies of Lillian Russell's earlier husbands, whether a girl educated at Vassar could ever really learn to love, the exact composition of chicken paprika, the correct tempo of the Vienna waltz, the style of William Dean Howells, what George Moore said about German bathrooms, the true inwardness of the affair between D'Annunzio and Duse, the origin of the theory that all oboe players are crazy, why *Löwenbräu* survived exportation better than *Hofbrau*, Ibsen's loathing of Norwegians, the best remedy for Rhine wine *Katzenjammer*, how to play Brahms, the degeneration of the Bal Bullier, the sheer physical impossibility of getting Dvorák drunk, the genuine last words of Walt Whitman.[54]

For anyone counting, that makes ten references to music, five to fiction, four to theater, and one each to painting, philosophy, poetry, cooking, brewing, women at Vassar, and hangovers.

"Allusive" is the word Mencken settles on to describe Huneker's "geyser of unfamiliar names, shocking epigrams in strange tongues, [and] unearthly philosophies"—his "chaos made to gleam and coruscate with every device of the seven arts." Huneker was "allusive in his books . . . [and] ten times more allusive in his discourse."[55]

In describing Huneker as allusive, Mencken is as well, especially if one hears in that allusiveness a tendency toward the illusive and the elusive, and Mencken's breathlessness comes from trying to run it all down. The breathless intensity and no-exit circuitry of this style thrived on both the multiplication and overextension of weak connections. The cynical claim about it would be that when faced with little of substance to say, Mencken took the route of verbal exponentiation. If there is little of substance to report, simply use more words to describe what is not there. The more substantive claim is that the tic was a stylistic reproduction of the tonal quality of these interests, an allusion to a community that made an art of this chaos of vaguely apperceived relations in a spindly network of aesthetic linkages. In other words, Mencken describes the impression made at the moment of their reception. He seems to be asking how one catches hold of so little but so intense a storm.

"Breathlessness" and "allusiveness" are linked terms characteristic of both a style of literary criticism in the *Criterion* but also the feeling one is likely to have if trying to take in the sweep of the bibelot movement. If Mencken is to be our guide, then we might surmise that developing a contemporary interest in the bibelots will depend on getting similarly swept up in the whirlwind of its short-lived vogue and the aesthetic frisson of its bedeviling allusiveness. We, too, will want to feel breathless in our race to take them all in—but it won't be easy because our flight is pinned in on either side by a well-established narrative of literary progress, constrained on the one hand by the dominant place held by Realism and Naturalism and on the other by the near-total disregard of the bibelots by the Modernist avant-garde. Let us catch flight, then, with a turn on the *Lark* and the short-lived bibelot adventures of Burgess.

The first half of this book describes the vogue for ephemeral bibelots, its beginnings and its demise, in such a way as to make sense of how many of the characteristics of early Modernism that we most appreciate are produced in the late nineteenth century by the fad-driven development of relational aesthetics. The second half considers what happens when we reposition canonical writers who are typically taken to be waypoints in the constellation of American Realism and Naturalism within the bibelots' constellation. Accordingly, analysis extends from largely unknown writers like Stuart Merrill, an American poet who was part of Mallarmé's circle, unfamiliar to American scholars because he wrote in French and to French scholars because he was American; and Gelett Burgess, editor of several key bibelots who coined the word "blurb" in 1907; to such well-known authors as Henry James, Kate Chopin, and Stephen Crane. Spanning fields and the turn of the century, this analysis of print culture incorporates discussions of pragmatist philosophy; popular women writers who got their start in the bibelots like Juliet Wilbor Tompkins and Carolyn Wells; the graphic artists Will Bradley, Louis Rhead, and John Sloan; the dancer Loie Fuller; and twentieth-century figures like H. L. Mencken, Amy Lowell, and Anita Loos.

The goal of the first chapter, "Gelett Burgess and the Flight from Reality," is to establish the significance of the bibelot vogue for the history of American literary and visual Modernism by way of a case study of its most significant editor and artist, Gelett Burgess. The first move is to disorient the received nationalist narrative about Realism and Naturalism that to this day structures our understanding of American literary history in the second half of the nineteenth century. I do so by turning to Paris, where the first bibelots appeared in the late 1870s alongside countercultural art movements of Les Incohérents and the Hydropathes. The second move is to shift attention away from the *Chap-Book* and the *Yellow Book* to the hundreds of other bibelots being published at the same time, and to the productive nature of their interactions. And the third move is to look in some depth at Burgess's work in the *Lark* and *Le Petit Journal des Refusées*. One finds in Burgess's contributions to these bibelots examples of what would later be called Dada, Surrealism, automatic writing, Cubism, and Primitivism—all of it unnamed as such by Burgess. The chapter concludes by looking at Burgess's work after the bibelot vogue in order to better understand the structural dynamics of its evanescence.

The second chapter, "What Travels? What Doesn't? The International Movement of Movements," delves in a more theoretical fashion into the international scope of the bibelot craze and the character of its movement across national borders. How do movements move? What travels when the magazines, themselves, do not? The chapter examines the vogue in terms of the circulation of iconographic images and puns, poetic and literary forms, and ideas about Modern art from one journal to the next. It includes a discussion of Anton Chekhov's writing as a young man in *Oskolki*, translated as "fragments" or "shards of glass," a Russian little magazine modeled on the ones in France, and asks what relation that might have to material appearing in small-town American bibelots, like the *Clack Book* of Lansing, Michigan, and the *Philosopher* of Wausau, Wisconsin.

The third chapter, "Relating in Henry James," uses the serialization of *What Maisie Knew* in the *Chap-Book* to begin a wide-ranging discussion of what I describe as the relational era in Modernist aesthetics. James frequently refers to "relations" and "connections" in a technical sense in his criticism and fiction. In *Maisie*, a novel ostensibly about the fracturing of family relations, James attempts to formally represent the nebulous, transitory situation between seeing a thing and knowing what it means. The chapter traces connections between *Maisie* and the fiction of Balzac, the cabaret dances of Fuller, the poetry of Mallarmé, the poster art of Will Bradley, the photography of Muybridge and the pragmatist philosophy of William James. It uses *Maisie* and James's later novel *The Ambassadors* to provide a theory of how and why art represents the between-space of the relation.

Chapter 4, "Butterflies, Faddishness, and the Iconography of Desire," juxtaposes the sexual politics of the bibelot vogue, which might be summed up simply as the desire for more of it in American literature, with the bibelot writing of three women writers. The most well-known of these is Kate Chopin; the other two are Juliet Wilbor Tompkins and Carolyn Wells. What I mean to suggest are the links between the bibelots and the emergence of popular, middlebrow Modernism in the early twentieth century, culminating with a brief story about how to trace the steps from the bibelots to Anita Loos. But I am also interested, here, in the fact that because the bibelots were associated with faddishness, which was largely an attribute of the way their treatment of sexuality and their reception were feminized, they were largely written out of literary history.

Finally, in chapter 5, "The Edginess of Stephen Crane at the End of the Relational Era," I try to explain how the bibelot vogue contributed to making relational aesthetics unappealing to mainstream Modernism in the 1920s. In order to recuperate Crane's poetry for Modernism, Amy Lowell felt the need to extricate it from the history of the bibelot vogue. Most of his lines had been published in the *Philistine* in the 1890s, and Crane was intricately linked into the movement. Burgess singled him out in the important locater-poem in *Le Petit Journal des Refusées* (1896), "Our Clubbing List," where "S is for Stevie Crane, infant precocious / Who has written some lines that are simply ferocious." Lowell, however, finds it important to dissociate Crane from the club and insist, instead, that he was essentially an original, a "man without a period . . . [who] sprang from practically nowhere." This chapter uses the disconnect between the reception of Crane's lines in the 1890s and 1920s as a way of distinguishing between the "relational era" of proto-Modernist bibelots and the Modernism of Lowell and T. S. Eliot, which emphasized singularity and wholeness. The story told is that of the end of the bibelot vogue but also the end of the art of association.

In all of what follows, I would like to suggest that the dry, dusty bookshelves housing the bibelot craze provides a useful perch from which to consider the new critical paradigms for approaching the literary past. Lasting for only a decade but spread over at least four continents, the bibelot vogue draws our attention to the relational field and the dynamics of circulation we have at times associated with the experience of watching and reading Modern art. It is my hope that reconnecting with the bibelots will also remind us of why certain historical modes of artistic experimentation and reception, and in particular the bibelots' ardor for association, may be newly attractive to our thinking about art and aesthetic publics today.

1 Gelett Burgess and the Flight from Reality

> To her sisters, *The Chap-Book*, *The Lotus*, *The Philistine*, *The Bibelot*, *The Lark*, *The What-not*, etc. (accidental order of precedence), *THE QUARTIER LATIN* offers a warm greeting, and she hopes (we know she does) that the fact that she was born away off in Paris will not cause them to entertain towards herself any distant feeling. Why should it? We cannot all be fortunate enough to be born in Kansas City.
>
> The *Quartier Latin* 1:1 (July 1896)

Gelett Burgess, the most iconoclastic bibelot editor of the late 1890s, had only middling success as a middlebrow humorist in the first few decades of the twentieth century, and he has now been forgotten by all but a few chroniclers of bohemianism and eccentricity in San Francisco.[1] When mentioning him to friends and colleagues over the last few years, I have found that some recall reading or seeing copies, when they were kids, of *The Goops*, his humorous series of illustrated children's etiquette books. First published in 1900, the volumes featured formless, rounded creatures with long arms, "the goops," known for cheating at marbles, picking their noses, and scribbling on fences and walls.

> The Goops they lick their fingers,
> And the Goops they lick their knives;
> They spill their broth on the tablecloth—
> Oh, they lead disgusting lives!
> The Goops they talk while eating,
> And loud and fast they chew;

And that is why I'm glad that I
Am not a Goop—are you?[2]

Along the same lines, I have met an occasional eccentric, and in particular one or two with connections to Williams College, who have known something about "the purple cow," the nonsense quatrain that the *New York Times* used as the headline and lead for his obituary in 1951. Williams adopted the oddly colored cow as its mascot in 1907, presumably because students there would just as soon *be* as *see* one. Most everyone I have talked to has been surprised to learn that Burgess coined the word "blurb" as an advertising slogan for his book from the same year, *Are You a Bromide?*, a volume propounding a "sulphitic theory" to explain the pathologies of bores and businessmen. And no one seemed to know that Burgess published one of the very first appreciations of European Modernist painting, "The Wild Men of Paris," in the *Architectural Record* in 1910. As one might expect, Burgess took on Matisse and Picasso from the point of view of a humorist: "I realized for the first time that my views on art needed a radical reconstruction. . . . And ever since, I have been mentally standing on my head in the endeavor to get a new point of view on beauty so as to understand and appreciate this new movement in art."[3] While not taking the new movement altogether seriously, he was, at least, on the scene well before the famed Armory Show of 1913.

Even though most people don't know Burgess today, he was, for a brief stint in the late 1890s, at the absolute forefront of the spread of Modern art in America. He was the country's most significant figure in the craze for ephemeral bibelots, and the buzz about his work would not have been dissimilar from what he had to say of the French Modernists. It was a source of bewilderment. He was the editor and main creative talent behind the *Lark*, *Le Petit Journal des Refusées*, *Phyllida: or, the Milkmaid*, and *L'Enfant Terrible*—all of these, and especially the first two, being at the very center of the tightly networked coterie of the aesthetic public sphere. That Burgess has been so completely disentangled from the history of American avant-gardism leads me to want to argue that one of the most interesting things about him is his inconsequentiality. He is, at the very least, the most inconsequential major artist of America's fin de siècle. In this chapter, I want to consider what it might mean to recuperate him as the country's first, albeit largely forgotten, self-identified Modern artist.

As we will see, the eclecticism of Burgess's work in the bibelots antici-

The *Lark*, no. 18, October 1896, showing the primary editor, Gelett Burgess, at work amid the detritus of other ephemeral bibelots, including the *Philistine*, the *Echo*, the *Chap-Book*, *Le Petit Journal des Refusées*, and the *Bibelot*

pates to a surprisingly large extent many of the different strands of early twentieth-century Modernism, including nonconceptual abstraction, automatic writing, Dada, and Surrealism. And yet the trace of his connection to the history of the period's innovation has grown so faint as to have almost entirely disappeared. So on the one hand, Burgess's story gives us a way to catch the evanescent traces of early American Modernism in the bibelot vogue during its brief éclat, while on the other, it also says something about the structure of the bibelot movement, as a movement, that made it prone to historical evanescence. The particularities of Burgess's life can be used to tie the American bibelot fad to the countercultural artistic trends of the Parisian cabarets, to which critics have long turned to stage the early development of the Modernist movement. But his work in the bibelots also signals the particularity of the aesthetic élan developed therein—what I have been referring to as their relational aesthetics—that made it subject to being forgotten. One sees in Burgess's work the shift of attention away from the work of art and toward the scene of its reception, classically understood as the shift in Modern art to a reflexive mode of questioning the category of art as such, and finding its apotheosis in the anti-art impulses of Duchamp's ready-mades and Dadaist provocations more generally. And yet, as with Dada, because Burgess's art was so dependent on a public capable of taking in the trace relations of his allusions, and being jazzed by them, it was structurally prone to falling out of sequence with the march of literary and artistic history. It is nearly impossible to maintain the level of attention needed to be able to catch the connections.

The model for my thinking about Burgess comes from the fact that it is now something of a commonplace to acknowledge that Dada grew out of the spirit of Montmartre of the 1880s and 1890s. Dennis Cate and Daniel Grojnowski, for instance, have pointed to work like Alphonse Allais's *Album Primo-Avrilesque*, with its humorously subtitled monochromes, and Eugène Bataille's illustration of "Mona Lisa with a Pipe" (1887) as clear precursors to Duchamp's own work, most obviously in the latter case with *L.H.O.O.Q* (1919).[4] We know that Duchamp caught the aggravated strain of absurdist art originating in Paris; what I want to draw attention to is the related development of this line in the United States, and, especially, to why it has stayed so spectacularly submerged in accounts of the period.

The thing about Burgess's inconsequence, today, is that it seems ridiculously obvious: his work depended so heavily on the sets of relations established in the allusive play of artwork as it passed between bibelots, often in the shape of nonsense and parody, that losing the thread was an absolute given. The up-to-datedness of the work came from the sense it gave that the thread had *already* been lost—and, perhaps, had *always* been lost.

Mary Shaw makes a significant point about the history of aesthetic inconsequence of this kind when she insists on the particularity of thinking of the material generated during that originating, Montmartrean moment as a group phenomenon. Shaw argues that within the group, artistic elements functioned not only to signify breaks with literary and artistic traditions but also to form links "for initiated readers with a network of other contemporary, subversive, avant-garde texts." As she points out, "when this work is rediscovered . . . it is less because our attention is captured by the particular merits of a certain writer's work than because of the work's manifestation of a given writer's inextricable involvement with the general spirit of these avant-garde groups."[5] Regardless of the content of the work, the very fact that its uptake depends on this group-phenomenon aspect of the bibelots makes thinking about it very different from thinking about the kind of thing more familiar to mass media, say a novel in serial, because the mode of transmission in the bibelots entails quite a different circulatory dynamic.

When thinking about the mass public of magazine or newspaper readers, we tend to imagine a loose relation among strangers who need share relatively little in common beyond whatever it is they are reading or watching together at the time. A blockbuster novel or movie is enough to bring such a public together, and the sense of being a public on such an occasion actually depends on limiting the extent to which one needs to establish any kind of sociability with others in the group. Imagining yourself part of a community on the basis of magazine reading necessarily means overlooking all the differences between you and everyone else in the group, differences that could conceivably include everything except the magazine, book, movie, or radio broadcast in common. In contrast, the coterie public I am describing depended on a structural arrangement with a heightened reflexive sense of being part of the group capable of catching the in-jokes, and also of a feeling of timeliness, as if the jokes were going to get past them if they did not keep leaping ahead. In its reflexive self-designation, the coterie public resembles what Michael Warner calls a "counterpublic"; and in its sense of being timely but also prone to unraveling, the coterie public is what Gary Fine describes as being, in the technical sense, a "wispy community."[6] The public cultivated by the bibelots carried an aesthetic charge, a frisson or tinge of recognition, in which the point of focus shifted from works of art to the network of relations swirling around them. Value was placed on references and allusions so many times removed as to be imperceptible to the uninitiated, and the excitement came from recognizing oneself to be among the cognoscenti. Indeed, the relational dynamics might explain why the movement was said to have felt upbeat and light but not substantive, faddish and fashionable but not real; and it might also suggest why the bibelot craze seemed to have a lot of geographical range, it being easy to spread a rumor, but also to have very little consequentiality over time, there being relatively little taken to be of actual substance to preserve.

The Flight from Reality

Links in the coterie public of the bibelot fad constitute movement, the circulation over space and time of individuals, ideas, books, images, and a general sensation of the artistic life. However, the links to the ephemeral bibelots have been curiously disentwined from those we have to our literary and artistic present. What Burgess's story shows is how a movement, no matter how rapid and far-flung, from cabarets of Montmartre to Russia Hill among the bohemians in San Francisco, can build up into a little storm and then be forgotten. In later years, Burgess never put too much weight on the *Lark* or any of his other writings, never risked upsetting what Johanna Drucker aptly described as the "deft soufflé" of his "winks and plays at the expense of the posturing Bohemians."[7] And yet, if only he had given himself a bit more credit, if he had continued on in the way of the *Lark* and his outrageous, one-issue bibelot, *Le Petit Journal des Refusées*—if he had generated the links that others have made to material very much like his from the 1910s and 1920s—then he could well have been something like a Marcel Duchamp . . . or a Mina Loy, or a Gertrude Stein. Here was material generating breathlessness and movement all around, and then it was gone.

In the draft of his autobiography, Burgess muses that psychologists would probably call the pattern of his mental action a "flight from reality."[8] He grew up in a middle-class family in Boston, where his father was the proprietor of a small painting company that employed thirty men. The fourth of five children, he was not close to his older brothers but shared an elaborate imaginative life with his two sisters, to whom he dedicated what he thought of as the best of all his books, his 1902 collection of essays *The Romance of the Commonplace*. It was with his sisters, he wrote in the dedication of that work, that his "philosophy had been proven."[9] His mother was rigorously strict, and he felt that his move to California signaled his liberation from her restrictive mode of thought. "I was the first generation of my family, that is the eighth generation, to effect a complete break with puritanical thought and contact."[10] He was not Harvard educated, nor was he independently wealthy, which already distinguished him from a large portion of the American literary establishment. A graduate of the Massachusetts Institute of Technology in 1887, he began writing and publishing after working for several years as a draftsman for the Southern Pacific Railroad and a drawing instructor at the University of California, Berkeley.

When he started the *Lark*, he was twenty-nine years old, and the key idea for our story is that his biography confirms the Francophilia one would expect of an American bibelotist. In particular, he had spent time in Paris in the spring of 1891. While there, he had a romance with an older woman, the amorous details of which are recorded in the unpublished diary in which he describes a flirtation that sounds very much like the one he developed in stories for the *Lark* featuring a carefree young woman named Vivette. Both of them read, today, like original types of the manic pixie dream girl, free-spirited, vibrant, unconventional, hopelessly attractive, and forever unattached. What is of interest is the fact that Burgess learned, then, about bohemian Montmartre. As we discover from the notes for his unpublished autobiography, the *Lark* had been modeled not only on the *Chap-Book* and the *Yellow Book* but also on *La Revue Blanche*. The other Anglo-American magazines were "all morbid or decadent," he wrote, but ours was "Renaissance," which is to say, without saying it, that it was like *Le Chat Noir*, which also considered itself in these terms.[11] The cabaret was dedicated to the Middle Ages and to Louis XIII, and its journal delighted much more in the frolics of Montmartre than the Decadence of the Left Bank. Burgess wrote in the autobiography that the *Lark* would play with "French Forms and Tours de Force," including "Triolet, Rondeau, Ballade, Sonnet, Vilanelle, Rondeau Redouble, Pantoum, Virelai, Sestina, Chant-Royal, [and] Glose." Moreover, it was also to feature "form and type from France," taking up the look and feel of a French *revue éphèmere*.

What might Burgess have gotten from France? To start, perhaps the term itself, "ephemeral bibelots." One of the first to use it was Stuart Merrill, an almost entirely forgotten American Symbolist poet who happened, ironically, to have been a wayward acolyte of William Dean Howells, America's foremost Realist and a regular whipping boy of the bibelotists.[12] There is no record of Burgess and Merrill meeting, but their artistic paths are deeply intertwined. Merrill had been under Howells's wing as a young man but left the United States in 1891—the same year Burgess first went to Paris—to become part of Mallarmé's circle in Paris. He had already published two important volumes of poetry in France, and he edited the first English-language anthology of French Symbolist authors, now almost entirely forgotten, *Pastels in Prose* (1890), for which Howells wrote a surprisingly warm and appreciative introduction. Merrill used the term "éphémère revue"—and not merely a *revue éphémère*, with the adjective following the noun, as one would normally expect grammatically in French—in an appreciation of Oscar Wilde published in the French literary review *La Plume* in 1893.[13] He was referring to Dante Gabriel Rossetti's little magazine, the *Germ*, a small journal of the Pre-Raphaelite Brotherhood published at the beginning of 1850, his point being to say that Wilde, who Merrill understood to be the head and founder of the "Esthètes" in England, had matriculated in the Pre-Raphaelite school when he was a student at Magdalen College.

Everything about Merrill's 1893 use of the term "éphémère revue" links into the small world developing around Burgess and the bibelots in the next few years. Like many of the bibelots, the *Germ* was designed in the Arts and Crafts publishing tradition, beautifully constructed with heavy paper stock, deckled edges, and specialized typography. It only lasted for four numbers in 1850, but it was reprinted in the 1890s by Thomas Mosher, a Maine fine arts publisher who kept many of the British aesthetes in print in a little magazine he had founded in 1895, which was titled, most fittingly, the *Bibelot*.[14] That the *Germ* comes up in an article on Wilde not only helps situate the counter-Realist aesthetic impulses of the movement but also initiates what will quickly become a spiraling web of allusion to the queerness of the bibelot movement. Merrill goes on to draw in Poe, the actress Sarah Bernhardt, and the suggestion that she would be the one to bring Wilde's adaptation of *Salomé* to life, just the person to "ressusciter pour notre joie et notre terreur la sanguinaire princesse qui baisa sur les lèvres le chef décaptité du Baptiste!"[15] That the article was published in a French journal by an American poet about a British playwright sets the international coordinates that would come to distinguish the bibelots from the pronounced localism of many of America's more ardent Realists. Contrast Merrill and Burgess, for example, to Hamlin Garland, who was at the same point in time making the countervailing claim that what American literature needed was to become more native.[16]

Much of the humor that Burgess is known for in the bibelots seems to have been catalyzed by countercultural currents that trace back to France and the antecedents of *Le Chat Noir*. There was a tradition of scandalous little magazines there that Burgess seems to replicate in the United States in the 1890s. For example, there was the frequently censored four-sheet, weekly journal *La Lune* (1865–1867), which featured political and social caricatures by André Gill. Upon being shuttered in 1867, *La Lune* metamorphosed into *L'Eclipse* (1868–1876), still featuring Gill, and then again, after another round of censoring, into *La Lune Rousse* (1876–1879) and *La Petite Lune* (1878–1879). It might be noted, appropriately given the type of punning going with these titles, that Gill, at the center of all of these endeavors, had also started a little journal called *Parodie* (1868–1869). Among the various ways that Gill's sequence of journals connects to *Le Chat Noir*, one is by way of his association with that cabaret's Montmartre neighbor, Le Lapin Agile, which got its name in 1875, when Gill painted a sign for it that featured a rabbit jumping out of a saucepan. Local residents began to refer to the iconoclastic sign as Gill's rabbit, "le lapin à Gill." Le Chat Noir opened its doors six years later, in 1881, and in so doing made numerous points of reference to Le Lapin Agile. Dennis Cate remarks that when the journal *Le Chat Noir* first appeared, edited from 1882 to 1884 by Emile Goudeau (this fact becomes important in just a moment), it signaled its arrival with an image subtitled "Ne bougeons plus!," which he reads as a direct reference to Gill's nimble rabbit, an image working, as does all parody, both as a sign of historical difference and continuity.[17] And it may be no mere coincidence that for its own signage, Le Chat Noir perched its black cat in the crescent of "*la lune*." At any rate, Le Chat Noir quickly became a rival to its neighbor, and one begins to see the passing of the avant-garde from Le Lapin Agile to Le Chat Noir, and from Gill to Goudeau and the new cabaret's founder Rodolphe Salis.

Another line of antecedents might be imagined stretching back to 1878, when a group of bohemian artists headed by Goudeau established a literary society known as the Hydropathes; they, too, had an *éphémère revue* of the same name, *L'Hydropathe* (1879–1880). Different explanations of the name have been proffered, but, in keeping with the punning style, it would seem to be a play on Goudeau's name, "*goût d'eau*," and perhaps the salon where they first met, the *hôtel Boileau*.[18] Water made them suffer. The journal was very much a seminal instance of the type, featuring, again, the same style of oppositional caricature and ambiguous punning, "defiant laughter" in Julian Brigstocke's formulation, which Gill had established with *La Lune*.[19] Within a few years, the Hydropathes numbered in the hundreds, and the story goes that when he decided to open Le Chat Noir, the cabaret's founder, Salis, convinced them to move their operations from the Left Bank to his new location in Montmartre.

When their activity shifts to the new cabaret, the *quartier* as a whole is refashioned as a kind of country unto itself, a "Chatnoireville," the center of the modern world out of which bohemian explorers would be sent to report on what they find down the hill in foreign lands, like Paris. The humorous frolics of such excursions, like the brand of humor seen in *La Lune*, continued to depend upon an extreme form of parody, which came to be known as *fumisme*—a style that Georges Fragerolle described at the time as having the goal of "cutting open the smug sky under which we live."[20] Daniel Grojnowski has argued that *fumisme* bequeathed to Modernism its "sneer and renunciation of the ideal": "The *fumiste* avoids discussions of ideas, he does not set up a specific target, he adopts a posture of withdrawal that makes all distinctions hazy, and he internalizes Universal Stupidity by postulating the illusory nature of values and of the Beautiful, whence his denial of the established order and of official hierarchies."[21]

There are no direct lines connecting Burgess to *fumisme*. He did not, for instance, write about Goudeau in any of the manuscript materials I have been able to locate. And yet knowing this history helps clarify the trajectory of his adventures in little magazine editing in the second half of the 1890s, as we can see most clearly in the run of the *Lark* and in the single number of *Le Petit Journal des Refusées* published in 1896.[22] What also helps are the few clues we can glean about Burgess's awareness of his coconspirators in the bibelot movement from his notebooks. In them, one can further trace the connections to Montmartre, and the aesthetic and artistic trends of the emergent Parisian avant-garde. By the time the eleventh number of the *Lark* came out, he knew of at least fourteen other bibelots being published in the United States. Burgess lists them as "brownie books," and they include the *Chap-Book*, *Chips*, the *Philistine*, the *Bibelot*, the *Black Cat*, the *Bachelor of Arts*, the *Lotus*, the *Bauble*, *M'lle New York*, the *Echo*, the *Fly Leaf*, *Miss Blue Stocking*, *Paragraphs*, and *Kodak*. He was exceptionally pleased to have been reviewed in 1896 by the German little magazine *Pan*, where the *Lark* was singled out alongside the *Chap-Book* as being representative of a new movement in American magazine publishing. And he had concluded that the way to literary fame was through brevity. He pegged the magic number at 350 words and worked to limit all of his articles to that length. Interestingly, the editor of the Russian "skinny magazine" *Oskolki*, which translates as *Fragments*, in which Anton Chekhov had published much of his very early fiction, had come to the very same conclusion. I will have more to say about what these international connections represent in the next chapter, but the point to take for now is that Burgess had a fairly sophisticated sense of what was happening around him aesthetically. These are the coordinates for the brief flight of the *Lark*, *Le Petit Journal des Refusées*, and Burgess's other work with the little magazines.

Three Unwritten Modernist Manifestos

Burgess never wrote a Modernist manifesto, feeling, perhaps, that it would have ruined the quick feint and lunge of the *Lark*, the light touch of artistic inconsequence of *Le Petit Journal des Refusées*. But, if so inclined, we could do so from hindsight with relative ease. Here are three possibilities: Primitivism, nonsense, and Dada.

The first number of the *Lark*, May 1895, is invested in situating children's drawings as the genuine expression of Modern art—a "Primitivism" of the fin-de-siècle variety. (For links to the full run of the *Lark*, readers are directed to https://sites.rutgers.edu/bibelots.) In "Some Phases of Primitive Art," Burgess pairs a discussion of "the ideal of art [being] the perfect expression of a thought" with reproductions of children's drawings: a tiny man in a top hat leading a gigantic horse; a farmer and his rectangular dog wandering toward a horizon punctuated by a setting sun and a cow as big as the trees. These were, Burgess wrote, the line drawings of "child-thought" at age six, "the untrammeled expression of a stage at which the mind and fingers are equally developed." The *Lark* seems to dare readers to take it seriously, with Burgess explaining, with an earnestness that belies the subject, that the children's pictures "do not scale with the observer": "the child strikes hard at the central idea, unhindered by tradition of rendering." These images, in turn, set the tone for many of Burgess's own verses and illustrations in the *Lark*, most of which are childlike and cartoonish. Most famously, this includes his quatrain on "The Purple Cow," in the first number, but short, nonsensical lines of verse accompanied by comic drawings are a regular feature of every issue, for instance "The Invisible Bridge": "I'd never dare to walk across / A Bridge I could not see, / For much afraid of falling off, / that I should be." His original "goop" drawings, which in the 1900s were used in a series of books on manners and morals for children, also made their first appearance in the *Lark*.

The idea of children's drawings and verse as a kind of "Primitive art" was hardly original to Burgess and the *Lark*. As Jonathan Fineberg has pointed out, the notion found broad cultural footing starting in the late eighteenth century with the Romantics.[23] By Burgess's time, Baudelaire had developed the idea in "The Painter of Modern Life," where a discussion of Poe leads him to compare the man of genius to the child, whose "sensibility is almost [his] entire being": "The child sees everything in a state of newness; he is always *drunk*. Nothing more resembles what we call inspiration than the delight with which a child absorbs form and color."[24] In *The Elements of Drawing*, Ruskin had similarly argued that the "whole technical power of painting depends on our recovery of what may be called the *innocence of the eye* . . . a sort of childish perception of these flat stains of colour, merely as such, without consciousness of what they signify,—as a blind man would see them if suddenly gifted by sight."[25]

For many during the fin de siècle, childhood was given as the definitive answer to the malaise of overcivilization and gangrenous decay of Western Europe. At precisely the same time that Burgess's article opens the flight of the *Lark*, the link between children's artistic development and the primitive was being made in books by Alfred Lichtwark and Carl Götz in Germany, as well as in England in James Sully's *Studies of Childhood*. Even more famous representative examples are to be found in Darwin's evolutionary theories, Nietzsche's affirmation of Dionysus, Gauguin's artistic self-exile to Tahiti, and Freud's excavation of the unconscious. The Modernist apotheosis of the idea arrived in America with Alfred Stieglitz, who organized a series of children's art exhibitions at his "291" gallery in New York between 1912 and 1916.

My point about Burgess is not that he was entirely original. Rather, he was plugged in and on the mark; and it seems worth saying that he not only anticipated Stieglitz by two decades, but also Wassily Kandinsky and Franz Marc's much more famous but not entirely dissimilar reproduction of children's drawings in *Der Blaue Reiter Almanach* in 1911. Proof that Burgess had coordinates like these in mind can be found in the first number of the *Lark*, which pushes toward this more radical interpretation by linking the children's pictures of oversized cows to the Italian Primitives. As a supplement to the first number, Burgess reproduces a photograph described in the caption as being of "Pico Della Mirandola" the Italian Renaissance philosopher, by "an unknown Tuscan master," the relevance of which for us comes from recognizing the significance of such painters to the development of the idea of Primitivism. Edith Wharton, for instance, describes the craze for Italian Primitives most poignantly in her novella from *Old New York*, "False Dawn." In this story, the son of an overly successful American businessman is sent to Europe in the 1840s to collect old masters but befriends John Ruskin and collects the Primitives instead, the value of which are only appreciated decades later, in the early 1900s. A bit like the character in Wharton's novella, although much poorer, Burgess had likely picked up the reproduction of "Pico Della Mirandola" during his travels in Europe a few years earlier. It came from a small, commercially produced albumen photograph, and we

Gelett Burgess, "The Goop (*Verse and Cartoon*)," the *Lark,* no. 22, February 1897

now can ascertain that the "unknown Tuscan master" was in fact Botticelli.[26] Burgess was intrigued enough by the Italian Primitives to make the link between them and the modern phases of the primitive to be found in children's art, a precocious move that situates Burgess very much on the cutting edge for 1895.

A second manifesto might have been for nonsense—or, perhaps we should say *fumisme* given the preceding discussion of the influence of Montmartre. Burgess's quatrains, like "The Purple Cow," are fine examples of nonsense in the style we know from Edward Lear, Lewis Carroll, and Frank Baum. But so, too, were the Goops, at least before Burgess transformed them for his etiquette series for children. They make their first recurring appearance in the early numbers of the *Lark* and come to be described in April 1897 as "a failure of the skeleton to ossify," or "the projection upon a warped surface of a semi-solid, whose periphery is a curve-in space 2y = a (3byx + 7)." In order to draw one, "[t]he artist must first know the anatomy of the human figure to the minutest detail. The Goop is the result of carefully excluding every effect of this knowledge."

The point is that Burgess's impulse with the Goops parallels that described by Susan Stewart, who has argued that the intertextual inversions and language play of the period's nonsense ran counter to the logic of the dominant discourse of Realism.[27] As opposed to the burden of history carried by Realism, nonsense like that Burgess offers in the *Lark* offers the lightness of inconsequence; to Realism's standardization of time, nonsense gives dreamlike flights of fancy; to Realism's ideological commitment to commonsense reasoning, nonsense commits to reversals, inversions, and rearrangements, to play with boundaries and simultaneity.

In 1901, the Frederick A. Stokes Company collected material from the *Lark* and other sources for a magnificently illustrated anthology, *The Burgess Nonsense Book* (1901), which Burgess dedicated "To her who in the hammock lies/And, bored with Ibsen, Burgess tries."[28] The Goops appear frequently in that volume, most notably in a frontispiece where he identifies the goop as "the muse of nonsense": "Her Figures have nor Rule nor Joint/And so it's Hard to See the Point." The next year, Carolyn Wells, one of the few women to have been published in the *Lark*, edited *A Nonsense Anthology*, which not only includes Burgess but is dedicated to him as above all "a nonsense lover."[29] In his unpublished autobiography, Burgess described the *Lark* as being the "Crystallization of a plicy [*sic*] Purpose. The rejuvenation of nonsense and optimism."[30]

All of this would lead us to want to situate Burgess at the forefront of nonsense writing in late nineteenth-century America, but not only did he not make the kind of claims for himself along these lines that he might have, he even appears to have been quite ambivalent about his success in that vein. By 1900, he was thinking of the Goops as hackwork, a way to keep from having to move back home with his mother in Boston, for lack of funds, which he had done briefly after his European tour at the end of 1899. In a letter to Claude Fayette Bragdon dated August 1, 1900, he complains about having to accept a commission from the *San Francisco Examiner* for a Goop comic every Sunday: "The Goop page will probably appear next Sunday, and the verse is rotten, the colour worse. I don't give a dammmmmmmm. I am trying to do more freak work, though I loathe it, and hate to go back to nonsense. But I am pulling down the &&&&&$$ I got $110 the first payday, so that consoles me."[31] He goes on, of course, to milk the Goops for all they are worth, but the career he makes with them comes to seem increasingly pathetic. There is a random letter in his archives at the Bancroft Library from Random House in 1951, when Burgess is in ill health, expressing their reluctance to publish yet another volume of new Goops. While bold and bewildering in 1897, the Goops and Burgess's writing more generally become middlebrow shortly after 1900, and thus it is only as a humorist and a children's author that he is remembered. It could have been otherwise.

Finally, that brings us to *Le Petit Journal des Refusées*, which would seem to carry us beyond the shores of nonsense and *fumisterie* to its most obvious twentieth-century counterpart, Dadaism. The *PJR* was almost certainly the most eccentric of the American little magazines, only sixteen pages in length and with only one issue ever published, in the summer of 1896. Printed on old wallpaper, not a single edition was exactly the same, with extant copies collected in research libraries across the country varying widely in color from mostly black and white with decorative perforations at Princeton to brilliant gold at Rice, various greens with flowers at the Huntington, and even a startling purple at Harvard (see plates 2 and 3). It was cut in an odd, trapezoidal shape, which Drucker has wittily described as being designed to make it stand out in any library, tipping forward off the shelf on its angled pages. Its shape "destabilizes the object," as she writes, setting it apart from "the upright stance of better-behaved publications," which knew how to stand straight on shelves.[32] When opened up, it looks rather like a butterfly, which is fitting, metaphorically, since *Le Petit Journal des Refusées* was nothing if not a social butterfly. It was a nonsensical romp of inside jokes shared with other exemplars of the so-called freak magazines, "the *reductio ad absurdum* of the 'freak' journal" as Burgess later put it.[33]

Drucker suggests that *Le Petit Journal des Refusées* is amusingly, deftly, even uniquely an exemplar of what we might call the "middlebrow modern"—that vast terrain of fine art that was neither fully avant-garde in its critique of the mind-numbing dross of the culture industry, nor ideologically recoupable as a resistant or subversive mode of mass culture. And for her, that is its main provocation to critical studies of Modernism, which have had no place for this middle ground. The *PJR*—with its stimulating touches of proto-Cubist and proto-Dadaist visuals, absurdist doggerel, and unrelenting parody of the social and aesthetic milieu in which it circulated—is certainly modern. But the paradox Drucker points to is that it cannot be slotted into the "critically acceptable traditions" of Modernism because it has "not a single impulse to 'subvert,' 'resist,' 'overturn,' or 'intervene' in the culture of which it is a part."[34] Rather, its modernity registers in terms of the way that its artistry is produced from the scene of its reception. Its innovative combination of image and text on the page was not original but intricately "networked, with publicity machines and transatlantic culture industries of literary, lifestyle, and artistic publication working at full tilt and in active exchange with each other."[35]

And yet, the more we are able to catch *Le Petit Journal des Refusées'* allusions and jests and link it to the buzzing of the bibelot network internationally, the harder it is to keep Burgess's soufflé in the oven. The relentless cross-referencing of other bibelots, both in words and in its circulation of iconographic imagery, could have made *Le Petit Journal des Refusées*, in hands more ambitious than those of Burgess, less an exemplar of the vast terrain of the middlebrow than of the first aesthetic salvo of the Modernist movement. How many degrees of separation are there, after all, between the *PJR* and, say, Marcel Duchamp's rather more famously staged refusal of the *Fountain* in 1917? As already noted, connections have been made between Duchamp's famous parody of Mona Lisa with a moustache and the fact that Bataille, a regular figure in the French *éphémères revues*, had published a copy of his own parody of Mona Lisa smoking a pipe in 1887. Whether or not Duchamp had the Bataille in mind is not clear, but it is very likely that he had known many of the French bibelots associated with the cabarets in the 1880s. And when Duchamp went to stage the refusal of the *Fountain*, he chose to do so by publishing Alfred Stieglitz's photograph of the urinal in his own little magazine, the *Blind Man*, alongside a punning article by Louise Norton and poem, "For Richard Mutt," by the American painter Charles Demuth. The original urinal gained notoriety in a little magazine, not a museum. It was a networked ploy that made more sense in a bibelot than anywhere else.

By my count, that puts Duchamp and Burgess at no more than two degrees of separation because we know, from evidence in *Le Petit Journal des Refusées*, that Burgess was parodying *Le Chat Noir*. The screaming black cat motif that borders "The Ghost of the Flea," itself a parody of William Blake, with its phallic tail and bulbous eyes, appeared frequently in the journal *Le Chat Noir*—and it's the very one on the cover of *Vogue* (see the prologue). It seems entirely appropriate to describe the art of *Le Petit Journal des Refusées* in terms of Goudeau's *fumisme*, and, if we do, then its significance may come not from anything in particular in its pages but for the way in which it remodeled the aesthetic public sphere in America, *fumiste* parody depending upon networks of like-minded aesthetes who could detect and

Gelett Burgess, "The Purple Cow," published in the first number of the *Lark* in May 1895

redirect the obscure references. It is for this reason that the networks of which Drucker writes are particularly important, because what Modernism does is shift our attention from the work of art to the networks of its reception. It seems perfectly fair to say that the ephemeral bibelots began to establish the circuitry initiating that shift.

And anecdotally, I'm not alone in making this assertion. In 1914, the *New York Times* reported on a charity fundraiser at the Biltmore ballroom, "The Cubist Ball," where colored lights turned dancers "Post Impressionist" and "Futurist," and where the room was decorated like "a Cubist landscape with such realistic details as a purple cow."[36] And then in 1936, *Vogue* published a tongue-in-cheek article on Surrealism that makes a visual pun on Burgess's purple cow in order to describe the delirious art of Salvador Dali, whose full-page portrait appears on the facing page.[37] Curiously, then, Burgess was on the scene of the Modernist revolution as it took shape in Paris; he was at the forefront of elaborating upon it to a coterie public of bohemian avant-gardists in America in the mid-1890s who were ecstatic about his work in the bibelots; and he was still entirely aware of what was happening on the Modern art scene when he introduced "The Wild Men of Paris" to American audiences in 1910. But somewhere along the line, his own writing and illus-

Artist Salvadore Dali, looking to one side, holding fencing equipment. Cecil Beaton, *Vogue* © Condé Nast

SURrealism

or the purple

by M. F. Agha

"Oh, the same people who think that Einstein would never have achieved such a tremendous popularity if the editor of the *New York Times* had not been an amateur mathematician. You do not have to pay any attention to such disparaging remarks. They overestimate the imaginative powers of the press. Even the most sensational newspaper could not have invented Dali."

"But newspapers write about Surrealism all the time. Why?"

"Because, beside being a movement of a considerable cultural importance (please do not laugh—I really mean it), Surrealism has a great news value. You know the old formula: 'Man Bites Dog'—only in this case the Dog has paranoia, and the Man is really a couple of other guys. Or, as Surrealists put it, a Double Image; that is, a 'Representation of an Object, which, without the slightest change in its appearance or anatomy, is at the same time a Representation of Another Object, totally different.' Thus, according to the Surrealists, 'an image of a Woman can be, at the same time, an image of a Horse.'"

Photo and illustration accompanying M. F. Agha, "Surrealism, or the Purple Cow," November 1, 1936. *Vogue* © Condé Nast

tration fell to the wayside, leaving him with the paltry reputation that he himself seems to have thought his work from that earlier period deserved.

Disentangling Vivette

A manifesto might have helped Burgess's reputation. He could also have used some friends who understood the work he was doing. Instead, his most influential collaborator was Frank Norris, who was also his loudest critic. They were both San Francisco writers, running in the same literary circle, and appearing to have had no personal animosity toward one another. And yet, Norris excoriated the bibelots in general and his friend Burgess in particular. In the *Wave*, he published a screed that took the ephemeral bibelots and him directly to task.

> Yes, there are Les Jeunes [the punning name had been adopted by the *Lark*'s editors after an early review in the *New York Times* had called them "les Jaunes," a cross between "young," which they were, and "yellow," as in the *Yellow Book*], and "The Lark" was delightful—delightful, fooling, but there's a graver note and more virile to be sounded. Les Jeunes can do better than "The Lark." Give us stories

> now, give us men, strong brutal men, with red-hot blood in 'em, with unleashed passions rampant in 'em, blood and bones and viscera in 'em, and women, too, that move and have their being, people that love and hate something better now than Vivettes and Perilles and Goops.[38]

Norris took the same disparaging tone a few years later in his sprawling Naturalist story of wheat, *The Octopus* (1901), where the ephemeral bibelots are placed in the trembling hands of Annie Derrick, a lost and terrorized cultural dilettante from the East who had become the wife of one of the novel's major industrial farmers. She and her beloved "little toy magazines, full of the flaccid banalities of the 'Minor Poets,'" are ridiculed by Presley, the would-be epic poet of the struggle between California farmers and the railroad monopoly who serves as the artistic center of the novel; he submits the bibelots as a class to "savage abuse and open ridicule [for] their neatly phrased rondeaux and sestinas and chansonettes."[39]

Norris's novel even caricatures a prominent protégé of Burgess, the Japanese poet Yone Noguchi, who published for the first time in the *Lark* and who, we now know, exerted a significant influence on Ezra Pound's development of the idea for Imagism.[40] At a cultural gathering attended by Annie Derrick, a Noguchi-like "Japanese youth, in the silk robes of the *Samurai* two-sworded nobles, read from his own works." The novel groups his lines of poetry with an eclectic mix of foreign or freak performers, "now a civilised Cherokee with a mission; now a female elocutionist, whose forte was Byron's Songs of Greece; now a high caste Chinaman; now a miniature painter; now a tenor, a pianiste, a mandolin player, a missionary, a drawing master, a virtuoso, a collector, an Armenian." Following a gendered script familiar to Naturalism, Norris dismisses them all as "the Fake, the eternal, irrepressible Sham; glib, nimble, ubiquitous, tricked out in all the paraphernalia of imposture, an endless defile of charlatans that passed interminably before the gaze of the city, marshaled by 'lady presidents,' exploited by clubs of women, by literary societies, reading circles, and culture organisations."[41] It is hardly a flattering review, but it is by no means a bad description of the American bibelots if, instead of dismissing them, one values such things.

Just as the vogue for ephemeral bibelots can be traced by Burgess's youthful enthusiasms, its end follows his abandonment of it. By the end of 1897, he had published in *Life*, *Harper's*, the *Chap-Book*, the *Black Cat*, *St. Nicholas*, the *Century*, *Little Folks*, *Munsey's*, *Truth*, and *Bookman*. By 1901, he could add to these *Queen*, the *Criterion*, the *Smart Set*, and *Ladies' Home Journal*. His first novel had come in 1897, *Vivette, or, The Memoirs of the Romance Association*; two more books featuring versions of the Vivette character would follow, *A Little Sister of Destiny* (1904) and *Lady Mechante* (1909). Within the decade, he went on to publish two collections of essays, *The Romance of the Commonplace* (1901) and *Are You a Bromide?* (1906); several volumes of Goops books on children's manners, starting with *Goops and How to Be Them* (1900); a couple of satires, *The Rubaiyat of Omar Cayenne* (1904) and *The Maxims of Methuseleah* (1907); and two popular romances, *The White Cat* (1907) and *The Heart Line* (1907). While clever and appealing, none of this work captured the imagination of serious Modernist artists in the way that his work in the ephemeral bibelots might have.

Burgess's move away from the bibelot form was also a move away from the late nineteenth-century Modernist networks of the aesthetic public sphere. The last volume of the *Lark* was published in April and the *Epi-Lark* in May of 1897, and a swell of excitement seems to be building up around Burgess's successes—not only with the *Lark* and "The Purple Cow," but also with *Le Petit Journal des Refusées* and other bibelot adventures. After a three-month editorship of the *Wave*, he moved from San Francisco to New York and then, in the summer of 1898, to London, where he lived for over a year on funds provided in large measure by his friend, the architect and designer Bragdon, while writing for the British magazines *Sketch*, *Black and White*, and most lucratively for the *Queen*, which he described as a "fashionable fashion and ladies' paper."[42]

His letters from this time to Bragdon have been preserved, and we can read of his success at penetrating the coterie of English aesthetic arts writers. "I have been to Henry Jameseseseses to tea, and met Cable, Barrie Fawcett, and I go to Henry Harland's tonight,—(ex-ed. *Yellow Book*) and Gleeson White, .ex-ed. *Studio*, tomorrow night. Have yet to see Harold Frederic and J. Ralph, and next week, I am to be taken to call on Marriot Watson, and Wells. So you see I am doing it up, while I have the chance."[43] He also writes of having dined with Edmund Gosse, who, like Stephen Crane and Harold Frederic, impressed Burgess by the complication of his domestic ménages: "He is not divorced, and has two grown-up children, but in Kenley he is with this perfectly charming, sweet, gentle woman, and has a family of three children!"[44] Perhaps most intriguingly of all, we have, from the same letter, a glimpse of Herbert Stone, who was planning to relocate to London permanently. Stone, he writes, "had cabled to stop the *Chap-Book*, he was disgusted at their war numbers, and I dn't wonder! This is of course strictly under the rose, all of it, and that he expects to start a paper here with Justin McCarty, (and perhaps me) this winter. There are many schemes afloat. If I can hold on a year, it will be fun to see what comes. 'The Butterfly' is to begin again. Did U ever see it?"

All of which is to say that Burgess hardly disappears from sight. And yet, the tenor of his work out of the bibelots is quite different than it had been in them. Maybe the best example of that comes with his first novel. The stories making up *Vivette, or, The Memoirs of the Romance Association* had been developed in the *Lark*, but a good part of their effusive strangeness is lost when transposed to book form.

Vivette is a sprightly and romantically adventurous woman, younger on the page than in real life, but characterized in both instances by the vitality of her epistolary flirtations. In the *Lark*, but not in the novel, this vitality is replicated by the odd way that the running heads change from page to page, offering commentary on the story as it unfolds in the text below. Vivette only makes her way from the headers into the stories themselves in the second volume, after an entire year of hints about her mysterious character, appearing in the running heads long before she becomes a character in the text.

Vivette's first appearance in the headers comes in answer to a macabre two-page story in the August 1895 number about a woman who perfects herself by giving away her own body parts, giving her foot to a lame old man and her arm to a boy with his in a sling, while replacing them with parts from other people whom her lover, the narrator, finds particularly attractive. We are introduced to Vivette in the running head atop the first page of the story with the ironic quip "'SHE HAD A KIND HEART,' SAID VIVETTE." On the facing page, when the woman takes the pretty eyes of a young girl and the rosy mouth with pretty milk teeth of another, the header offers an equally dark reply, "'SHE HAD A GOOD HEAD,' SAID I." The banter between the editor and Vivette is continued the next month when Burgess contributes a modern fairy tale about a princess who is tricked into falling in love with a lonely shepherd. Over the course of three pages, the running heads read: "'I DON'T LIKE IT,' SAID VIVETTE. / 'FOR IT HAS A MORAL.' / 'BUT NOT FOR US,' SAID I." A few numbers later, for December, Burgess publishes a brief story about an elevator romance—a chance encounter involving a sleeve-link caught in a gown and, a burning blush, an eternal love, and the parting of ways once the elevator door opens. The header reads, "'NOW, WHAT IS THE SHORTEST POSSIBLE TIME?' SAID VIVETTE: 'THIS LASTED JUST TWO MINUTES,' SAID I." From one issue to the next, the delightfully playful headers establish something like the framing stories of Scheherazade's tales, all the while giving hints as to whom Vivette is supposed to be. It is as if we are overhearing the development of a romance between the magazine's editor and the mysterious Vivette, but their placement in the headers alters the relation of normal reading.

If I am not mistaken, Vivette was partially modeled on Burgess's lover from his European trip back in 1891, and the headers in the *Lark* replicate something found in Burgess's diary entries from the time. Throughout the diary, there are responses scribbled in a different hand beneath Burgess's entries, presumably notes from his lover. Notebook #3 (of 71), at the Bancroft Library, for example, interweaves Burgess's light poetry with his lover's equally witty responses, as in one titled "M'lle Couche Toute Nue":

Last night you came at 2 oclock
And, glorious sight to see—
This time, you didn't have your frock
Not e'en a robe de nuit!
But you and I together there
Though I suppose
Were just as satisfied a pair
As though we had our clothes
For hugging one another so
Is something to enjoy
For I can touch you then with no
Old corsets to annoy.

[Reply in another handwriting in the margin]: I never wear them anyway.

[And then, on the back of the page]
Her reply:
I hardly like to write upon so dangerous a theme
For I have suddenly grown very good
It makes me blush and tremble to know that in a dream
I behave as proper maidens never should.
You see I've lived some longer than you have my dearest child
And I know that some results can be avoided.

Much as with the diary entries, the formatting of the magazine asks us to read multimodally, the headers whispering reactions to the tales from the top of the page. It is an airy, flirtatious experience, voyeuristic but fresh and unexpected.

The same cannot be said of the stories once put into novel form. When transferred to the novel, the romantic element shifts directly to the body of the text itself. This version starts with Vivette and the narrator as real people engaged in a manic flirtation, whereas the *Lark* strung things out by alluding to the possibility over the course of many issues. In fact, the two are married before the book version is even halfway through. The result is rather deadening, making the story depend entirely on the absurd exigencies of the complicated situations the two lovers get into as the directors of an association dedicated to fulfilling other people's fantasies. The peculiarity of bibelot form had been a major focus of attention in the Vivette story as it was divulged piece by piece in the headers of the *Lark*, whereas there is no real center of attention in the freewheeling novel. The book version tries to replicate the *Lark* by having the running heads change from page to page, but they are without the same magic.

Even Burgess seems to have recognized the problem. One of his marketing coups was to convince the *Chap-Book* to publish a negative review of *Vivette*—a review that he wrote himself. In it, he argues that the stories were "all very well while she appeared in the yellow paper of the *Lark*" but failed to work as a novel; he then followed it up with a complaint about the review in a later issue.[45] The fact is, however, that he was right the first time. The interplay of text and header is almost entirely lost when resituated in the novel, *Vivette*, and, perhaps to his credit, he seems to have recognized as much. The romance had much more spark when carried along in the headers of the ephemeral bibelot.

Within two years of the *Lark*'s end, the entire coterie public of which it had been a central part came largely undone, and with its undoing our ties to it as scholars of the art and literature of the period were also severed. *Le Chat Noir* ceased publication in 1895; the cabaret's owner, Rodolphe Salis, died in 1897; and the new owner changed its name in 1899. The *Yellow Book*, the *Chap-Book*, the *Echo*, the *Bauble*, the *Lotus*, and *M'lle New York* had all ceased publication by 1898. Aubrey Beardsley died that same year. Stuart Merrill was established in France and writing even more rarely in English. It is true that the bibelot fad catches a second wind at the start of 1900, but magazines like the *Blue Sky* (1899–1902), the *Muse* (1900–1902), and

Ye Quaint Magazine (1902–1904) never achieve the network centrality of the key magazines of the whirlwind fad's first wave.[46] Without Burgess and the half-dozen or so other leaders of the *Tendenz* there as points of reference, interweaving the strands of the group movement together, making the coterie recognizable to itself, the revolutionary little vogue for ephemeral bibelots was on its way to being forgotten.

Even though I would argue strongly in support of the notion that the ephemeral bibelots have a claim to being the origin point for the Modern art movement in the United States, there is no denying that the complicated web of allusions, upon which the aesthetic public sphere that sprang to life in the 1890s depended, was exceptionally quick to disentangle. Whereas one might be tempted to think of the bibelots in terms of experimentation and innovation, Burgess's work reminds us something about the leading edge of new artistic movements in general, namely, that their newness is not new but rather emerges from repetition through particularly tight-knit, highly recursive publics. When that public unravels, it leaves very little of consequence behind.

Today, our ties to Burgess have come almost entirely undone, and it seems unlikely that a new edition of *Vivette* would do anything to change that fact, for it is almost impossible to recover an artist at the center of a group phenomenon, even one as innovative as he, without recovering the group as a whole.

2 What Travels? What Doesn't? The International Movement of Movements

> International exchanges are subject to a certain number of structural factors which generate misunderstandings. The first factor is that texts circulate without their context.
>
> Pierre Bourdieu, "The Social Conditions of the International Circulation of Ideas"

We know that Gelett Burgess had been looking to the French little magazines for inspiration when he started the *Lark* and *Le Petit Journal des Refusées*. But what does it really mean to say that the *vogue* for ephemeral bibelots in America started with *Le Chat Noir* in Paris, or that Burgess's work was part of a *group movement* spreading not only across this country but also much of Europe, Asia, and South America when we know that almost none of the American ephemeral bibelots and very few from other countries actually circulated across international borders? What travels when the magazines don't? How do we get from a black cat in Montmartre to the one on the cover of *Vogue*—or, as we will see in a moment, to a poem in the style of Verlaine, titled "Verlainesque," in the first volume of *M'lle New York*, or a genre of parodic blurbing held in common by *Le Petit Journal des Refusées* and a little magazine publishing juvenilia from Anton Chekhov in Russia a decade earlier? From there, how do we get to the idea that there's a movement afoot? How does a vogue catch its wave? How does a movement move? And what is left of Paris, the acknowledged capital of modernity, by the time the wave makes its way to the smaller towns and villages of middle America? When a taste for a particular kind of publication spreads, what spreads with it—and is it still the same taste?

I have been arguing that a key tenet of what would come to be known as Modernism was established in the bibelots, namely, the idea that the intensive circulation of material within a tight publication network could constitute the aesthetic project as such. That, after all, is essentially Dada, and as we saw in the last chapter, it was what Burgess began doing in the *Lark* and *Le Petit Journal des Refusées*—even if he did not come up with a name for it. We can thus use the bibelot vogue to mark the historical advent of this moment at which the self-reflexivity of *l'art pour l'art* began to achieve the intensity that later comes to be called the *avant-garde*. A second way to think of this transformation would be in relation to particular locales of urban artistic revolt, and so books have been written on "the spirit of Montmarte," or of the Secessions in Munich in 1892 and Vienna in 1897, and Decadent culture in the United States grouped around particular cities, New York, Boston, Chicago, and San Francisco.[1] The internationalism of the bibelot vogue suggests a third strategy. Instead of thinking about place, we can turn to circulation; and instead of concentrating on the movement within local contexts, we can emphasize the transformative significance of the diffusion of art beyond its points of origin.

However, there would seem to be a significant problem with this third line of argument. The idea of the bibelot vogue as a group movement is in tension with what we know about the transformative appropriation and remediation of objects put into circulation beyond their points of origin. As Bourdieu put it, "texts circulate without their context," and it is thus to be expected that the bibelots did not circulate in a smooth or uninterrupted way when crossing international borders. What a black cat means on the cover of *Vogue* is inevitably different than what it means in a cabaret in Paris. And, indeed, more often than not, circulation was blocked—interrupted by differences in language, the challenges of distance, and the particularity of local circumstances. Low subscription numbers and the vagaries of the post, alone, would get in the way of any easy account of the bibelots' diffusion.

This chapter is about how barriers to the international movement of the bibelots, the structural dynamics of circulation, primed the bibelot vogue for recognition as something like an early instance of the Modernist avant-garde, even if that recognition never fully came. What I hope to show are the ways in which the blockages and gaps in circulation, the intermittences between connections, become the obstacles around which the mazelike meanderings and acrobatic traverses that we have come to associate with aesthetic innovation take shape. It is a structural argument, one in which the dynamics of circulation set the conditions for aesthetic innovation and establish the infrastructure of Modern art. But it will also give us a chance to delve into some of the more exotic examples of little magazine production, bringing an international perspective to the movement of the movement to the far corners of the United States.

Structural Holes and the Mechanism of Innovation

The American bibelots we have looked at so far confirm in large measure an observation made by Pascale Casanova that the literary world in the late nineteenth century was looking to Paris as the "capital" of "the universal republic of letters"—"a republic having neither borders nor boundaries, a universal homeland exempt from all professions of patriotism, . . . a transnational realm whose sole imperatives are those of art and literature."[2] Interestingly, however, at least one avant-garde German magazine was looking elsewhere. *Pan*, a renegade little magazine later known for having helped the spread of Art Nouveau throughout Europe, was looking instead to the United States.

Franz von Stuck, Cover of *Pan*, April-May 1895. Stuck had been the cofounder of the Munich Secession in 1892

In most respects, *Pan* was much like Casanova might have predicted, whimsically adorned in the spirit of Montmartre. And yet, it had picked up on the growing movement for what it winningly referred to as the "goblin literature" being published in the United States by a class of small magazines, not unlike itself, "fight[ing] a fresh and joyous fight against the *fin-de-siècle* attitude of complacent weariness":

> For about three years cheap small-sized bi-monthly magazines, in which young writers and artists endeavor to put up a new tune, have been published in the larger cities of North America. To take note of this phenomenon is worth it already for the simple reason that the American variety of modernity functions as a peculiar correlate to the common definition of "new" and "young." Given their tendency, one could define these pocket magazines as "periodicals of protest"—as one of them, *The Philistine*, calls itself—because the best of them are guided by the deep wish to counteract thoughtless and vulgar sensationalism thanks to criticism and autonomous artistic contributions.[3]

Pan's recognition in Germany of these "pocket magazines" in the United States, published alongside reproductions of pages from the *Chap-Book* and the *Lark*, is a pleasant surprise, but it seems worth redirecting its point of emphasis. The really curious thing is that small fads for this new form of little magazines were popping up all over the world at this time—in England, Germany, Austria, Russia, Japan, India, South America—and most of these had the oppositional aesthetics of Parisian nightlife largely in view as an ideal of the "new" in art and life. *Pan* may have been right that the "American variety of modernity" was playing a somewhat different tune than European versions of the same; and yet, what is perhaps even more interesting is not the difference but the fact that the phenomena of these little magazines devoted to the new was "correlate" at all, emerging in many disparate locales including both cosmopolitan centers and the provinces. Even within the United States, exemplars of the journal had flared up across the country—not just in New York and San Francisco, but also in places like Wausau, Wisconsin, and Lansing, Michigan.

Casanova's argument in *The World Republic of Letters* concerns literary value and transnational canon formation; whereas what interests me here is how circulation structures the different ways we value the innovativeness of art movements. When Casanova set up her Paris-centric thesis on "the republic of letters," she expanded a sociological model of value familiar from Bourdieu in which literary reputations are established by a work's circulation in a world literary system. Her argument suggests that works achieve value when they are taken up by the "sanctioning authorities" of universal judgment—consecrated by translations, critical studies, tributes, judgments, prizes, and verdicts. When this happens, literary works are in effect transmuted into a different category of being.[4] They cross over a metaphorical border, undergoing an "almost magical metamorphosis of an ordinary material into 'gold,' into absolute literary value"; they are annexed into the autonomous literary sphere of the universal.[5] This kind of model works particularly well for describing the good fortunes of individual authors, and her readings of Kafka and Faulkner, for example, have been singled out for praise. It is, moreover, almost certainly the case that many of the American bibelotists involved in the vogue for little magazines evoked Paris for precisely the reasons suggested by Casanova. They saw it as a symbol of the autonomy of art and the restorative ethos of universality, a counterpoint to the stultifying conservatism and consumerism dominating the American publishing industry.

As critics of Casanova's work have pointed out, however, there are other kinds of world literary systems at work than those fashioning literary canonicity.[6] The canonization of individual authors, or even individual styles, is of less importance to my discussion of movements than other processes of imitation and dissemination, for which we need to pick up on a different part of Bourdieu. The bibelots never got anywhere near canonization. What they had, instead, was the prestige of innovation, to understand which we need to attend to two different kinds of processes. The first is the imitation of Parisian models or ideas about Parisian culture outside of France. The second is the formation of in-groups through circulation. The first is about the circulation of items from Paris to other parts of the world. The second is about the circulation of items marked as Parisian within a group, where their capital is traded upon in a process of collective identity formation among a separate and smaller circle—a small group of the highly innovative. In the case of the American bibelots, this second process was dominant, but it cannot take shape without the first. Those producing and consuming the bibelots recognized themselves and each other as part of the "new" because they recognized their shared circulation of materials plucked from the streets of Paris.

We can be more particular about the structural mechanism of this recognition by borrowing from the vocabulary developed in sociology to consider the effect of "structural holes" in networks.[7] The fad for little magazines was an international print-circulation phenomenon with the peculiar characteristic of being conceptually global and practically local. There was clearly some kind of international network situation developing around the bibelot craze, with a shared style and mood and sense of moment in a widespread number of geographical locations. However, it was a situation defined in large measure by the autonomous emergence of tight clusters of magazines between which circulation was blocked or occluded, each cluster cut off from the structure of the whole like galaxies of stars floating in the darkness of empty cultural space.[8]

The structure of the bibelot clusters reflected various kinds of blockages. At times, clusters could be defined geographically, taking shape in particular national and linguistic regions with seemingly very little if anything bridging the spaces between them. At other times, clusters were geographically right on top of each other, publishing not only at the same time but in the same city, while still remaining unlinked, as if separate network domains were extending alongside each other in parallel, nonintersecting planes. This was the case, as we will see in just a moment, of an American magazine published in Paris called the *Quartier Latin*. But on occasion, and these were important, bridges were thrown across the structural holes, the result being articles like the one in *Pan* that made the connections between the United States, Germany, and Paris apparent and unavoidable—and that made *Pan* recognizable for being on the cutting edge of the new art scene. As we will shortly see in more detail, *Pan*'s cover design by a cofounder of the Munich Secession in 1892, Franz von Stuck, was the perfect match for the artwork by Burgess reprinted inside, a very successful brokerage of the structural hole between bibelot clusters that showered social prestige on both bibelots.

Structural holes are important for understanding the aesthetic frisson of the bibelots, and indeed, Modernism as a whole, because artistic and intellectual innovation seems to cluster at the bridges. I borrow this hypothesis from the sociologist Ronald Burt, who has shown in empirical studies that actors who span structural holes often accrue certain advantages, arbitrage opportunities, for instance, and the development of reputations, sometimes earned, for innovation. Or as he puts it, explaining why social capital accrues to those who broker structural holes, "people who stand near the holes in a social structure are at higher risk of having good ideas."[9] It seems obvious, perhaps, but people so situated have access to a variety of opinions and behavior from outside their own groups, which tend to be homogenous, and thus have a vision of otherwise unseen options; it is the advantage in vision that becomes "the mechanism by which brokerage becomes social capital."[10] Burt has shown, for example, that in a large American electronics company, "[c]ompensation, positive performance evaluations, promotions, and good ideas are disproportionately in the hands of people whose networks span structural holes."[11] The same is true with the print culture of our ephemeral bibelots, where we find that good ideas are typically borrowed and repurposed, not new. The creative brokerages of structural holes within the movement produce much of the effect of noncomplacency and revolt valued by the amateurs of the modern; it is how the bibelots get their feeling of youthful revolt.

Structural holes take many shapes, but there is perhaps no greater gap in print culture than that initiated by the entwined hydra of nationalized publication systems and different languages. Nothing else is as quick to stop circulation. Even within national borders, the American bibelots had hardly any circulation at all, and there is very little evidence of their actual physical circulation across national borders, either on a subscription basis or in any other formal manner. *Pan* may have reproduced images from the *Lark*, but I have found no evidence of German libraries ever archiving it. As for French libraries, they have only very limited holdings of the American bibelots, a couple of copies of the *Lark* and the *Chap-Book* and none of the others, and it is difficult to know when they acquired them. In a recent history of the *Chap-Book*, Giles Bergel cites anecdotal evidence from a letter to the magazine's publishers to the effect that it was "impossible to get *The Chap-Book* in Paris."[12] The same holds in the other direction of the French *petites revues*. As was the case with their American counterparts, the French journals only very rarely published as many as a thousand copies. In 1900, Remy de Gourmont compiled a bibliography of 130 French *petites revues* in which he wrote, comically but in all truth, that many were so *petite* that their titles had already become enigmas.[13] And as for archiving, according to the *Union List of Serials in Libraries in the United States and Canada*, 3rd edition, published in 1965, the most important of the French magazines, *Le Chat Noir*, was held by only 4 of the 956 American libraries it catalogued (UCLA, Harvard, Yale, and the New York Public). By way of comparison, the *Clack Book* and *M'lle New York* were both held by 12 American libraries, the *Lark* by 46, the *Chap-Book* by 60, and *Harper's Monthly* by upwards of 500.[14] These were not journals that circulated along the regular channels.

If nation and language are the biggest blockages, a far more surprising one comes when we recognize the dimensional aspect of the problem. Even those magazines most poised to have an international audience appear to have carried on very much parallel, but unconnected, existences—as if disseminating along parallel, nonintersecting planes. A most interesting case of this comes with the *Quartier Latin*, a bibelot brought out in English by the American expatriate community in Paris, which was published simultaneously in Paris, London, and New York from 1896 to 1899 (see plate 4).

Despite its international points of origin, the *Quartier Latin* positioned itself from the start in relation to the American, and to a lesser extent the British, art journal movement, not in relation to the French. In the announcement of the first edition, July 1, 1896, the magazine took leave to introduce itself by way of a nod to one of the forerunning American bibelots, *M'lle New York*, presenting its readers to "Mlle. Quartier Latin, a young *débutante*, who, after the manner of most *demoiselles (Américaines)*, will have lots to say for herself, and try, in an ingenuous sort of way, to amuse you." Its editor, Trist Wood, makes it immediately clear that she is not a Montmartre girl. He explicitly draws a link between "M'lle Quartier Latin" and her "sisters," the *Chap-Book*, the *Lotus*, the *Philistine*, the *Bibelot*, and the *Lark*, offering them "a warm greeting": "[M'lle Quartier Latin] hopes that the fact that she was born away off in Paris will not cause them to entertain towards herself any distant feeling. . . . [T]hough she gets *her* dresses in Paris—and where in the world is there better material for beautiful attire, or more cunning hands to fashion it?—she has no inclination on that account to put on airs or appear vain." Like many of the ephemeral bibelots, the *Quartier Latin* made a habit of reproducing blurbs about itself published in other magazines, but its lists of these citations are impressive for lacking any notices by French journals. Instead, it includes the *Chicago Inter-Ocean*, the *Philadelphia Inquirer*, the *New Orleans Times-Democrat*, and *New Orleans Picayune*, as well as the *East Anglican Times* and the *Sheffield Independent*. In each case, the reviews evoke comparisons to other English language journals. The *Westminster Budget*, for example, is quoted in the March 1897 number: "In some dim and distant way *The Quartier Latin* reminds one of the *Yellow Book*, but for our part we greatly prefer both the art and letterpress of the former."

The only conclusion would seem to be that the circulation of American and British little magazines ran largely on a parallel plane with the French *petites revues*—two planes expanding simultaneously but not interconnecting. Despite being "compiled in Paris," and regardless of the extent to which it was embedded in the Paris art scene, the *Quartier Latin* maintains an Anglo-Saxon identity and distribution network. It sets itself up as being both within and outside the main run of French art and culture, inside to the extent that its art is just as good, outside to the extent that its American and British sense of moral decorum is not compromised, just decoratively adorned at the edges.

Surprisingly, the bibelot vogue also ran very much on parallel planes to the mainstream magazine press in the United States; that is to say, one needs also to account for structural holes between the little magazines and the establishment literary monthlies like the *Century Illustrated* and *Harper's*. We can get a feel for this situation by considering the number of times the magazines cited each other, their citational networks. As we see with the quotes cited by the *Quartier Latin*, it was in the newspapers, not the monthlies, that one finds notice of the ephemeral bibelots. Perhaps both forms shared an urgency tied to their ephemerality. By contrast, my survey of fifty of the most prominent American bibelots shows that while they cited the mainstream magazines with some regularity, such citations were entirely unidirectional and, compared to their citation of other bibelots, quite thin. The *Century Illustrated*, for instance, registered as a fairly significant node, being cited by eight different bibelots, but they each only cited it once. That makes it quite different from the *Lark*, which was cited by seven different bibelots, but it was cited twenty times. The *Philistine* was cited by eleven different bibelots, and it was cited twenty-one times. The *Chap-Book* was cited by ten different bibelots, and it was cited thirty times. And it is absolutely striking how silent the major monthlies were about the bibelot vogue. *Harper's Monthly*, the *Century Illustrated*, *Scribner's Monthly*, and the *Atlantic Monthly*, together, cited the *Chap-Book* only once, ever, in a fleeting mention in an 1897 *Harper's* article about book illustration.[15] I have found not a single other instance of the direct citation of any of the freak magazines on the pages of their mainstream brethren, which is a remarkable fact given the numbers of bibelots being published and the significance of the authors publishing in them, including most notably Henry James, Kate Chopin, and Stephen Crane.

It is difficult to conjecture on the source of a silence. Were we following Bruno Latour's ideas about the nature of network associations to the letter, were we good ANTS, as Latour's "actor network theorists" like to call themselves, we might simply ignore this blockage. Since there was no link, there could be no transformation, according to Latour, and I take to heart his suggestion to move on to a description of the links that do exist, and thus make a difference, as opposed to lingering with ones that do not.[16] But there can also be useful speculation about silences. A few things seem clear—and they help to particularize the shape of the network assembled by the ephemeral bibelots. There are, of course, all of the ethical objections the monthlies may have had about the bibelots, that they were, say, untoward, perfervid, unserious, or foreign. The typical reaction, had there been any other reaction, would likely have been the one we noted in the previous chapter of Frank Norris, who complained that the *Lark* was "delightful, fooling, but there's a graver note and more virile to be sounded."[17]

Just as interesting, though, is the fact that the major monthlies rarely cited any other magazines. It is not simply that they are not citing the bibelots. Rather, and this is key, the kind of aesthetic they practiced was one in which citation did not play the same role that it did for the bibelots. The monthlies reviewed literary and artistic works, whereas, as we shall see, the bibelots, in effect, reviewed each other, linking together a shared aesthetic public by situating works within the field of publication they and their brethren were creating and defining, as *Pan* did when noting the goblin literature in the American bibelots. Art for the monthlies would stand on its own merits and meet the test of time, whereas for the bibelots art emerged as a product of circulation within a reflexive field of citation. Moreover, the monthlies sought an institutional permanence, where significance was demarcated by subscription numbers and the authority of the editorial presences. The bibelots, by contrast, were programmatically small and ephemeral, devoted not to permanence but to the fleeting traces of the contemporary moment.

The point to retain from this review of the bibelots' noncirculation is that it establishes the structure for the characteristic aesthetic element of the bibelot vogue, the thing that makes them "new" and "young" in the eyes of many, which is their intensively self-reflexive investment in the brokerage of structural holes. You cannot see this investment as clearly without first marking out the negative space. As we will see, disassociated from, if not entirely independent of, the genteel monthlies and the emerging mass-market magazines, the ephemeral bibelots demarcated their field of circulation in order to turn circulation itself into an object of artistic play. Unlike the other publications, which always imagined their audiences in the broadest and most open terms, the bibelots moved along much more precisely defined routes, with so few links across structural holes and between parallel plains that they are recognizable as a different class of publication. They moved along exceptionally tight and improbably self-reflexive networks, making it difficult for those from the outside world to connect with them, which is to say that just because there might have been flights linking the goblin literature in America's ephemeral bibelots to the avant-garde in both Germany and Paris, it does not follow that you could catch a connection from any of those points to other destinations. Access was limited to a coterie of up-to-date insiders, and those who wanted to be.

Links and Bridges: Citational-Circulatory Modalities

What, then, does circulate? If not print matter, what contributes to the acute sense that the ephemeral bibelots, together, constituted a movement, a fad, a phenomenon, a protest, the new? How are we to understand the bibelot movement as such, when, as a movement, the bibelots did not themselves move? I am going to suggest that the best way to think about this problem is in terms of an expanded definition of citational practice.

It might be useful here to recall my earlier discussion (in the introduction) of Daniel Tiffany's description of Parisian nightlife as a clandestine underworld for sharing the experience of partiality, where obscurity becomes the medium for a social world of "monadic communities which are at once inscrutable and reflective, discontinuous and harmonious, solipsistic and expressive."[18] Clandestine space is also sociable, and for all the sense of splintering, fragmentation, disorientation, and loss that comes with entering into it, so too does the desire for connection. To the extent that the historical situation of this bohemian underworld coincides with the artistic forms emerging from it, as manifest in the ephemeral bibelots, what one sees is a kind of mad grasping after associations, an artistic fascination with the trace of linkages. The blockage of circulation is only half of the dialectic, the other being the development of intense citation networks within the clusters and occasional bridges between them.[19]

The little magazines often read like elaborate in-jokes, several-layer deep parodies, and elusively biting commentaries about the movement itself. This is another version of print circulation, not the movement of print matter through the market but the movement of shared points of reference among the magazines. Circulation is not only about physical objects moving in geographical space but also about what moves in the citational space between the bibelots. Movement in this expanded sense could usefully be imagined as happening in the links, also called edges, between nodes within clusters, as well as in the bridges spanning the structural holes and jumping between parallel planes.

The point is that the network itself implies a modality of nonprint circulation, circulation without the movement of paper. And yet the situation is complicated by the fact that any kind of thing can be an edge, even other edges, as we will see below and in the next chapter. The broader question of how the movement moved is tied to these modes of citation. As we will see, our sense of the movement's movement is not tied to any one of these particular modalities but rather to a kind of scintillation effect, where a spark makes the jump from one plane to the next and is reflected and refracted in a variety of ways in a new network cluster.

a. Authors and Artists

Perhaps the most obvious links between magazines are the people who published in them. Authors and artists are circulated by magazines in the sense of the magazine being a vehicle for the dissemination of their work to the public, and we might then intuit their social interaction, and its influence on the shape of artistic movements, based on the venues in which they published.[20] A no less lively social interaction occurs, however, when these same individuals become entities mentioned by the magazines. Indeed, citation becomes at least as important as publication when we are interested in the question of how networked publics take shape. To think of citations, and in turn of the citation of citations, as links and bridges—as solutions to the blockage of circulation within and between magazine clusters—requires a rather different way of conceptualizing their circulation, one in which a network edge is equated with the activity of tracing circuits between magazines. Authors and artists in this sense not only gain a larger audience by being circulated by individual magazines, but they also become points of reference holding magazines together as a movement.[21]

Some interesting things happen when thinking of artistic production in this way. For instance, the publication of a story, poem, review, or illustration becomes the functional equivalent of any other form of citation. Authors and artists do not have to actually have their work published in the magazines to serve as a link. Their names merely need to be bandied about between them. They can, moreover, index movement between magazines regardless of the valuation placed upon them. A negative review can in some circumstances count the same as a positive one, just as a universally panned poem can play the same role as a good one. William Dean Howells never published in the American ephemeral bibelots, but he was cited by at least thirteen of them, almost always negatively. Robert Louis Stevenson was cited by over twenty of the bibelots in universally positive terms. And

Stephen Crane was not only reviewed widely both positively and critically by them, but he was also published in them regularly. Much of his poetry, for example, appeared at some point in the *Philistine*. The citation of all three of them—the shared negative comments about Howells, the positive valuation of Stevenson, and the mixed publication and reception of Crane—work to assemble the network in much the same way. When shared as a point of reference by more than a single magazine, authors and artists become citational indices indicating movement within a networked cluster.

b. Translations

The gold standard in Casanova's version of the world literary system is translation, and it is obviously an important process for moving authors out into citational space. Surprisingly, it was infrequently practiced among the bibelots. Among American magazines, the three most prominent for translations were surely the *Chap-Book*, the *Quartier Latin*, and *M'lle New York*.[22] Curiously, the *Chap-Book* was more prone to publish its French authors in French than to translate them, as it did with two pieces by Mallarmé; it also published the untranslated, French versions of his multipage review of the poetry of Arthur Rimbaud and his original poem, "Les loisirs de la poste."[23] The *Quartier Latin* was more ambitious in terms of actual translations, publishing more of them than any of the other American bibelots. For example, it ran a racy story by Joris-Karl Huysman, the quintessential French Decadent novelist, about an artist falling in love with his studio model, who turns out to have been a society woman posing for him on a dare. *M'lle New York* was perhaps the most aggressively international in its orientation; even the *Chap-Book* recognized the fact, noting that the best thing about it was its editor, Vance Thompson, who "knows something of new movements in literature: that he has undoubtedly read the writings of several Symbolists—and that he is clever enough in his notions of them to lead one to wish for more."[24] And yet translation was very rare in both the *Quartier Latin* and *M'lle New York*, coming much less frequently than one might expect; it was more frequent to find foreign work appearing in the original language, almost always French.

A related anecdote about the limits of translation concerns the poet Stuart Merrill, who, as we noted in the last chapter, was almost certainly the most important *fin-de-siècle* American writer who remains entirely unknown to American literary historians. At one time an acolyte of William Dean Howells, he moved to Paris as a young man and became a member of Mallarmé's circle of Symbolist poets, a regular fixture in the French *petites revues*, and the author of five well-received volumes of poetry. But he was never translated. He introduced Walt Whitman and Oscar Wilde to the French little magazines, and he translated many of the French Symbolists in one of the earliest English language editions of their poetry, *Pastels in Prose* (1890). In many ways, he was a bridge between the two national language clusters. But he also marks the limits of translation as a bridge, the very high bar it set. An untranslated American writing in French, Merrill was and has remained a marginal figure to both national literary traditions. His example suggests the limitations of using translation as the gauge of network circulation.

c. Genres (Blurbs and Stories-without-Words)

Genres can serve a citational role in much the same way as people. Genres of particular importance to the bibelots included several with particular histories in France at this time, including caricature and the prose poem. One might also say that the shared format of the bibelots—beautifully illustrated, deckle-edged, oddly shaped—constituted a genre in and of itself, and thus was inherently a citational practice. I want to detail two other genres, the blurb and the story-without-words, which seem to have developed particularly in the bibelots, and which are interesting because of the specificity of their treatment of citation.

The most straightforward opportunity for citation comes with critical reviews, and a particular version of this practice rose to the level of a new art form in the bibelots, which began republishing extravagantly punning, comical excerpts about themselves from other magazines and newspapers. These were similar to what we know today as "blurbs," which is the word I will use to describe them here, even though the meaning today is no longer quite the same, because it was coined in 1907 by none other than America's leading bibelot editor, Gelett Burgess. He first used the term on the advertising dust jacket for his book of essays, *Are You a Bromide?*, where he included a picture of "Miss Belinda Blurb . . . in the act of Blurbing"—"All the Other Publishers commit them. Why Shouldn't We?" The self-mockery of Belinda's blurb was the culmination of a form developed in the bibelots in the previous decade, in which editors culled short quips about their publications from other magazines and strung them together in long lists. It was a genre of auto-blurbing, of selfie-puffing.[25]

The *Bauble*, started in July 1895 out of Washington, DC, was entirely given over to such blurbs, its twelve-page issues doing little more than ridiculing other little magazines and their contributors. In the first number, its editor insists that the *Bauble* "is not modeled after that patent-medicine-needing publication known as the 'Chap Book'" and goes on to berate its editors for being "a lot of hobble-de-hoys who have been drinking and dancing, and affecting cynicism and crazyisms of every kind until they have been attacked by a species of brain-fever."[26] In the next number it parodies the *Chap-Book*'s editor Bliss Carman with a lyric by "Cliss Barman" about a cabbage tossed out in the waste, as well as Henrik Ibsen with a mock tragedy in one act by "Henri Kibson" called "The Deaf and the Dumb." Among other bibelots, it takes on *Chips*, the *Black Cat*, the *Lark*, *Le Petit Journal des Refusées*, *Kit-Kat*, the *Lotus*, the *New Bohemian*, and the *Magpie*. Complaining of the "idiotic eccentricities" of *Le Petit Journal des Refusées* in October 1896, the editors claim to have originated the idea of publishing rejected manuscripts but concede "generously . . . that *L. P. J. Des R.* has printed much worse stuff than I dared to perpetrate."[27] Visually, with its title in red lettering and a subtitle in black rubricated letters of the familiar Arts and Crafts type, the *Bauble* looks very much like Thomas Mosher's *Bibelot* and Will Bradley's *Bradley, His Book*. And while decrying the publication of posters "the latest foolish fad," it too publishes a poster—described in the number for December 1895 as being "superbly printed on thin paper, trimmed edges, and . . . called 'A Physick for Fools.'"[28] By the third volume, it has a running column titled "Condemned Contemporaries," in which it features obituaries for deceased freak magazines.

Burgess, himself, provides numerous other examples. In the fifth number of the *Lark*, for instance, he blurbed his own magazine by publishing the following self-send-up, in French:

> C'EST une assez modeste Créature que THE LARK; elle ne se mesle pas de *Personnalités*; étant un Oiseau *matineux*, elle s'occupe du *Ver*. Elle ne pousse cependant pas *l'Insouciance* jusqu'à ne pas écouter les Notes louangeuses des *Cages* d'en-bas habitées par les Autres. THE LARK n'est pas *ingrate*, et elle remercie le CRITIC* des Renseignments sur sa *Circulation*; le BOSTON JOURNAL† qui la trouve *un peu sauvage*; le CHAP BOOK‡ qui l'appelle *intime*; le NEW YORK TIMES** qui voit en elle une Menace à la *Modernité chicagoenne*, et le NEW YORK TRIBUNE†† gentil Savant de la LARKEOLOGIE, qui la nomme L'OIE, sans doute à cause de ses *Oeufs d'Or*.[29]
>
> * "-One bookseller tells me that he has sold 100 copies." (!)
> † In an editorial comment, remarkable only for its length and the fact that it calls *The Lark* an "ornithological specimen," and its opening article an "epilogue."

‡ "It is an assertion of the right of the artist to be wayward, and indulge in innocent drollery. Its friends will be appreciative, but there will not be many of them."
** "Incredibly, even impossibly, 1895; written by *les jeunes*, and delightfully young they are."
†† "One more hysterical magazine—from a realm remote from the moorings of intelligence."

While not so witty, in general, as this one, a remarkable number of the bibelots published pages of auto-blurbs of this kind for themselves with each issue, often in the form of short comments or notes reviewing what was happening in other little magazines. Thus even more directly than when citing authors and artists, the blurbs establish explicit citational links between the bibelots themselves.

Another blurb example comes in the Russian bibelots—one that admittedly raises a number of questions about how far we want to trace these connections. Very early in his career, Anton Chekhov wrote ephemeral pieces for a number of journals known to Russian literary historians as "skinny magazines"—among them *Sverchok* (*The Cricket*), *Budil'nik* (*Alarm Clock*), and especially *Oskolki* (*Fragments*, or sometimes *Splinters*)—the more serious literary monthlies being known there as "fat magazines."[30] It is perhaps less surprising than it might have been, therefore, to see that Chekhov had produced something very close to Burgess's long-form auto-blurb for an article for *Oskolki* in 1883:

> Don't read the *Ufa Province News*: you won't find any information about Ufa province in it.
>
> The Russian press has many sources of light at its disposal. It has *The Komarovo Light*, *The Rainbow*, *Light and Shade*, *The Ray*, *The Little Light*, *Dawn*, etcetera. So why is it still so dark then?
>
> It has *The Observer*, *The Invalid* and *Siberia*.
>
> The press has *Entertainment* and *Little Toy*, but it does not follow that it has much fun . . .
>
> It has *The Voice* and its own *Echo* . . . Yes?
>
> Whatever is ephemeral cannot boast about its *Century* . . .
>
> *Rus* has little in common with Moscow.
>
> *Russian Thought* is sent . . . in a strong envelope.
>
> Then there is *Health* and *The Doctor*, but meanwhile, how many graves there are![31]

Cottin's "Comment on devient anarchiste," published in *Le Chat Noir*, July 2, 1892

We know that Chekhov had worked with at least a few of the papers he blurbs here, his brother having noted his association with *Light and Shade*, and at the very least his grouping of them together suggests their coherence as a class of magazines, a Russian bibelot vogue. It seems very clear that Burgess did not read Russian and knew nothing about *Oskolki*, which, at any rate, predated his own bibelots by a decade.[32] The point would be for us to hear the echo between Chekhov's version and Burgess's, linked via the elaboration of the genre of the blurb in the French bibelots. I come back to this problem in the conclusion.

One other shared genre prominent in the little magazines was the pictorial narrative, or story-without-words, undertaken in an infantile manner and often telling a macabre story. The genre was initiated in *Le Chat Noir* by artists like Théophile-Alexandre Steinlen, Willette, and Caran d'Ache, and one sees it carried over with great regularity in the American bibelots. For example, Eugène Cottin's "Comment on devient anarchiste" in *Le Chat Noir* clearly resembles Burgess's "Elliptical Wheels on a Cart" from the *Lark*, sequential line drawings coupled with a droll sense of knowingness. The

Second page of the article by A. Warburg, "Amerikanische Chap-Books," *Pan* 2:4 (October 1896), which reproduces pages from the *Lark*

genre's existence as such is confirmed by *Pan*'s decision to represent the *Lark* in its article on the American chap-books with this same image. The use by the magazines of this genre is not directly citational in the way of the blurb, but as with reviews, they establish the trace movement between magazines, such that one expects that a "linked in" reader of the *Lark* would sense that Burgess was indexing Paris with his elliptical wheels image, much as if he had commented on, say, Mallarmé. *Pan*, then, was doing the same twice removed. Genre citation thus works as a link in much the same way as author citation. It can be judgment-neutral, sharing the same form without necessarily sharing the same meaning, the magazines' judgment being irrelevant to their ability to help construct and reiterate the network.

d. Style (*Fumisme*)

In the examples I have given up to now, I have avoided suggesting anything so ambiguous as "style" as an example of a citational practice. Here, though, is a crucial point: the bibelots' style can best be thought of as that which develops along the citational lines themselves, a more subjective feeling or mood emanating from the sense of connection. There is, to be sure, a shared sensibility with both blurbs and stories-without-words, though as

I have tried to point out with all of the examples up to now, there is also a way in which a citational force offers the trace of movement regardless of whether it shares a meaning. In this last example, I want to show the citational effect of a shared style that operates independently of the genre in which it is enacted. More than the others, it emanates from the connection itself and is dependent upon readers capturing the trace of movement.

Parody is one of the oldest citational practices, and it has had, of course, a special place in French letters since the time of Molière. In the late nineteenth century it developed into the pointed, oppositional style known as *fumisme*, described in the previous chapter, a group movement that could be imperceptible to the uninitiated. The *fumisterie* most visible in the American bibelots took shape around certain iconic images, like the black cat made famous on the pages of *Le Chat Noir*. Parodic iterations of that image appeared all over the bibelots, on the head of the *Vogue* cover-girl and in the margins of an absurdist prose poem in *Le Petit Journal des Refusées* (see my previous discussion of the black cat in the prologue). Always the same cat, but with some parodic refunctioning, the ubiquitous *chat noir* indexed Paris and also the group of readers linked into the network who would recognize the play on that image.

Another example comes with a "purple cow" that Burgess made famous in one of the early numbers of the *Lark* (see chapter 1):

> I never saw a purple cow,
> 	I never hope to see one.
> But I can tell you anyhow,
> 	I'd rather see than be one.

"The Purple Cow" went on to achieve a kind of epigrammatic fame, with a variety of punning retakes quickly showing up in competing bibelots. For instance, the *Lotus*, from Kansas City, only half-facetiously recommended Burgess for a laureate position as our national bard before offering Arthur Grissom's parody of the lines:

> "I never saw a purple cow,"
> 	A bardlet wrote to get a laugh;
> If he had used a looking-glass,
> 	He might have noticed a green calf.[33]

James Huneker had a much darker take on the "Purple Cow" in *M'lle New York*, where he published a horrific dream tale about a purple turtle, "The

Ghost of a Turtle: A Fable for Naughty Nurses."[34] It starts with an invitation in the margins, "Why should an etiolated Lark alone be naif? Let us all be naif. Let us be Humperdincked and rejoice with childish laughter at Purple Cows and Chortling Turtles." The story then paints an age-warped scene in which a five-year-old boy named Goo-Goo, dressed in a brown velvet Fauntleroy suit, smokes cigarettes and drinks brandy while torturing a "very, very old lady," who sits trapped in a high-chair playing toy blocks. He threatens to bring in his "purple turtle" if she doesn't tell him the name "of the animal that gives us milk." The story culminates after a page with Goo-Goo "annoyed" that the nurse has died of fright, but giving a "delirious dance of joy": "Why, Maddy, do you know that you are dead? How jolly! Maddy will soon be a Skellack! Maddy, you look like a Skellack." The boy, we are told, grows up to be a great actor, "a marvelous portrayer in Ibsen's sorrowful dramas." The story is so dark as to take away just a bit of the surprise we experience upon finding in *M'lle New York*, just four numbers later, the first reproduction in America of Edward Munch's *The Scream*, redrawn, presumably by *M'lle*'s editor Vance Thompson, from an earlier woodcut in the French little magazine *La Revue Blanche*. Munch was making various versions of the image in paintings and pastels between 1893 and 1910, and the fact that this one showed up in an American bibelot in 1896, having passed first through the French arts press, is astonishing. We have moved quite far from Burgess's purple cow, which was already at some distance from the black cat; and yet, particularly given the historical development of *fumisterie* as an avant-garde style, it seems clear that the citational index to both of them remains.

From Paris to Lansing, with Love

All of these citational modalities—people, translation, genre, and style—establish indexical relations among ephemeral bibelots, *petites revues*, and skinny magazines. The bibelot movement in effect moves through these links. We might summarize with three quick remarks.

First, the movement moves in little pieces. The issue is not the dissemination of the entire class of magazines but rather the assemblage of the class by way of individual links.

Second, the sense we have of the movement as such, as a coherent phenomenon and not merely random coincidences, comes by way of the swarming multiplication of these minor links. The feel for individual magazines as being part of a movement is not dependent on any kind of direct association between their editors, or any statistical characteristics of their actual circulation in the literary marketplace. Rather, the sense of the movement moving comes by way of the linking of links, and so what we are really talking about is an expanding assemblage of connections. These connections, moreover, do not circulate evenly or randomly, like a drop of dye in a glass of water, but rather they are distributed through unevenly weighted hubs; and they constantly change, the arrival of nodes and links continually altering the topology of the network.[35] As suggested in the article in *Pan* with which we began, the network circulated through hubs like the *Chap-Book* and the *Lark* to an exponentially higher degree than through the smaller magazines; and yet their presence allowed the smaller magazines to link in to the circulation of the movement as a whole.

Finally, the movement moves without geographical centers, happening as easily in small towns in America as in Paris, given that all you need to establish a relation is to pick up a book. Just because the American bibelots were looking to Paris does not mean that the circulation of black cats between them had anything to do with the geographical space of Paris. The "world republic of letters" was a citational point of reference for the bibelots, not a geographical one.

What would it really mean, however, to say that the movement circulated to the small towns of, say, the American Midwest? The freak magazines of the 1890s may have been ephemeral, and they may have been broadly dispersed; however, the tightly clustered network configuration assembled by way of these modalities of citation helps us better understand what it means to talk about the Modernist refashioning of the aesthetic public sphere. It is the space of a different kind of artistic circulation, and small towns were well represented. We cannot tell much of this story from currently available resources on the history of reading. For example, one new resource is gathered in an electronic database, "What Middletown Read," which documents the reading habits of public library patrons in Muncie, Indiana, during the height of the bibelot vogue, from 1891 to 1902; not surprisingly, the database does not record any of the ephemeral bibelots having even made it to the public library.[36] *The Union List of Serials* is not much more helpful. Its regional coverage can be spotty; nonetheless it does not list any holdings of the bibelots in the Midwest. What can be said is that magazines of this kind were published in many American cities and small towns across the entire country, for example, the *Optimist* (Boone, Iowa, 1900–1901); *Pot-Pouri* (Fremont, Ohio, 1898–1899); the *Ishmaelite* (Indianapolis, Indiana, 1897–1899); the *White Rabbit* (Oberlin, Ohio, 1897); and the *Kiote* (Lincoln, Nebraska,

1898–1901). As with the *Chap-Book*, which was started at Harvard before relocating to Chicago, many of these were coming out of university towns. What allowed these magazines to jump the track, as it were, assembling the traces of links across structural holes and nonintersecting dimensional planes, was the expanding assemblage of this avant-garde public sphere.

So let us conclude in two small towns with the *Clack Book* from Lansing, Michigan, and the *Philosopher* from Wausau, Wisconsin (see plates 5 and 6). What is so striking about both of these magazines is the number of citational links circulating between them in their very first numbers.

The *Clack Book* came out first, starting in 1896, and it is evident from the *fumisterie* of its first cover—a fairly self-evident mash-up of the *Lark* and the *Chap-Book* suggesting, idiomatically, that one or the other of them had "laid an egg"—that it means to enter directly into the fray of the American goblin literature. Perhaps just a bit further afield, it would even seem to index *Le Mirliton*, a French *petite revue* started by Aristide Bruant on the tails of the success of *Le Chat Noir*—*Le Mirliton* being the name of the new cabaret that Bruant started in the building that Le Chat Noir occupied before moving to a bigger space. To the extent that it is an Americanization of the French, the origin of its title points us toward "*claque*," the organized group of hired applauders that became a regular part of opera performances in the 1830s. The *Clack Book* is full of such applause in a self-satirical mode, making regular citations in the early going to authors and artists central to the bibelot network, and to other freak magazines, including the *Echo*, Percival Pollard, the *Lotus*, Stephen Crane, the *Philistine*, Aubrey Beardsley, Will Bradley, *Bradley, His Book*, Yone Noguchi, and Gelett Burgess; and it demonstrates the citational circulation of the movement by linking to the *Iconoclast* of Waco, Texas, and the *Optimist* of Detroit. Two months after the arrival of the *Philosopher* on the scene, the *Clack Book* gives it a blurb: "There is a new Philosopher among us—a new exploiter of the world's very old philosophy. . . . It is not a very hot Philosopher as yet, this new arrival upon the arena, but since in the same breath it lauds the legacy and damns the Gilder family, to say nothing of omitting periods in punctuation, something may come of it."[37] The next month, the *Clack Book* would lament the passing of the *Lark*, which had ceased publication after two years, with a stylistically similar blurb anthropomorphizing the bibelot's title: "The poor Lark! did she soar too high or did she sing to deaf ears?"[38]

What is significant for understanding how the bibelot movement moved is that the *Philosopher*'s opening numbers make so many of the same connections, eliciting so many of the same citations. The *Philosopher* typifies not only an American bibelot but also the movement of the bibelot movement, by the swarming multiplication of links one finds in it. As noted by the *Clack Book*, William Ellis sets out the project of his "booklet" in contradistinction to "the Gilder family," who "have hamstrung the literature of our land enough, what with their Century Magazine, and their Critic, and the cheap-john receptions, and all the flapdoodle in which they delight."[39] (Recall that *M'lle New York* had started in the very same way, sharing the negative citation through Gilder.) The *Philosopher*, too, notes the passing of the *Lark* and cites Yone Noguchi and the *Philistine* in the same section of notes; it even sends out a blurb to the *Clack Book*, "Michigan being the state where good celery comes from, and celery being an excellent sedative."[40] The point of all of which was to ensconce the magazine in the ethos and the aura of the bibelot movement, which in effect meant assembling its citational credentials, circulating a shared set of references. It joins itself to the assemblage and in multiplying the links accelerates the movement's movement.

Moving, then, out from Wausau and Lansing, what one sees happening with the repetition of this citational mode is its reformulation as an aesthetic form in its own right. The bibelot vogue is moving, and also assembling an aesthetics of movement. The links and bridges, figured as such, are not merely the traces of a literary-social network; rather, they are, themselves, developing into the subject of aesthetic elaboration. They become new genres and encourage new styles. It has been typical to say of Modernist texts that their engagement with other works of art signals their exclusion of, or retreat from, material and political concerns that had preoccupied both sentimental and Realist fiction. While it may well be that the bibelots are no less hermetic in their insistent reflexivity than the works of Modernist art they in many ways anticipated, they nonetheless circulate dramatically, worldwide, in tightly clustered networks. The notion of structural holes and nonintersecting planes structuring this new aesthetic public sphere should help us reconsider their relation to the public at large. Not just a production of Paris, London, and New York, the bibelot vogue took shape from the surging citational waves being actively assembled in the proverbial Lansings and Wausaus (and St. Petersburgs) of the world. *Pan*, in the end, may have been exactly right to be looking in such places for the "fresh and joyous fight against the *fin-de-siècle* attitude of complacent weariness."

3 Relating in Henry James

This is the age of esoteric magazines, published for the few, "The Remnant," as John Eglinton calls them in that little book that comes from Whaley, in Dublin.

The conservative man thinks these periodicals the apotheosis of foolishness, and the fulcrum of the logroller.

Dear conservative! The gods give him joy. Some of the rest of us enjoy them.

The *Chap-Book*, March 15, 1895

The history of the bibelot vogue in the United States inevitably leads to the *Chap-Book*, which, in turn, typically finds itself staged as Herbert Stone's Chicago-based knock-off of Aubrey Beardsley's London-based *Yellow Book*. Neither magazine is a particularly good example of a bibelot on its own. The *Chap-Book* may have been called the "pater familias / Of magazines started by many a silly ass" in *Le Petit Journal des Refusées* and the *Critic* may have identified it as "the first of these fad papers."[1] But it is an odd representative of the class, being too sober, too ambitious, with too many contributors, too many pages, and too big a circulation.[2] Similarly, the *Yellow Book* was, by reputation if not content, almost too resolutely Decadent to count, even if it hadn't garnered so much attention because of Beardsley's scandalous drawings and its association with Oscar Wilde, who never even published in it. What these two magazines represent is not so much the ephemeral bibelot as *a type*, but the mass of the bibelots taken together as *a group movement*—with a stress on movement. The *Chap-Book* and the *Yellow Book* became something like transit hubs in the diffusion of the bibelot fad, catalysts speeding up the flow of new trends and points of reference for other bibelots, which could orient their own forays into the international territory of the modern and the new merely by citing them.

Nor is Henry James, who published in both magazines, a particularly good representative of the typical bibelotist—except to the extent that the sets of associations he evoked, both by reputation and in the style of his writing, served a similar purpose in orchestrating the bibelots as a movement.[3] Although certainly attuned to the literary trends in both London and Chicago, although probably more so to the former than the latter, James never seems to have developed a clear sense of the little revolution in print that his association with them helped catalyze. The *Yellow Book* opened its first number with his short story, "The Death of the Lion," but only a month later he wrote to William that he hated "the horrid aspect and company of the whole publication," even though he continued to publish in it until 1897.[4] It is even less clear what he was thinking when he decided to serialize his novel *What Maisie Knew* in the *Chap-Book* in 1897. It may have been the money. Stone went out of his way to make sure James was happy, once even stranding himself in England when using his own reserves to make sure James got paid on time.[5] But there is no record of James having any kind of attachment to the magazine, and my point, really, is to use his presence there to pursue an altogether different problem.

The gist of this chapter is that we can read the appearance of *What Maisie Knew* in the *Chap-Book*, and the development of its themes in *The Ambassadors*, as a theoretical encapsulation of the wispy connections described in chapter 2. In other words, I want to read James as a theorist of the period's relational aesthetics—an aesthetics that keyed the rapid expansion and dissipation of the bibelot vogue but which also reached beyond it into other arts and ideas.

What Maisie Knew is James's novel of relating. Thematically, the little girl at its center is the link holding together a cascade of complicated adult relations—marriages, divorces, deceits, and love affairs—which fall apart and come together all around her throughout the course of the novel. Stylistically, it is also by way of the slow reveal of Maisie relating that the novel unfolds, the novel being delimited to Maisie's point of view in such a way as to focus our attention on the mystery of the process by which Maisie links the outrageous things she sees to the claptrap of words she had stored away to explain them. Its tension develops from the unevenness of this relating; Maisie often sees more than what she can understand, and on occasion understands more than what she can see; being just a little girl, she does not make the connections we do as readers, but on occasion she sees and connects even more than we do—and there is the real magic. As with James, I will argue, so too is relating the key to taking in the aesthetic of the bibelot vogue all the way down its many intersecting lines. We see this aesthetic not only in James's *Chap-Book* novel but also in the materials chosen by the *Chap-Book* editors to accompany the novel. Attending to James can help us more clearly establish the essential stylistic aesthetic of the bibelot vogue, the way the movement depended on having readers follow along in an exercise of apperception that worked by encouraging them to make more, and more sophisticated, connections.

Paterfamilias

The thing to keep in mind about the *Chap-Book* and *Yellow Book*, especially with regard to their mutual publication of James, is not only that they shared so much in common but that they played a similar role in shaping the queer and wispy coterie public taking shape around the bibelots. The historical tendency has been to do otherwise, to distinguish between them. It has been typical, for example, to say that the *Chap-Book* derived from the *Yellow Book*, as did the critic Percival Pollard when looking back on the movement in a memoir published in 1909, even though they began publication within a month of each other in 1894. Pollard, an accomplished bibelotist himself, who contributed to the *Fly Leaf*, the *Goose-Quill*, *Whims*, the *Anti-Philistine*, and the *Chap-Book*, situated the *Yellow Book* at the head of these because of his bitter sense that the movement had been a failure in America, which he blames in part on the *Chap-Book*'s lack of commitment to the modern.

According to Pollard, the problem with the *Chap-Book* was that it reflected the country's antipathy to continental art. America preferred the raw to the cooked, choosing Hamlin Garland's "ploughboy prose" and the "great cosmic crudity" of Jack London over the stylistic brilliance of Ambrose Bierce, who "wrote with as crystally cold an art as De Maupassant" and thus was held in vague distrust and considered "in no wise 'American' as an artist." With the exception of Bierce, Pollard suggests that American writers of the fin de siècle had little to show when compared to Verlaine, Rimbaud, Laforgue, Dowson, and Symons: "That entire, considerable school of art which, according to the temperament of the critic, has been dubbed decadent, symbolistic, impressionistic, romantic or merely Young, had but slight American equivalent."[6]

In direct contrast to that record of failure, Pollard puts forward the *Yellow Book* as the model, calling the British little magazine "a bilious explosion of long smoldering revolt against conservatism in English art and letters" with Henry Harland as its editor and Oscar Wilde as its "main cargo"—even though Harland was an American expatriate and Wilde never published in the magazine. According to Pollard, it was the *Yellow Book*'s scandalous success that planted the seed for "a crop of strangely fashioned periodicals, preaching fantastic doctrines, uttering weird thoughts, but all expressive of youth and of dreams of non-commercial art," not the *Chap-Book*'s.[7]

In many respects Pollard was right. By the time he was writing, the bibelot movement in America had ended and been largely forgotten, and with it most traces of the nineteenth-century Modern art movement in America (see chapter 5). And yet, for most readers grasping after the coterie public of the bibelots, the *Chap-Book* and *Yellow Book* must have seemed, at the time, to be painting from the same palette. To give but a taste of the similarities, one might note that they both drew inspiration from the same Arts and Crafts sources, especially the British magazine the *Century Guild Hobby Horse*, and that the editors of both magazines had cut their teeth in the literary atmosphere of Harvard.[8] The *Yellow-Book*'s editor had spent time at Harvard in the 1880s before moving to London; the *Chap-Book* was founded by Harvard undergraduates Stone and H. J. Kimball. They were also of similar interest visually, although for different reasons. The *Chap-Book*'s unusual format drew much of the early attention to it. An article in *Leslie's Weekly* in 1895, remarking on the fad for the "bijou magazine," suggested that the class was "distinguished mainly by its finical daintiness of contents, its homeopathic size, and its loyal adhesion to purely literary traditions and decadent and non-perspective art."[9] In its first two years, the *Chap-Book* was published in a diminutive duodecimo page size, only 7.5 × 4.5 inches, with red and black ink, old-style Caslon type on artisanal paper, and uncut pages. The *Yellow Book* was not so small, but it was also known by sight. It published in hardcover and was known for the line drawings of Beardsley, who had become famous for his illustrations of the English edition of Wilde's *Salomé*, and for the color yellow, styled after the yellow wraps of French novels that had become code in the English-speaking world for adult content.

Moreover, while Beardsley is most often associated with the *Yellow Book*, he was prominently featured throughout the first volume of the *Chap-Book* as well, which is another way of saying that the *Chap-Book*'s interest in the artist coincided with his editorial position with the *Yellow Book*. Not only is there a tribute to Beardsley, complete with a self-portrait, to open the notes section of the first number but also a two-page spread featuring a Beardsleyesque nude by the period's other major illustrator of Oscar Wilde, Charles S. Ricketts, in the third number (June 15, 1894). In the second volume of the *Chap-Book* Beardsley's style is reproduced by John Sloan in his pre-Ashcan School incarnation as an aesthetic arts illustrator; the list of illustrators would later grow to include others working in this same style, most notably E. B. Bird, Frank Hazenplug, Claude Fayette Bragdon (a close friend of Gelett Burgess, see chapter 1), and Will Bradley. Then, of course, there were the *Chap-Book*'s extraordinary posters, most of which were by Bradley, but which also included a famous example from Henri de Toulouse-Lautrec, which takes us right back to the nightlife of Paris.

That said, the American little magazine was guilty of a certain tentativeness due to its attempt to square the major themes of European Decadence, Symbolism, and Aestheticism with a desire for commercial success. MacLeod suggests, correctly, that the *Chap-Book* attempted to turn an "elite coterie form into an affordable aesthetic commodity"; it is, perhaps, in this respect, above all, that the *Chap-Book* wanted both everything and nothing to do with the *Yellow Book*.[10] Its creators were clearly wary of the British magazine's association with the gendered and sexual coding of Decadent aesthetics. The *Chap-Book* found itself both uneasy with and utterly enmeshed in the queer crosscurrents of fin-de-siècle culture. Like the *Yellow Book* and a vast majority of the other American bibelots, it depended upon the logic of what Rita Felski identifies as an "aestheticized and feminized modernity . . . a self-conscious textualism which defined itself in opposition to the prevailing convention of Realist representation, turning toward a decadent aesthetic of surface, style, and parody that was explicitly coded as both 'feminine' and 'modern.'"[11]

Wilde and Beardsley are only the most obvious examples of this feminization in the *Chap-Book*. James would have provided more of the same. And just as recognizable, surely, would have been such elements as the monocled dandy on its frontispiece, a figure later taken up by the *New Yorker* in its cover design for Eustace Tilley; the lyric sensibilities of a significant group women writers recruited for the early issues, which included Louise Imogen Guiney, Gertrude Hall Brownell, Maria Poole, Alice Brown, and Louise

Chandler Moulton; and the extensive space given over to French Symbolist poets, especially Verlaine and Mallarmé. Pollard's contributions to the *Chap-Book* also fall in line here. For instance, he contributed a story titled "For a Jest's Sake" on June 1, 1894, that was based on two of the most famous icons of the French cabaret scene, the devilish clowns Pierrot and Pierrette, who would have been associated with the same sexual coyness.

But at the same time, the *Chap-Book* consistently held itself apart from the *Yellow Book*'s more outré self-presentation, as well as from many of the other American bibelots. One of the first direct mentions of the *Yellow Book* by the *Chap-Book* came in a veiled quip about the British magazine's publication of Arthur Symons's erotically explicit poem, "Stella Maris," which includes the lines

> Oh! No oblivion, for I feel
> Your lips deliriously steal
> Along my neck, and fasten there;
> I feel the perfume of your hair,
> And your soft breast that heaves and dips,
> Desiring my desirous lips,
> And that ineffable delight
> When souls turn bodies, and unite
> In the intolerable, the whole
> Rapture of the embodied soul.[12]

The queering of masculine desire in the poem—with its delirium, perfume, and rapture—epitomizes the sexual logic of the male avant-garde, which Felski describes as a "masking" that was not necessarily feminist, but which risked effeminacy in order to counter the dominant narrative implied by the reigning discourse of American literary Realism.[13] We are far, here, from the prurience of William Dean Howells. The *Chap-Book* sidles up to this position but ultimately places itself apart from Symons's extravagance, noting bemusedly, and not a little disingenuously, that it was surprising to find Arthur Waugh's "Reticence in Literature" in the same number: "But I suppose the Yellow Bookmakers call that broadmindedness."[14] Similarly, in an article length review of the *Yellow Book* the next month, August 1894, Pierre La Rose reassures readers of the *Chap-Book* that despite the quarantine one might worry was necessary because of the yellow covers, there had now been "two harmless numbers" of the *Yellow Book*, the "quiet, pervading charm" of which was to be found in "its brazen inessentiality." Appreciative of the contributions of Henry James and Aubrey Beardsley while dismissive of much of the rest, La Rose concludes soberly that "[i]n the long run, the ancient love of simple dignity and self-respect in literature and in art will probably prevail again; meanwhile, *The Yellow Book* is winning a well-deserved popularity."[15]

The following year, the *Chap-Book*'s editors likely felt themselves chastened alongside the *Yellow Book* by the prosecution of Wilde in the spring of 1895, which may explain a later editorial from February 1897, "The Decadent's Progress," in which Stone approved of the more conservative direction taken by the *Yellow Book* under the direction of its editor postscandal, Ethel Reed. The *Yellow Book* as it had begun, "was extremely 'young and curly'": "There was something essentially annoying in the persistency with which these young gentlemen forced their plans for a new code of immorality on the world. They were just a bit too strenuous about it. Their cheeks were too rosy, their voices too loud. They had too plainly read themselves into a pose. We were grateful when the *Savoy*—the Pink'Un of Decadence—entered the field and stole the ground from them."[16] Again, the note seems strangely disingenuous given the prominence of Beardsley to the early numbers of the *Chap-Book*, not to mention the posters produced for it in his style by Will Bradley and in the style of the French cabarets by Toulouse-Lautrec. And yet, as time went on, the *Chap-Book* became more and more like the establishment periodicals it had set out to displace. In April 1897, with the financial backing of his father, who had been pushing him to make the magazine profitable, Stone enlarged the *Chap-Book* to the size of the English weekly reviews and began to cover the release of important new books. He tastefully limited its illustrations to "portraits, pictures of literary interest and purely decorative designs," and he added James to his contributor's list, outbidding the *Yellow Book* for *What Maisie Knew*.[17]

The change was met with derision by many of the other bibelots. One of them, the *Clack Book* of Lansing, Michigan—its title a noticeable parody of the *Chap-Book*—complained that the "*Chap-Book* has ceased to be ephemeral, at least it has taken on the form of a substantial and critical magazine—a conservative ruler of opinions who dresses his shop windows soberly and puts behind him the days of the bargain and remnant counters."[18] Another taking the *Chap-Book* to task was the *Red Letter*, a stunningly beautiful bibelot edited by Harry Draper Hunt and illustrated by E. B. Bird that ran from September 1896 to April 1897. "*The Chap-Book* announces an important change in its size and form. Henceforth it is to assume a place with the many.

Alas that this should be! From the time when it began to print the work of that inveterate hack, Mr. R. Harding Davis, we foresaw the end. 'It wishes to invite criticism as a literary and critical journal of the first rank.' Doubtless its wishes will be granted, and the 'criticism' will be forthcoming. Next, we expect to see *The Lark* take up the function of a homiletic review. God save the mark!"[19]

Some literary historians have argued that the change in format did not significantly alter the intellectual content of the *Chap-Book*, which was never "the radical proponent of the avant-garde that some critics would like to make it out to be in its early days."[20] And yet this suggestion belies the significance of the *Chap-Book* to the network of American ephemeral bibelots, even if it had previously resisted assuming the role of paterfamilias.[21] By the time *What Maisie Knew* began to be published in it, the *Chap-Book* had become less of an ephemeral bibelot than it had been, the change in format signaling the end of the first and most significant phase of the bibelot vogue. Even after that time, however, the *Chap-Book* served as the most central hub in the bibelot movement, enabling the breathless accumulation of velocity between bibelots around the country. Turning now to the novel James published in the *Chap-Book*, we can get a much better feel for the character of the new relational aesthetic that occasioned such breathlessness, an aesthetic that is neatly represented by the novel.

Externalizing Relations

My thinking about James in this context falls not far from the mark of Sharon Cameron's *Thinking in Henry James*, which beat a path away from the psychologizing of consciousness in James's fiction by instead externalizing it, insisting that consciousness be "represented spatially as being situated not 'inside' the single self but rather 'outside' 'between' persons."[22] In the section that most concerns us here, Cameron points out a contradiction at the heart of James's conception of consciousness. She notes that, in the prefaces to the New York edition, James put forward an argument for human consciousness as coming from somewhere within his characters and, indeed, from within his own consciousness as the author of his novels. However, this psychologized notion of consciousness was a revision of his fictions' more regular portraiture of consciousness as being external to the characters themselves. In the novels and stories, consciousness takes shape in the intersubjective relays and gaps between them and their relations—

relations both to other characters and to things, and more complexly to other characters by way of things, as well as by way of the plethora of images and scenes with which they come into contact.

Cameron's reading of consciousness in James's fiction is characteristic of phenomenological approaches to James. Consciousness, in these accounts, is not the production of a coherent, unified subject, or of a Freudian unconscious; rather, it is assembled, over time, and often belatedly, from experiences linking the self to things external to it.[23] In the prefaces, Cameron sees James revising, unconvincingly, the relentless representation of consciousness in the novels as something taking shape "not in persons [but] rather between them," not below the surface but in relations external to the self. She argues, correctly in my view, that despite what he wrote in the prefaces, James framed consciousness in the novels in terms similar to those used by his brother William, whose essays on radical empiricism rejected the notion of a consciousness anterior and interior to experience (77). For William, the logic of this externalization led to the thoroughgoing redescription of consciousness in terms of a psychology of experience. Cameron maintains that, very much like William, Henry was exhilarated in his fiction by the idea of consciousness as something extricated from the duality of mind and body, of subject and object, and shaped instead in the space of the relation.

Bruno Latour makes an argument about society analogous to that of Cameron about Jamesian consciousness, and to the extent that Latour's "actor-network theory" looks to extend phenomenology's disruption of the Cartesian split between subject and object, this similarity should not be a surprise. Both were coming straight out of William James's radical empiricism, for which the idea of the relation was essential.[24] And just as Henry can be read in phenomenological terms, so too is his work amenable to the concerns raised by Latour. Over the last decade, Latour has argued for thinking of society not as a homogeneous matter of fact, but rather as "a trail of *associations* between heterogeneous elements," not as a "special domain, a specific realm, or a particular sort of thing, but only as a very peculiar movement of re-association and reassembling."[25] In much the same way that, in Cameron, Jamesian consciousness is "disseminated," and that thinking is "interactive, fleeting, and ultimately interpenetrated" (77, 59), the social in Latour takes shape in the process of "mediation," "translation," and "association" (124–132). James might have found the particular word "networks" unartful; but it is only to the credit of our comparison that Latour discredits the word as well, favoring instead the more descriptive language of an inveterate Jamesian, describing networks as "flows of translations" or "the trace left behind by some moving agent"—and, in the end, as "a benchmark of literary quality" (132, 132, 131).[26]

Indeed, Latour would seem to imagine his fellow relational sociologists, whom he affectionately refers to as "ANTs" (for their obsessive perseverance, a pun on "actor-network theory"), to be engaged in the authoring of an altogether Jamesian fiction. "Can the materiality of a report on paper, a story, or rather a fiction—there is no need to abstain from a word that is so close to the fabrication of facts—*extend* the exploration of the social connections a little bit *further*?" he asks, and we might imagine the creator of Strether nodding in agreement (128). Could anything better describe, say, the hero of *The Ambassadors*, and never more so than when Strether finally comes to understand what he saw when seeing Chad and Marie de Vionnet in a rowboat on a river in the French countryside? Strether only gets himself into relation with their "virtuous attachment" (another relation) by way of going one step further, relating them to a painting, an exquisite little Lambinet, which he had almost bought many years before in his youth, and which he had been thinking about all day during his stroll.[27] The social for Latour, like consciousness for Cameron, is nothing less than Strether's process of tracing those relations.

What is striking is the particular resonance that obtains between the language with which both Cameron and Latour describe the all-important matter of the "relation"—language that, I will argue, is provocatively elaborated in James's fiction in ways that signal the beginning of a relational era in Modernist aesthetics—an era taking shape in America in the *Chap-Book* and other ephemeral bibelots looking to it for clues to the new aesthetics. Apart from the important work of understanding how the relation can serve as a solution to the subject-object divide, a solution cultivated both by phenomenology and Latour's science studies, the task of simply describing the externalized, temporally bedeviling, between-space of the relation is confoundingly difficult. When in Latour (and as we will see in Henry James), the relation is not only between people but also between things, the description becomes even harder. And yet the metaphorics of the relation have become increasingly important not only in philosophy and sociology but also in literary criticism for the assessment of Henry James and for reimagining the sociality of the novel. It is thus to the project of describing the language of the relation that my work here is directed.

For let us be clear, relating has been the fulcrum for many of the most important pieces of James criticism in the last thirty years, and not only those with phenomenological approaches. This fact has been most especially true among those attending to questions of the social in late James, starting with Leo Bersani's promise to offer a "most resolutely superficial reading of texts . . . [that] would trace the continuous disappearing and reappearing of relations and forms."[28] The peculiarity of the Jamesian relation manifests in the various critical attempts to describe and recontextualize the gaping absences around which so many of James's fictions circle—the figure in the carpet, the beast in the jungle, the crack in the bowl—whether it be, say, in Eve Sedgwick's seminal reading of a queer James in "The Beast in the Closet" (1986) or Robert Pippin's very different account, *Henry James and Modern Moral Life* (1999). For both critics, meaning assembles around the formal gesture of James imbuing "a lack" with content: the "apparent gap of meaning . . . far from being a genuinely empty one . . . is no sooner asserted as a gap than filled to a plenitude" (in Sedgwick); "an equally radical claim about the intersubjective and unstable nature of subjectivity itself" (in Pippin).[29] J. Hillis Miller's recent deconstructive reading of the indeterminacy of the effect of Caspar Goodwood's kiss of Isabel Archer at the conclusion of *The Portrait of a Lady* also turns to the problem of the gap, the between-space of relation. The problem for Miller is that we never know what the kiss between them helps Isabel decide, or why; we are given, instead "the hiatus, the elision," "the connection, the bridge," "the blank place in the language," "the gap," and "the absence of the verifiable ligatures the reader would need, with a clear conscience, to fill in a blank like that between Caspar's kiss and the knowledge it gives."[30] And for Miller, we find ourselves inhabiting the same blank space as Isabel when deciding the "what" and the "why" of her decision, James having cleverly overdetermined the indeterminacy of the space of our relation not only to Isabel but also to his novel.

The critical energy directed at the relation can be explained by how terribly hard it is to describe a gap in meaning, or a transitive space between two nominal poles. Most often, we turn to giving it a name. How do we represent the connection between two people, between people and things, the subject and the object? Most of our conventional terms are abstractions: love, desire, ethics, art. But what about the metaphorics of the relation itself? My interest in describing it, here, is motivated by the kind of work I associate with Latour, which might be linked more generally to the move currently afoot to reinvigorate the field of literature's sociality by letting go of "contexts" in favor of assembling a more flexible and imaginative notion of historical and cartographic literary relations.[31] If the history of the novel pushed us toward consciousness, might we conjecture that the history of the novel's sociality may be pushing us more fully toward the confounding temporal and spatial complexity of the between-space of the literary relation? Cameron remarks that the interest of understanding consciousness in James came from the place he holds as epitomizing the central concern of analysis of the novel with the representation of psychology, as the author of "the psychological novel par excellence" (1). We could certainly follow this observation with one about the "extreme perspectivalism" of the novels and stories, their most salient stylistic trait, noting as does Peter Brooks that it is "not things and persons and happenings that matter so much as the way they are perceived by a certain consciousness."[32] But as both Cameron and Latour would seem to suggest, there is something to be said for resisting not only consciousness but also set ideas about the social when tracing histories of the novel. What might it look like to settle with the transient externalities of the relation, the art of associating, which in James is a thing no less curious and even more difficult to describe? How does the language of relating in the James novel help us think about relating to it as a novel? How do these relations, in turn, help us think about relating to the bibelot vogue?

Relational Aesthetics

The relation in late James is a constant; it becomes visible thematically by being broken and stylistically by being opaque. If the window is the mediating object in James's house of fiction, the window gets cracked in the later James so that we actually perceive ourselves seeing through the glass, instead of just looking through an open frame. We might note that it would seem to be in recognition of something like this general formula that Latour becomes most Jamesian in his descriptive approach to the social. For a network sociologist, Latour is largely uninterested in network visualizations of the kind that have begun to appear in recent literary studies.[33] These would seem to offer an "open window" onto the social world of literature, a neat and clear view of, say, the citation and publication networks linking authors to each other and to their publics. Even if his ANTs initially sharpened their edges on networks in the technical sense—subways, the Internet—Latour has always been interested in eliciting a more literary sense of the ongoing movement of networking, movement which network graphics tend to lock in place. The visualizations to which networks lend themselves can all too easily capture a static image of a network in time, but what Latour is after instead is the evolution of relations over time. The network relation, in Latour's words, "is not made of nylon thread, words or any durable substance but is the trace left behind by some moving agent" (132). So, too, literary relations can move beyond immediate historical contexts, be they publication histories or political ideologies, and I take it that the project of the humanities in its most ambitious formulation is that of tracing new relations to older ones.

The fiction of James's late period is full of the traces of such movement, traces visible because of broken relations. One of the clearest examples is *What Maisie Knew*, which I will suggest in what follows offers a blueprint for the later fiction by using the shattered social relations of a nasty divorce to make visible the relational character of how a little girl comes to know. In *Maisie*, a novel all about extenuating relations, the issue is made explicit. The sense of relations is doubled in *Maisie*, for just as she literally functions as a relation between people, she also knows what she knows by the slow process of tracing the connections between things she sees and hears. This process is explained at the start of the novel in terms that are particularly apt for this discussion. From the beginning, Maisie was to be educated in "opposed principles" and "she was to fit them together as she might."[34] Her little world was like a "magic lantern"; it was "fantasmagoric—strange shadows dancing on a sheet" (*CB* 6:5, 215; "phantasmagoric" in *NYE*, 9). As time went on, "she found in her mind a collection of images and echoes to which meanings were attachable . . . like games she wasn't yet big enough to play," and the novel progresses by way of her increasing ability to make the attachments, and especially to relate those attachments to words (*CB* 6:5, 216; *NYE*, 12). One of the great delights of *Maisie* comes from the troubling mismatch between what she knows and what we know. What she knows is quite often a delicious surprise for us, both in those moments when what she knows is not as much as what we think she ought to know, but even more so in those moments when she comes out with something in excess of what we know, for example, the name of her mother's lover, Lord Eric, or the club where her father spent the night, the Chrysanthemum. We did not know either of these names when she throws them out. Lord Eric and the Chrysanthemum were outside our streams as readers, and for this reason, they send our heads spinning. We feel we ought to know them, but in fact we have no way of knowing them because we have not been told. We are given the answer without having been asked the question, which only produces the delirious sense that there is really so much more that we ought to know, so many more relations that we ought to be able to trace.

Maisie is a novel about social relations, but were we to imagine its author invested in the contemporary moment as a theorist of social networks, he would surely have been more interested in their illusoriness than their promise. James's fiction in today's terms would be interested in the social dysfunction of Facebook, Tumblr, Twitter, and Snapchat—the overlaps and silences and misperceptions that, so it would seem, make such ephemeral connections so perversely addicting. An emphasis on consciousness in James misdirects us from what the late James stories and novels are all about: the failure of social relations to apprehend themselves. James's formal experimentation with perspective may center *What Maisie Knew* on the consciousness of the little girl, but the story in the end is that of the failure of her relation to all the adults of the novel. In the same way, his other late fictions are most ostensibly about broken relations: between Lambert Strether and his new friends in Paris, between Millie Theale and Merton Densher, between Maggie Verver and Prince Amerigo, and between John Marcher and May Bartram. As a metaphor for the relation, nothing is quite as apt as the crack in the golden bowl, and as critics we have delighted in describing the broken relations that crack signifies. If we are to reconsider the history of the sociality of the novel, then the fractured and fractal character of so many of these relations in James's fiction would seem to impress upon us the interest in not losing the feel for the benchmark of literary quality of social networks. Networks need narrative. They are the novel's art, the tracing of relations both subtle and direct, in and out of context, and with a curiously uneven and asynchronous relation to time. We can think through a theory of networks with James, but, even more, we can turn to him for a description of the impossible-to-describe art of associating.[35]

Relations are the product of movement, and once put in motion, relations have a tendency to multiply over time. This understanding of motion and multiplication over time is suggested in a particularly interesting way by James when he wraps up his 1905 lecture on "The Lesson of Balzac" with something of a variation on the frequently noted theme of the preface to *Roderick Hudson*: "[r]eally, universally, relations stop nowhere."[36] To sum up his discussion of Balzac's permanence in the literary imagination, our relation to Balzac being an evolving constant without which the art of fiction could not go on, James ends with the following paradox:

> There is none the less such an odd condition as circulating without motion, and I am not so sure that even in our own way we do move. We do not, at any rate, get away from him; he is behind us, at the worst, when he is not before, and I feel that any course about the country we explore is ever best held by keeping him, through the trees of the forest, in sight. So far as we do move, we move round him; every road comes back to him; he sits there, in spite of us, so massively, for orientation.[37]

It is interesting that James puts Balzac's influence in such relational terms; the description would almost seem to suggest what the sociologists Duncan Watts and Steven Strogatz call the "collective dynamics of 'small world' networks," as if Balzac were a hub in a heavily clustered network, his presence there part of a dynamic system enabling "enhanced signal-propagation speed, computational power, and synchronizability."[38] So, too, in "The Lesson of Balzac," does James circle around this unfathomable problem of how Balzac's "immediate presence causes our ideas, whether about life in general or about the art they have exemplified in particular, to revive and breathe again, to multiply, more or less to swarm," while at the same time Balzac himself remains "fixed by virtue of his weight," marked by an "inaptitude largely to circulate" (116, 138, 139).

It is through—and thanks to—Balzac that relations multiply. But as James intuits, the fixed nature of that hub, upon which any network graph would depend, is an illusion. There is no relation without circulation, and there is no circulation that is not moving through time. We cannot produce a graph of Balzac's importance; we can only keep graphing, tracing the continuous disappearance and reappearance of relations, as they multiply and shift around him, over the course of literary history.

This paradox James identifies with Balzac between the swarming multiplicity of thought over time and the illusion of the fixed image, "the odd condition [of] circulating without motion," brings to mind any number of well-known moments in his fiction, especially in its later phase, where a suddenly glimpsed object gives way to swarms of "connexions"—a word used twenty-three times in *Maisie* and forty-two times in *The Ambassadors*.[39] Lambert Strether offers many of the best examples, as with his belated understanding of Chad and Madame de Vionnet's appearance together in the rowboat, but also, much earlier in *The Ambassadors*, with the many associa-

Plate 1. Cover of *Vogue*, January 31, 1895, "LE CHAT NOIR"

OUR CLUBBING LIST—refused by THE COMPLETE ALPHABET OF FREAKS

A is for Art of the age-end variety;
We Decadents simply can't get a satiety.

B is for Beardsley, the idol supreme,
Whose drawings are not half so bad as they seem.

C is for Chap-Book, the pater familias
Of magazines started by many a silly ass.

D is for Darn it—it's awfully shocking
Your Dekel-edge Hosiery, Mistress Blue Stocking.

E is for Editor; what does it mean?
Everyone now runs his own magazine.

F is for Freak: see the great exposition
Of freak magazines—5 and 10 cents admission

G is for Goup; I would much rather be
A nice Purple Cow than a G-O-U-P.

H is for Humbug attempts to be Horrid!
(See Mlle. New York, she's decidedly torrid.)

I am an Idiot, awful result
Of reading the rot of the Yellow Book cult

J is for JENSON the TYPE of the day,
Some people can't read any other, they say.

K is for Kimball, assistant of Stone;
I wonder how he will get on all alone.

L is for Lark, and the fellows who planned it Say even they cannot but half understand it!

608824·25

Plate 2. "OUR CLUBBING LIST—refused by THE COMPLETE ALPHABET OF FREAKS," from *Le Petit Journal des Refusées*, 1896. RB 608825. The Huntington Library, San Marino, California

Plate 3. *Le Petit Journal des Refusées*, 1896. AC9 B9125 896pb (A). Houghton Library, Harvard University

Plate 4. Henry Fangel, Cover of *Le Quartier Latin* 4:20, March 1898. The journal was edited by young American artists living in Paris and published simultaneously in Paris, London, and New York between 1896 and 1899. Rare Book Division, Department of Rare Books and Special Collections, Princeton University Library

Plate 5. The *Philosopher*, February 1899, published out of Wausau, Wisconsin. Little Magazines. Rare Book Division, Department of Special Collections, Princeton University Library

Plate 6. The *Clack Book* "lays an egg" on its cover for April 1896, a self-deprecating pun on sister magazines the *Lark* and the *Chap-Book*. Little Magazines. Rare Book Division, Department of Special Collections, Princeton University Library

Plate 7. John Sloan's poster for *Moods: A Journal Intime*, 1894. Special Collections and University Archives, Rutgers University Libraries

Plate 8. Stephen Crane's "I stood upon a High Place," illustration by William Denslow, back cover of the *Philistine* 8:4, March 1899

tions he attaches to a velvet neck band worn by Maria Gostrey, which becomes for Strether "a starting-point for fresh backward, fresh forward, fresh lateral flights," for "[a]ll sorts of things [that] in fact now seemed to come over him, comparatively few of which his chronicler can hope for space to mention" (21:51, 52). It is by way of the velvet band that we learn, for example, of the death of Strether's wife and child; but it is less that fact than the Balzacian swarming of "fresh backward, fresh forward, fresh lateral flights" that holds particular interest for the novel as a whole.

Joan Richardson, pursuing a similar vein of interest in linking both Henry and William James to contemporary advances in cognitive science, has recently suggested that the "mental space created by this kind of contemplation is not linear but n-dimensional, connections radiant, multiple, constellated, superpositioned, a 'sea of spuming thought,' requiring navigation" and that navigating it "is Henry James's singular writing project."[40] Writing along the same lines, Paul Grimstad describes "the ambassador effect," in which "relations are as real as, and external to, their terms."[41] I would agree and go further. The traces left behind by the moving agent of Strether's streaming consciousness as it circulates between Maria's neck band and the memory of his past not only describe the narrative modality of *The Ambassadors* but also the novel's reason for being. The novel is about Strether relating, about the exponential swarming of relations linking in all of the backward, forward, and lateral flights of Strether's attention, and our attention to it. As with Balzac, relations beget more relations, multiplying over time to the nth degree.

The Maisie Effect

The relation is centrally important to any representation of movement in fixed forms, be they network graphs, paintings, or novels. Following Jonathan Crary's insight into the fin-de-siècle transformation of understandings of perception, I would suggest that the relation in this sense was an integral part of the cultural field most often associated with the disintegrative forces of the modern world, and that it can be found in everything from William James's radical empiricism, to Henri Bergson's work on the mind, to Eadweard Muybridge's sequential photographs of horses' movements.[42] The resonance between modes of perception and the development of Modernist aesthetics is one I want to emphasize, here, by turning back to analogous instances of relational aesthetics in the *Chap-Book*.

As we have seen, relations in and between these magazines more or less swarmed in the most Balzacian of senses, drawing on an interest in the ethereal aesthetics of movement that was, at the same time, taking shape among the Symbolist poets and artists of the shadow theater shows in the cabarets of Montmartre—cabarets so risqué and cutting edge that most Americans seem never to have frequented them, not even those among James's characters who were most in sympathy with Paris. *The Ambassadors'* most bohemian characters, Miss Barrace and Little Bilham, for instance, never get much further than the artist studios of the Latin Quarter. The French literary historian René Taupin remarked in his seminal study of the influence of French Symbolism on American Modernism that 1895, the year before *Maisie*, marked the apex of American attention to the French Symbolists and their progeny, notable by the crush of the "little revolutionary magazines in the style of the French Symbolist journals and dedicated for the most part to French propaganda [petites revues révolutionnaires imitées des revues symbolistes françaises et consacrées pour la plupart à la propagande française]."[43] As I have been arguing, it would seem that any young bohemian traveling through Paris at the time would return home with the idea of starting an ephemeral bibelot of his or her own. James's fictional character, Lambert Strether, would have been part of this group, for what is it that he does in Woollett if not rekindle the lost Parisian years of his youth with his editorship of his little *Review*, with the cover of "the most lovely shade" of Art Nouveau green, the best of his "tremendous things," and Mrs. Newsome's "greatest fad" (*NYE* 21:64, 66). James's model for the *Review*, though unmentioned, must most certainly have been one of the ephemeral bibelots, and perhaps he had something like John Sloan's cover decoration for *Moods* (1894) or Will Bradley's for the *Echo* (1895-1897) in mind when evoking the green of its cover (see plates 7 and 8).

The fad for the bibelots depended upon the relations developed between them, which came to register as what was "modern" in art. As the reviewer for the German avant-garde magazine *Pan* noted, "the *Chap-Book* is turned towards getting its readership in touch with the most modern creations of the world" (see chapter 2 for a discussion of *Pan*).[44] We need an art of networks, an art of associations, to describe the feeling of those relations. Network visualizations are quite useful for representing the swarming multiplication of relations that characterized the fad for these bibelots, but they have a great deal of trouble with the representation of circulation over time. It is possible to produce network visualizations that track the number of times one ephemeral bibelot cited another (you can see a few of them at

Loie Fuller dancing, ca. 1900, a photograph by Samuel Joshua Beckett that had been in the possession of the sculptor Theodore Rivière. The Metropolitan Museum of Art. Gilman Collection, Purchase, Mrs. Walter Annenberg and The Annenberg Foundation Gift, 2005

https://sites.rutgers.edu/bibelots), and one sees in such images the relations swarming to connect with the *Chap-Book*, which was cited more than any other bibelot over the three years of my survey. But the image freezes those relations in time, a snapshot rendering of Latour's "traces of movement." They miss what Richard Hocks, following William James, has called "ambulatory relations," and what Jonathan Levin, following Emerson, refers to as the "poetics of transition" characteristic of the period's engagement with the French Symbolists' notion of "correspondences."[45] For this notion of relations, we need a finer and more nuanced art than the network graph, as the bibelots themselves seem to have known.

The artworks associated with the bibelot network, as suggested by three examples from the *Chap-Book*, can be seen to be grappling with the paradoxical problem of representing "circulation without motion": a series of images of the American dancer, Loie Fuller, who was enjoying a meteoric stint in the Parisian cabarets with her development of a dance form that put light in motion; the publication of French Symbolist poetry by both Verlaine and Stéphane Mallarmé; and the serialization of *What Maisie Knew*. In each instance, the paradox of representation swirls around the problem of the artistic rendering of the relation as it multiplies over time.

Loie Fuller's success in the Parisian cabarets in the early 1890s generated a swarm of interest in her work among the American bibelots, and nowhere is this more apparent than in the early numbers of the *Chap-Book* shortly before its publication of *What Maisie Knew*. Fuller is known for the dances she developed at the Folies Bergère, especially the Serpentine Dance and the Fire Dance, in which a central torque of her body sent yards of silk expanding into the periphery, lit from underneath by colored lights that produced what would later be known as a strobe light effect. Her dance became one of those Balzacian objects around which relations multiplied as she captured the imagination in France of the poster artists Jules Cheret and Henri de Toulouse-Lautrec and sculptor François-Rupert Carabin.

The challenge, and delight, of picturing Fuller comes from her embodiment of the paradox of representing circulation, and as such it is particularly telling that representations of her seem emphatically to stress the between-space of the relation—between Fuller in one instance and Fuller in the next.[46] She is reported to have inspired Mallarmé's famous description of the mystery of the ballet, which he outlines in precisely these terms with talk of the "ellipses or élan": "The dancer *is not a woman dancing*, for the juxtaposed causes that *she is not a woman*, but a metaphor summarizing one of the elementary aspects of our form . . . suggesting, by the miracle of ellipsis or élan, with a corporeal writing that would necessitate paragraphs of prose in dialogue as well as description to express. . . . [She is] a poem disengaged from all writing apparatus."[47] The dance scholar Ann Albright clarifies what was so profoundly new about Fuller's dance in these same terms. "For the first time," she writes, "audiences were asked to attend not to the poses at the end of a musical phrase, but rather to the motion between phrases, not to the decorative arrangement of arms and legs, but to the sequence of movement from center to periphery and back again." Rather than a series of "poses linked together by graceful transitions," Fuller's work "used the body sequentially, constantly initiating the movement with her spiraling torso, flowing out through the arms into the wands and fabric, then looping back into the center in order to start the cycle all over again."[48] The serpentine swirls of her dress confused the conventional ways of looking at dance by taking out poses and leaving only movement.

Will Bradley, "The Serpentine Dance," published in the *Chap-Book* 2:2 (December 1, 1894): 62

Will Bradley, "The Ballet," published in the *Chap-Book* 2:2 (December 1, 1894): 59

In his illustrations of Fuller for the *Chap-Book*, Bradley develops two different strategies for representing Fuller in motion: he either shows the flow of her dress swirling back on itself, or he superimposes one dancer upon the other in a sequence. The latter choice resembles something like the famous paintings from the Modernist exhibitions of the subsequent decade, most notably Marcel Duchamp's *Nude Descending a Staircase* (1912), which has been linked to Muybridge but seems equally related to the theatrics of Fuller and the representations of Bradley. It is also like William James's description of the stream of consciousness from the early 1890s, and particularly to his distinction between "'substantive' and 'transitive' states of mind."[49] In much the same language that Mallarmé uses to describe the ballerina, William James compares the stream of our consciousness to a bird's life with "an alternation of flights and perchings," where the stream is like the flight "filled with thoughts of relations" (159, 160). Bradley's illustrations seem to struggle to come to terms with such relations, to the visual description of the conjunctions between Fuller's poses. They are a visual register of William James's transitive mode, and like James we might say that the images register "a feeling of *and*, a feeling of *but*, and a feeling of *by*, quite as readily as . . . a feeling of *blue* or a feeling of *cold*" (162). When James goes on to describe the "feelings of relation" in terms of "psychic overtones, halos, suffusions, or fringes," we might be led to wonder what the stream of consciousness is, after all, if not Bradley's depiction of Fuller's serpentine dance (168).

The *Chap-Book*'s fascination with this kind of material is further suggested by its publication of a poem by Mallarmé, "Les loisirs de la poste," which appeared exclusively in the American magazine before being collected posthumously in 1920 in *Vers de circonstance* (the *Chap-Book* published it in French). The poem gives us something of the same attention to the transitive mode, the "postal pleasures" mode, in a series of twenty-seven quatrains making figurative allusions to the addresses of artists familiar to readers of the ephemeral bibelots, including Whistler, Dégas, Vielé Griffin, Balzac, Manet, and Verlaine. Indeed, the poem was headed by a note from Mallarmé explaining that he started the verses after noticing the "rapport" between the size of an envelope and a quatrain, and that their numbers "multiplied over the course of his relations [Il les multiplia au gré de ses relations]."

> Leur rire avec la même gamme
> Sonnera si tu te rendis
> Chez Monsieur Whistler et Madame,
> Rue Antique du Bac 110.
> Rue, au 23, Ballu.
>
> J'exprime
> Sitôt Juin à Monsieur Degas
> La satisfaction qu'il rime
> Avec la fleur des syringas.
>
> Monsieur Monet qu l'hiver ni
> L'été, sa vision ne leurre,
> Habite, en poignant, Giverny
> Sis auprès de Vernon, dans l'Eure.[50]

The poem engages movement on many levels, the pleasures of the post coming not from what is substantively in the poems but from their evocation of transit. It would be an obvious choice for thinking about networks, in which sociality is often metaphorized in the exchange of letters, the only thing better being, perhaps, the draping of wires from telephone poles. Like

Bradley's images of Fuller, however, the emphasis is on the transitive mode: Mallarmé gives us not the substance of the letters but their addresses. The pleasure of the quatrains themselves come from the suggestiveness of their allusions, which are specific enough to index a link between the poet and his artist friends while still vague enough to evoke a mad multiplication of relations on the part of readers trying to puzzle them out. These are addresses that must circulate without motion, a kind of movement-in-stasis that makes drawing attention to the gaps all that much more essential. The movement is as much of a paradox in print as it is visually for Bradley, where the element of time struggles against the fixity of the page. Is it any wonder that the aesthetic frisson of such a paradox would be of interest at a moment in the history of art struggling with modernity?

Having drawn James into relation with these materials, we should find it less of a surprise that James's *Chap-Book* novel imagines its main character, Maisie, knowing in precisely these relational terms. As James wrote some years later in the preface, "The infant mind would at best leave great gaps and voids; so that with a systematic surface possibly beyond reproach we should nevertheless fail of clearness of sense. . . . To that extent then I settled—to the question of giving it all, the whole situation surrounding her, but of giving it only through the occasions and connexions of her proximity and attention" (*NYE* 11, x). The issue of these connections over gaps and voids, moreover, has a particularly interesting temporal dimension. The delightful pacing of the novel's first half is made possible by the streamlining of relations to those of the sexual liaisons of a French melodrama. The connections Maisie makes at the beginning of the novel are restricted to those between her parents and stepparents, but as the novel moves forward, adding such names as Lord Eric and Perriam and the Countess and Tischbein, Maisie comes to make out in ever greater detail the "fine network of [their] relations" (*CB* 7:1, 17; *NYE*, 203). The more she knows, the more she is able to disentangle her parents' complicated relations, and better understand her role in making them possible.

But the novel moves along so quickly that we rarely know what Maisie feels. When Ida has one of her outbursts over Maisie's so-called treachery—which ends with the child being called a "clammy little fish" and a push that sends her "flying across the room into the arms of Mrs. Wix"—Maisie "was not even frightened enough to cry" (*CB* 6:8, 329; *NYE*, 89). Rather, she is "more than anything else, curious about the opinion mutely expressed" by her companions, and, over the course of the next several sentences, learns that opinion to be simply that "her mother was no longer in love" with Sir Claude (*CB* 6:8, 329; *NYE*, 89, 90). It had only been fourteen pages earlier that Maisie had put two and two together and learned in the first instance that her mother was in love with him—and "passionately" so (*CB* 6:7, 293; *NYE*, 68). All of this is tracked through the enlarging relations that Maisie takes in, the way she comes to make the connections with more and more certitude. But while we get more of her relating, we get so little of her feeling that one might come to wonder if she feels anything. Is she but a machine for knowing?

If the first half of the novel moves very quickly through an indeterminate number of Maisie's early years, the second half slows to a crawl, taking place over a couple of days in Boulogne, on the coast of France, during which time, to borrow from James's language on Balzac, all of the old connections Maisie had made begin to "revive and breathe again, to multiply, more or less to swarm." Particularly at the end of *What Maisie Knew*, when Maisie has mastered the "art of not thinking singly," the language of relation multiplies in ways that recall both Mallarmé's problematic description of Fuller's dancing, a poetics "disengaged from the apparatus of writing," and William James's ideas about "psychic overtones" and "halos" (*CB* 7:1, 23; *NYE*, 222–223). James is attempting to portray not simply relations but the relation of relations to other relations, the echo of the trace of relations over time.

Nowhere is the exponential multiplication of relations more apparent than around the possibility that what Maisie comes to know is that she has the power to make Sir Claude "afraid" (*CB* 7:7, 199; *NYE*, 326)—and, of course, what he has always been afraid of is his susceptibility to seduction. As they sit having buttered rolls and *café au lait*, just prior to not taking a train to Paris, Maisie comes to understand the meaning of his "jesting postponing perverting voice" as "a relation that had wholly changed, a relation that she had, with her very eyes, seen in the act of change" (ibid.). If the relation in the first instance had been to the difference between this moment and their "old London playtimes," the relation in the second was to a vision from "the day before [when] in the salon Mrs. Beale rose suddenly before her" (ibid.). A proper relation only comes belatedly, and then exponentially. Maisie knows at that moment that the relation between Sir Claude and Mrs. Beale, who had traveled to Boulogne both "free" but also "alone," was still in flux—they had not yet connected (*CB* 7:5, 129; *NYE*, 290, 291). That realization leads, in turn, to a fantasy about the possibility that she and Sir Claude might connect—a possibility that even makes Maisie "afraid of herself," and that informs her plea to Sir Claude that he go on to Paris with her alone, that he take the train tickets—"Prenny, prenny. Oh prenny!" (*CB* 7:7, 202, 204; *NYE*, 338, 345). Maisie seems to understand that Sir Claude now realizes that she is a problem because she is infatuated with him and will pose continuing problems between him and Mrs. Beale as well as in regard to his already troubled social status. The aura of the illicit in Maisie's relationship to him is part of the "relation." This multiplication means that nothing is straight at the end of the novel; the end is a maze of possibilities, and even after they miss the train to Paris, "they had not gone straight" back to the hotel (*CB* 7:7, 204; *NYE*, 346).

What comes back over and over again is the language of connection. "'You're a nice one,'" Mrs. Beale complains to Mrs. Wix near the end:

> "—'discussing relations'—with your talk of our 'connection' and your insults! What in the world's our connection but the love of the child, who is our duty and our life, and who holds us together as closely as she originally brought us?"
>
> "I know, I know!" Maisie said with a burst of eagerness. "I did bring you."
>
> The strangest of laughs escaped from Sir Claude. "You did bring us—you did!" His hands went up and down gently on her shoulders.
>
> (*CB* 7:7, 208; "connexion" in *NYE*, 359)

Of course, with each iteration of the "connection," the relation itself changes, building upon itself over time, and meaning different things for each of the characters involved. What breaks Maisie free from this mess at the very end is nothing other than Sir Claude finally severing the relation, cutting the tie that had bound them all together, when he tells Mrs. Beale, "We *can't* work her in. It's perfectly true—she's unique" (*CB* 7:7, 208; *NYE*, 360). Sir Claude then turns Maisie out, sending her back to England with Mrs. Wix, who still is no good for straightening: Mrs. Wix can only give Maisie "a sidelong look" and "wonder at what [she] knew" (*CB* 7:7, 209; *NYE*, 363). In the end, what Maisie knew was the sum of the connections she was able to make with what she had seen and stored away. The novel draws attention to these things by troubling both Maisie's relations to them and our own, all along the way.

The Artwork of Networks

With its attention to the art of relations, *What Maisie Knew* offers a blueprint not only for the bibelot movement but also for James's late novels, and none more so than *The Ambassadors*. One might be pushed to argue that this novel is the legate of the bibelot movement, the bibelots, as we saw earlier, having defined the dreams of Strether's youth. Strether is almost certainly the most *Chap-Book*-like of James's late fictional characters, although the novel camouflages the problem of "how Strether knows" more artfully behind the cover of what he knows about the "virtuous attachment" of Chad and Madame de Vionnet than did *Maisie* with the story of her family's broken relations (*NYE* 21:182). We can read both novels by interweaving two lines of interest, following by way of extreme perspectivalism not only what the main characters know but also how they know it. But there is also a crucial difference between the two novels, which explains an evolution in James's novelistic construction of how the linkage between what and how registers as art. Whereas *Maisie* traces the story of a little girl learning to disentangle the maze of relations swirling around her, attaching names to the things she had seen, heard, and stored away with the toys in her closet, *The Ambassadors* is about something like the opposite of that. Not disentangling but entangling, not naming but learning to unname, not linking two things together but linking everything to everything else, the art of *The Ambassadors* is to be found in such a mad multiplication of relations that the lines of connection are lost to sight. As Strether says when trying unsuccessfully to argue Marie de Vionnet's case to Sarah Pocock, "[e]verything has come as a sort of indistinguishable part of everything else"—and whereas in *Maisie* such lack of clarity would be a problem to straighten out, here it is taken as a sign of cultivation (22:201).

The passage with Sarah Pocock, where "everything has become an indistinguishable part of everything else," is one around which we can further stage a progression in the relational aesthetic. Both Richard Hocks and Paul Grimstad have read this passage as being emblematic of William James's radical empiricism, but each emphasizes different aspects of William's argument. Whereas Hocks reads the Sarah Pocock passage for an affirmation of the movement of consciousness through time, which he describes in terms of the "ambulatory relation" and the "transitional nature of ideas,"[51] Grimstad reads it for how relations are externalized, materialized, and gathered "into a large loose bundle and thrown . . . into his [Strether's] face."[52] Hocks gets to the heart of what seems important to *The Ambassadors* as a novel of process, where the interest is in the unfolding of Strether's understanding of the situation, which in my own reading is determined by his ability to multiply relations, attaching more and more things together, and eventually everything to everything (although Strether is jumping the gun in thinking he has done so here, when talking to Sarah). Grimstad's observation about the external materiality of the relation, relations being made of the same stuff as the things they relate, and on and on, is similarly important in linking the novel to radical empiricism, and more so for an interpretation informed by Latour that attempts to get beyond the resilience of the subject in phenomenology.[53] Grimstad helps us understand that the reason relations multiply for Strether is not because there are more things in the novel to be related: we never get more than Chad, Madame de Vionnet, and their assemblage of friends. The reason relations multiply is that they become related to other relations, and each new relation offers new opportunities for relating. Moreover, the question of a consciousness relating to things is externalized, relations being the stuff of everything.

Putting Hocks and Grimstad into conversation, I would suggest that the contrast between Sarah and Strether is not that of which character is right or wrong in their perceptions of the attachment between Chad and his lover; rather, the contrast is between who relates more and who relates less. Sarah can only attach one thing to another: "virtuous" can only mean one thing for her. It is this limitation that confines her to Woollett, which makes her unable to appreciate either Chad or, even, Paris. She is clearly not headed out to the red-light district with her husband, who is likely going to the cabarets to take in one of Loie Fuller's risqué performances. One is reminded of the explanation Henry gave William when the latter objected to the verbosity of the late novels. Henry complains that William seems to want him to follow a less interesting path and write like a schoolboy adding up columns of numbers, a "two-&-two-make-four system on which all the awful truck that surrounds is produced"—whereas he holds out for "the art of the brush . . . to recover whatever may be still recoverable of its sacrificed honor."[54] Sarah is adding up numbers on a slate; Strether is painting with a brush. In "The Lesson of Balzac," Henry had noted that one of the most difficult and fascinating aspects of the art of the novel was "the mystery of the foreshortened procession of facts and figures, of appearances of whatever sort, which is in some lights but another name for the picture governed by the principle of composition" (136). What he seems to be after with this talk of "the foreshortened procession" is how the novel could reproduce the visual effect of painting—the distortion of objects to give the impression of depth and plenitude—by using a literary style of multiplying the relations of relations to yet more relations.

Of course, as readers of the novel, our own lines of relation often run at cross purposes to Strether's, and only as the novel goes on does Strether catch up to us, our own situation corresponding more readily (or so it seems to me) to Maria Gostrey, Madame de Vionnet, and Chad's sophisticated Parisian friends. When Strether allows himself the thought, toward the start of the novel, that he "had wanted to put himself in relation, and he would be hanged if he were *not* in relation," we know quite well that he ought to be hanged (*NYE* 21:93). He still has many more connections to make, and the relations still need to multiply and swarm for him to get himself into relation with "the fundamental impropriety of Chad's situation, round about which they [Chad's friends] thus seemed cynically clustered" (*NYE* 21:116). But as the novel moves on, Strether is increasingly able to get into relation with the sociality of his Parisian surroundings, and in so doing he in effect lets go of the substance of his preconceptions in favor of a new assemblage of associations. He is "brought . . . into relation with Miss Barrace" at Gloriani's Sunday afternoon, where she explains to him that "in the light of Paris one sees what things resemble" (*NYE* 21:203, 207); he visits Marie de Vionnet's drawing-room, and "by a turn of the hand she had somehow made their encounter a relation" (*NYE* 21:249); he confesses to Chad that he has gone so far in his appreciation of Paris that he now no longer wants to return to Chad's mother, and we are told that the "change of position and of relation, for each, was so oddly betrayed . . . that Chad laughed out as soon as he had uttered it—which made Strether also laugh" (*NYE* 22:34). By the time Sarah Pocock arrives on the scene, he is so far gone that he is subject to the "perverse law" that "he should affect Mrs. Pocock and Waymarsh as launched in a relation in which he had really never been launched at all" (*NYE* 22:94). Strether even manages to get "into relation" with the young Mamie Pocock when he becomes aware of the fact that, alone among the second wave of ambassadors from Woollett, she had taken in the "deep still things" of Paris and thus "knew what had become" of Chad (*NYE* 22:151).

Strether finally gets into a proper relation to the attachment between Chad and Madame de Vionnet, in a scene that has been a favorite for analyses of this sort, by way of a painting, the little Lambinet.[55] James's treatment of that painting, I want to suggest, is very similar to Will Bradley's rendering of Loie Fuller in the *Chap-Book* because of the way James replicates the multiplier effect. The language of the scene is altogether that of the bibelots' group movement; what is really quite enchanting, as it unfolds, is not the substance and not the relation, but the trace of the relation, the enchanting, hallucinatory projection of a relation that is in many instances only a virtual relation, unnamed, or only belatedly perceived. It could be disconcerting to us, as literary critics, that when Strether finally gets there, awaiting the row-boat reveal of Chad and Marie de Vionnet, he is not wandering in a novel but in a painting. But to be more precise, he is in a novelization of a memory of a painting he never bought—as if literally in relation to "the trace left behind by some moving agent," that agent being his younger self. Strether is so completely in relation with his memory of the Lambinet that, unlike Maisie, he knows what is there even without having to worry about naming it, even if he could, as if it were any one thing:

> The oblong gilt frame disposed its enclosing lines; the poplars and willows, the reeds and river—a river of which he didn't know and didn't want to know, the name—fell into a composition, full of felicity, within them; the sky was silver and turquoise and varnish; the village on the left was white and the church on the right was grey; it was all there, in short—it was what he wanted: it was Tremont Street, it was France, it was Lambinet. Moreover, he was freely walking about in it. (*NYE* 22:247)

Unlike Maisie (and Flaubert), Strether does not worry about getting just the right word to describe the sky. The point is the relation. The sky is both "silver and turquoise," and it is also, more peculiarly, "varnish"—the clear color of paint that one both sees and sees through. The varnish recalls our discussion of the broken window, insisting by its presence that we see the connections Strether is making between past and present. The relations swarm and overlay temporalities simultaneously—"it was Tremont Street, it was France, it was Lambinet"—rendering the novelistic version of the Lambinet rather more like Bradley's *Chap-Book* depiction of Loie Fuller in sequence, and perhaps even more like Duchamp's Cubist *Nude Descending a Staircase*, than like what one supposes the original painting by Lambinet to have been.

To really get into relation with this scene, we would have to keep in mind that it is about more than how or what Strether knows. It is also about how the scene has been experienced since its publication. Metaphorically, the Lambinet must be meant to function like *The Ambassadors* itself, and also like one of James's favorite Balzac novels. These are objects around which our "ideas, whether about life in general or about the art they have exemplified in particular . . . revive and breathe again." They are the substantive spots from which "fresh backward, fresh forward, fresh lateral flights" take off. That role as a hub in an expanding network of relations is one the Lambinet plays for Strether, that the *Chap-Book* and *Yellow Book* play for other ephemeral bibelots, and that James would surely have *The Ambassadors* play for us, though even more fully. This version of relating suggests what it would mean to understand "internal" and "external" relations as being coterminous, and thus what it would mean to reassemble its sociality in network terms.

So how does the art of the Lambinet work for Strether? Having arrived at the Cheval Blanc, a picturesque hotel situated along the nameless river that Chad and his lover will shortly drift down in a rowboat, and having finally understood that he had gotten into relation with everything, Strether ultimately understands the relation in terms of "a text," not a painting:

> "The" thing [the arrangements for dinner at the Cheval Blanc] was the thing that implied the greatest number of other things of the sort he had to tackle; and it was queer of course, but so it was—the implication here was. Not a single one of his observations but somehow fell into place in it; not a breath of the cooler evening that wasn't somehow a syllable of the text. The text was simply, when condensed, that in *these* places such things were, and that if it was in them one elected to move about one had to make one's account with what one lighted on. (*NYE* 22:254)

Strether inhabits these relations purely in the transitive mode: all his "observations fall into place" because he seems finally to know that "to move about one had to make one's account with what one lighted on." Where, though, is he moving about? He is moving about in "the text"—from one "syllable" to the next.[56] And, of course, so are we, only with different points of reference, as we read from one sentence to the next, from one James novel to another, and then back to Balzac, and then on to Ann Albright's account of Mallarmé's attachment to a ballerina, which we might want to connect to the *Chap-Book* and Loie Fuller. If we are to move about in "these places," we need to make our "account with" what we find there, namely, other texts, other fictions, other relations.

Moreover, the sociality of *The Ambassadors* evokes both literary and nonliterary relations, and its Balzacian centrality to our thinking depends on both. We can follow these traces further, from "text" to "life," just as Strether does with both the velvet band and the Lambinet, though perhaps with diminishing returns. The novel can bring us into relation with other readers of James, as in the scholars I cite in the endnotes, and with you as readers of this book. In a rather different mood, but now as part of the same assemblage, the novel can be brought (and bring us into) other kinds of experiences. I had a copy of *The Ambassadors* in my bag on a day in February 2013, when, having just served as an outside reader at a dissertation defense chaired by Ross Posnock at Columbia, I received a phone call from home in which I learned that my mother had taken very ill. Who would have guessed that Posnock, and, relatedly, his book about the James brothers, *The Trial of Curiosity*, would find its way, at ever so many removes, linked to this phone call, with which it will be connected for me moving forward? And who would guess that Posnock's book, which does not pay any attention whatsoever to the bibelot vogue, might nonetheless be connected to the curiosity of the vogue's evanescence. When such relations happen is of little consequence. It could have happened later, when I was looking for a fitting conclusion to this chapter. With regard to my mom, it could even have been made up, though I do remember it quite clearly, for as William James was fond of pointing out, the idea of the book in the mind is every bit as open to relations as the book on my desk.[57] It could be a relation those of you reading this now have despite your wishes, a disjunctive instead of conjunctive relation. Quite likely, you have no interest in getting into my stream, even if you do have an interest in James and the bibelot vogue.

The point is that *The Ambassadors* is there, "behind us, at the worst, when [it] . . . is not before," and our collective sense of it can be but the trace of moving relations. As we move to reimagine the sociality of the bibelot movement, we could do worse than to open a link to James as a theorist of the artwork of networks, for ultimately his novels are neither the residue of consciousness nor mere objects; they are, rather, part of the ever-swarming assemblage of relations. The more relations the better.

4 Butterflies, Faddishness, and the Iconography of Desire

> Gnats, beetles, wasps, butterflies, and the whole tribe of ephemerals and insignificants, may flit in and out and between; may hum, and buzz, and jarr; may shrill their tiny pipes, and wind their puny horns, unchastised and unnoticed.
>
> Samuel Taylor Coleridge, from Chapter VIII, "Remarks on the present mode of conducting critical journals," in *Biographia Literara* (1817)

In Shakespeare's time, a butterfly could refer to a "vain, gaudily attired person; a light-headed, inconstant person; a giddy trifler"; for Coleridge the butterfly's fitful flight joined that of the gnats and the wasps to make up a tiny-piped and puny-horned swarm of ephemeral magazines.[1] In the 1890s, the two connotations were linked together, and the butterfly's range of signification expanded to a new corner of the cultural imagination. With pen and ink outlines in an aesthetic arts style, and brightly colored wings careening decidedly toward Decadence and Orientalism, the butterfly was taken up as a liberatory sign of the new consumer culture that was aesthetic in style and pretention. It tied together commercial faddism and the aesthetic avant-garde. It connoted sexual desire in the public sphere, a symbol of flirtatious American girls and queer male cosmopolitans challenging the stale prurience associated with the Realism of William Dean Howells. And it hearkened to internationalism at a moment of increasing cultural nationalism, and to the fantasy of impermanence and seasonality in an era otherwise given over in literature to substantiating the real.

The meaning of the butterfly had been developing in the decades leading up to the advent of the bibelots. For followers of the French utopian Charles

Fourier in the 1850s, the butterfly passion had signaled the love of variety in both work and sexual relations. One of painted cardboard, now held by the Library of Congress, had been the point of focus of a well-known portrait of a relaxing Walt Whitman in 1873.[2] Around the same time, a butterfly with an implike little tail had been the enigmatic signature of the American painter James Whistler. The butterfly was central to the *Japonisme* of Pierre Loti's infamous novel of fin-de-siècle Decadence, *Madame Chrysanthème* (1887), which was taken up subsequently as "Madame Butterfly" in the 1898 short story by John Luther Long, the 1900 play by David Belasco, and the 1904 opera by Puccini. By the 1890s, *Vogue* was referring to its female readers as "the butterfly sex" with some regularity, for instance, on a cover for March 5, 1896, titled "Chrysalis and Butterfly," in which a model in an opera cloak is paired against one wearing an off-shoulder, décolleté gown. Butterflies made frequent appearances on the cover of the *Yellow Book*, and by way of association they were linked to Oscar Wilde, who was described by his friend, the *Yellow Book* contributor Ada Leverson, as "a giant with the wings of a Brazilian butterfly"; Wilde wrote to another friend that *The Importance of Being Earnest* had been "written by a butterfly for butterflies."[3] It was the original title of one of the more risqué novels published in the United States in the 1890s, John Lane Allen's coming of age story, *Summer in Arcady: A Tale of Nature*, which had originally appeared under the title *Butterflies* when it was serialized in the popular literary magazine *Cosmopolitan* from December 1895 to March 1896. The next year, Kate Chopin titled her second collection of stories, *A Night in Acadie*, the switch from Allen's "summer" to Chopin's "night" suggesting how much further she was willing to go in registering what transpires in the evening between adults. Closer to home for the bibelots, one finds butterflies on a poster by John Sloan for *Moods* (see plate 7), an early bibelot in which Chopin published in 1894, and in the *Quartier Latin* in an illustration for a reprint of Edgar Allan Poe's poem "Ulalume" as well as on a striking advertisement for the Parfumerie Oriza in Paris. (Many of these images can be seen at https://sites.rutgers.edu/bibelots.)[4]

With butterflies, we are in the grip of another circulatory fad, one gendered even more explicitly than that of the black cat and purple cow. The butterfly is figured as a most feminine insect, wayward in flight, buffeted by the slightest breeze, light, full of beauty, and terribly difficult to net—but then who but a Naturalist would want them pinned to a piece of cardboard? Butterflies represent well in illustration, being decoratively at home in the margins of print columns, on Art Nouveau posters, and in dress patterns

"Chrysalis and Butterfly," *Vogue*, March 5, 1896

and millinery. They are forever young, more flirtatious than matronly, both fragile and fashionably exotic. They are essentially ephemeral, fluttering around the garden or parlor on brightly lit summer afternoons, disappearing with the onset of fall without leaving so much as a trace. They are decorative and consumable. And, of course, the most notable butterflies are migratory, traveling with the seasons across international borders. The butterfly is the bow on the kimono of a Japanese maiden, but it is also "metamorphosed," in one memorable *Vogue* illustration, to the American maiden's spring hat.[5]

What I want to suggest in this chapter is that the fad for butterflies is particularly good at evoking the gendered political historiography of fads and faddishness as a whole, as well as the role women artists played in the passing storm of revolt represented by the ephemeral bibelots. As Jennifer Fleissner has argued, fads are paradoxical events from a historiographical perspective in ways directly linked to the emergent feminist movement in the late nineteenth century. They are entirely of the moment, even compulsively so. To say that something is a fad is to suggest an absence of human agency. Fads spin out of control, but no one actually does the spinning. They are determined by a situated matrix of cultural elements that are exceedingly timely, but not timeless, and as such, they are taken to be lacking in historical relevancy. In Fleissner's telling, the fad "operates as the limit of historical knowledge," representing movements that are so deeply embedded in history as to be illegible as anything more than a passing trend, a consumerist caprice.[6] To the extent that the fad is coded feminine, associated like the fluttering butterfly to visual spectacle and the ephemerality of the season's fashions, one can imagine the challenge posed when women's writing, not to mention women's politics, as in the suffrage movement, becomes associated with faddism. No one wants their art, their writing, or their politics to register as nothing more than a fad.

One place where the ephemeral bibelots reached out to mainstream American culture is around the faddish confluence of women's popular writing and the readjustment of sexual relations around the idea of the New Woman. Many of the cultural conventions structuring the modes of sexual subjectivity that have been codified as being "Modernist"—such as the relation between sexual sophistication and smartness, or between flirtatiousness and women's independence in public spaces—can be seen taking shape in the ephemeral bibelots. They bequeathed a combination of aesthetic and sexual provocation to the then emergent mass-market magazines, which catered in content and advertising to the new consumer-oriented women's culture. In many respects, they anticipate what Donal Harris and others have identified as the "deep affiliations of mass market magazines and literary modernism" in the early twentieth century.[7] Indeed, some of the American bohemian women writers who published in the bibelots found their way after the end of the fad to successful careers in the *Saturday Evening Post*, *Vanity Fair*, and the *Smart Set*. And yet, an association with the gendered faddishness of the 1890s has colored the historical reception of the ephemeral bibelots and early mass-market magazines alike, making it difficult for either to find a permanent place in the stories we tell about the history of American literature, Modernist aesthetics, or feminism.

This chapter argues that the ephemerality of the bibelots is usefully perceived by way of the faddishness of the butterfly. The bibelots were not particularly political except in their orientation to a sexual politics that was both queer and faddish. They were strong proponents of frankness in the discussion of sexual desire—sexual desire in marriage and out, between men and women and also between couples of the same sex. Moreover, neither marriage nor art were sacrosanct from the market. The bibelots and the mass-market magazines stopped trying to protect the ideal of womanhood from the market, instead accepting that marriage, for instance, was a money game that women should also play and win. So, too, motherhood, careers, and suffrage. And so, too, art. As we have seen, the bibelots were programmatically ephemeral; this chapter considers what a sexual politics built of the aesthetic frisson of such ephemerality might entail.

In order to work through this story, we begin by connecting the career of Kate Chopin in the ephemeral bibelots to her writing in the early numbers of *Vogue*. In its early years, *Vogue* had the look and feel of an ephemeral bibelot, and this chapter considers why. We then move to the story of two female contributors to the *Lark*, Carolyn Wells and Juliet Wilbor Tompkins, both of whom went on to have prolific literary careers in the early 1900s. Between them, they published scores of novels, stories, and verses with some of the period's most prominent literary houses, as well as in many of the most widely distributed magazines. I focus here on their work published in *Munsey's Magazine*, which no one would mistake for a bibelot, but which was entirely devoted, as its editors made sure to highlight, to the "fads and furbelows, fancies and frills" of the American fin de siècle.[8] The chapter concludes with a quick look at how the Modernist sexual subjectivities emblematized by the newness of both the bibelots and popular magazines in the 1890s became popularized by women writers in the 1920s, and at how certain ambivalences in economic history and feminist theory have shaped our reception of fad culture, frequently for good cause but with the effect of large gaps in cultural histories of the period.

Chopin's Vogue

At the height of the bibelot fad, Kate Chopin was trying desperately to be published in the *Chap-Book*. Writing to Herbert Stone in early January of 1896, she almost pleaded with him to take some of the stories or poems she had sent to him. "These things have not been printed. I would greatly like to see one of them—some of them—something—anything over my name in the Chap-Book."[9] It never happened. His publishing house brought out her most important novel, *The Awakening*, in 1899, but it only did so after the *Chap-Book* had folded, and only because Stone and Kimball had taken over the assets of the other Chicago fine arts publisher, Way and Williams, which had it under contract. The young Harvard graduate also declined to take up Chopin's cause after the sexually provocative novel stirred up the very response one might easily have predicted for it, rejecting what would have been her next collection of short stories, *A Vocation and a Voice*, which contained some of her most wickedly amusing and sexually provocative short stories. (The envisioned volume was not published as such until 1991.) For the *Chap-Book* itself, Stone had earlier rejected *Young Dr. Gosse*, a novel which Chopin tried unsuccessfully to have published throughout the 1890s, not to mention two of her poems and nine more of her short stories.

Which is all very odd, because by most other measures, Chopin was a bibelotiste of the highest order. In 1895, at the very start of the bibelot movement, she placed two pieces in the little magazine *Moods*, one of the very earliest bibelots, which had begun publication out of Philadelphia the year before. Chopin was ensconced in the literary bohemianism of St. Louis, her hometown, which she had returned to two years after the death of her Louisiana husband. She was good friends with William Marion Reedy, the publisher of the *St. Louis Mirror*, who was described in the important little magazine, the *Philistine*, as being "among the scant half-dozen men of our time who have the impersonal, unmoral, wide sweep of wing that qualifies them to rank as men of imagination."[10] She was also friendly with Sue V. Moore, editor of the society magazine known originally as *St. Louis Life*, which in 1897 moved to New York and was rechristened the *Criterion*, the late bibelot so admired by H. L. Mencken (see earlier discussion in the introduction). Chopin published in the *Criterion* after a mysterious Frenchman, Henri Dumay, replaced Moore. Under the pen-name "La Tour," she gave the *Criterion* two of her bolder short stories—"The Falling in Love of Fedora" and "Miss McEnders," both of which will be discussed in a moment—as well as six impressionistic prose pieces on contemporary international fiction and society. Dumay is said to have translated some of Chopin's stories into French, including her racy "The Story of an Hour," in which a wife finds herself strangely elated by a sense of freedom after learning that her husband had been killed in a freak train accident, only to die of heart failure moments later when he walks through the door unscathed.[11] Nothing came of Dumay's translations—they were never published—but the fact that he made them is telling of how Chopin's Maupassantian style might have made her stories recognizable in the context of nineteenth-century French Modernism. It was the newness of this aesthetic that was also being championed by the bibelots in the United States.

Chopin's rejection by the *Chap-Book* can be read in terms of Stone's wariness of fads. The aesthetic flare of her stories and the newness of her sexual politics played in the same register, one that Stone, who, as we saw in chapter 3, was trying to dissociate his publication from the fad magazines, would have wanted to avoid. By way of contrast, we could consider the exceptionally warm reception Chopin received in what, on the surface, might seem like a very different kind of magazine, *Vogue*. First published in 1892, *Vogue* published nineteen of Chopin's short stories during its first decade, making her something like its in-house fiction writer. It even went so far as to put her portrait at the very top of a page in December 1894 devoted to "Those Who Have Worked with Us." The contrast with the *Chap-Book* is striking and would seem to mark Chopin out for the women's magazines, but as anyone who knows either her wickedly indelicate stories or the early history of *Vogue* would know, there is nothing self-evident about such a classification. In the first years of its publication, *Vogue* was impressively avant-garde, pushing boundaries aesthetically and with regard to the role of women in society. The magazine and its chief fiction writer were perfectly suited for each other.

If the *Chap-Book* is not always the best exemplar of the little magazines of the 1890s, *Vogue* actually is, at least to the extent that it can be seen mobilizing key visual and literary elements that had been animating the bibelot fad. On the pages of *Vogue*, the politics of gender were explicitly brought into alignment with the aesthetic spirit that had awakened in Montmartre. Its editor was Josephine Redding, a fearless advocate for feminist causes who has been suggested as the model for Chopin's Mademoiselle Reisz, the angular piano teacher in *The Awakening* who schools the novel's heroine in the senses and the need for female self-sufficiency.[12] At the time, no other magazine was more devoted to the New Woman. Its editorial pages were given over to denouncing the moral hypocrisy of relations between the sexes, and especially of societal expectations for young women with regard to marriage and careers. The visual stylistics of the magazine also brought it much in line with the faddishness of the bibelots—even though

"Those Who Have Worked with Us," *Vogue*, December 6, 1894

its initial publication predated them by a few years and it has outlasted them by more than a hundred. In addition to fashion plates and sly editorial cartoons satirizing relations between the sexes, its margins were decorated with Art Nouveau drawings by the well-respected poster artists Will Bradley and Louis Rhead.

The distinction between Chopin's reception by the *Chap-Book* and *Vogue* is interesting because of what it suggests about the emerging relation between the fad for ephemeral bibelots and mass-market magazines, which were very much in tune with faddishness. The decade of the 1890s was crazy for fads. *Munsey's Magazine*, for instance, chronicled them in a monthly column, "Latest Fads." In the winter of 1896 to 1897, these included the collection of "poker chips, champagne corks, burnt matches, pipes and old hats"—"Oh, woman, in your hours of ease/How came you to be hoarding these?"[13] The problem is that faddishness could extend both to politics and artistic reputations. The New Woman could be both figured and dismissed as the fevered follower of such fads, as she also could be when dressed up in Art Nouveau as an athletically fashionable young person riding a bike in a magazine ad, or when pictured fencing, which was said to be the "fad of the hour among American society women."[14] By the same token, writers like Gelett Burgess figured the bibelots in similar terms, as "a craze for odd sizes and shapes, freak illustrations, wide margins, uncut pages, Jenson types, scurrilous abuse and petty jealousies, impossible prose and doggerel rhyme."[15] For both women and the bibelots, the problem comes from the fad being coded as dilettantish and unreal, tied to the commercial whims of consumer culture, and buffeted by gendered associations that multiply, like loose gossip or gloves in a shopping basket, but fail to take permanent hold of reality.

Chopin's reception in *Vogue*, then, highlights the interpretive problem for contemporary scholars when both fin-de-siècle aestheticism and feminism become associated with faddishness. What it exposes is a contradictory historiographical impulse between a critique of the culture industry that is tragic and an account of new sexual subjectivities emerging alongside it that is guardedly optimistic. For example, Richard Ohmann argues in *Selling Culture: Magazines, Markets and Class at the Turn of the Century* that women's magazines were designed to contain and redirect the impulse toward cultural feminism. They "offer up possibilities of meaning that seem untroubled, uncontested. And they must do so because their producers are constrained by their position between advertisers and audiences. . . . Readers must feel broadly content with their place in the world, so that the drift of their anxieties may be channeled into smaller concerns like the need for a healthy breakfast or for a laundry soap that won't shrink clothes."[16] Catherine Keyser suggests something similar in her history of popular women's magazines in the 1910s and '20s. There, she notes the bifurcated way in which the magazines produce a modern sexual subjectivity while at the same time redirecting it toward transitory, commercial ends, such that "the sexual voracity and independence that can serve as an emblem of the autonomous modern woman can also be co-opted and redirected by the sensuality of cosmetics and the allure of advertising."[17] Notably, something very similar was said of the ephemeral bibelots in the most complete cultural history of the American 1890s. In a chapter titled "The Tinkle of the Little Bell," Larzer Ziff argued that the problem faced by the little magazines was that the writers of merit they hoped to promote were unable "to divorce themselves from the mainstream of their commercial culture even while feeling oppressed by it"—a situation confining the bibelots to being nothing much more than "period pieces."[18] In all of these accounts, the links to commercial culture are seen to be tying the aesthetic impulse of the bibelots and the political impulse of the New Woman to the kind of faddishness that falls well short of the desired ends of revolution.

So the problem with fads is that, like consumer objects, they don't last. However, what seems to matter to both *Vogue* and the bibelots is the sense of newness that is engendered by faddish temporality. Butterflies are ephemeral, and here we have movements dependent upon temporariness—both the temporariness of an art growing up from the swirl and multiplication of allusions to things like black cats and butterflies, and the temporariness of sexual liaisons that might avoid the monotonous permanence of bourgeois marriage.

The background to this story of the alignment of fad aesthetics and fad sexual politics has to do with the elite literary monthlies, where Realist aesthetics were linked to a much more conservative take on how to represent issues of sexuality. William Dean Howells, as usual, becomes the scapegoat. Despite a relatively forward stance on the subject in his novels, his essays for *Harper's Monthly* stake out a position on representing sexual relations that was rejected vociferously by many of the bibelots and implicitly by *Vogue*. For instance, in June 1889 he wrote about the impossibility of an American *Madame Bovary*, arguing not only that the publishers of reputable American magazines had an obligation not to print anything that a father could not leave for a daughter to safely read on her own, but also that times had changed, and America simply didn't have many young girls like Emma Bovary. "Generally," he wrote, with humor but apparently not irony, "people now call a spade an agricultural implement."[19] This kind of thinking was written off by Vance Thompson in *M'lle New York*, who complained that Howells was a "male blue-stocking" suffering from "intellectual priggishness" and "moral snobbishness."[20] As we will see, a similar disregard for Howells's type of injunction can also be found in the openness of mass-market monthlies, like Chopin's *Vogue*, to a more adventurous treatment of the subject in both illustration and print.

The background also concerns the realignment of artistic styles from earlier in the century that had long been associated with women's writing and consumerism. In particular, one sees in the 1890s a retooling of the "highly wrought" prose and poetry of an earlier generation of women writers, which had served as a precursor to the decorative and Orientalist stylistics so common in the bibelots. Dorri Beam describes the highly wrought style as an intervention in literary Romanticism that emerged in contradistinction to domestic sentimentality at midcentury. The style embodied an alternative language of female sexuality, "a new version of the feminine," with florid, purple prose that valued intensely ornamental descriptions of flowers and mesmeric experiences.[21] In many ways a literary equivalent of pre-Raphaelite image making, the highly wrought style gave way in the 1880s and 1890s to the serpentine lines of Art Nouveau. The key change is that the aestheticized illustrations of women, more often than not nude and posed in risqué settings, served the symbolic function not only of challenging bourgeois sexual mores but also of connecting young illustrators and authors, male and female alike, to the French avant-garde. The highly wrought style of the 1890s was understood to have a very real connection to the street life and cabarets of Montmartre.

When put in circulation in the American bibelots, the visual and literary representation of women as both desired objects *and*, at least on occasion, as desiring subjects codified something like a countercultural poetics of revolt—codified it precisely because of the representation's self-evidence as a Parisian, and thus fashionable, and thus temporary, cultural commodity. Thompson's *M'lle New York*, for example, is entirely unsubtle about its own intentions to link the aesthetic avant-garde and newly public discussions of sex as a consumer good. The desired *mademoiselle* is right there in the bibelot's title, which recalls our earlier discussion of the titles of mademoiselle *Quartier Latin*, and the supposedly rejected women writers of *Le Petit Journal des Refusées* (see chapter 2). In a sketch titled "M'lle New York" in the inaugural number, August 1, 1895, she is introduced to "you"—the presumably male, likely collegiate, undoubtedly bohemian reader—as an actress or prostitute who had lovingly offered herself to you the night before, a young woman tinged by the inconstancy of the modern city itself. She is modern because undomesticated. Having been fashionably dressed in "high-colored, décolleté, with warm flesh, rose-white and red-gold in the gaslight," she appears differently at daybreak, her "rouge and powder are smeared . . . the throat you thought so white is pallid yellow; the lips are swollen with sleep and wine." You nonetheless accept her presence beside you in bed as a Decadent kind of sweetness, and you may even indulge in "the innocent depravity of her morning kiss"; but the time has now come to send her off, "Now ring the bell and bid your man bring a tooth-brush and a glass of water." The editors place an image by Tom Powers under the article showing the sunrise over the sullen city, a lonely carriage, and—is it any surprise?—a dozen black cats scattering back to the gutters. A quarter-page advertisement on the facing page advertises a restaurant, Le Chat Noir, the city's "finest table d'hôte, with wine" to be found at "the sign of the Black Cat." The easygoing freedom of French sexuality is the obvious backdrop to the elaborate metaphor that figures reading *M'lle New York* as akin to spending the night with her.

Crucially, however, *M'lle New York* does not withhold the pleasures of the new mix of aestheticism and sexuality from women or women readers. While far from a feminist magazine, its editor Thompson being a self-avowed misogynist, as we will see in a moment, it does not hesitate to suggest that women also play at this game of temporary love. In the next month's issue, the same story is told again with a significant change in perspective, in effect putting her sexual desire before his.[22] Powers once again provides the illustration, and the image caption repeats the concluding lines of the previous article verbatim, starting "M'lle New York is awake." This time, however, the bachelor addressed by the lines is still sleeping, as if nursing a hangover, his shoulders shrugged under the covers and hair in disarray, while the young woman is comfortably propped up on her pillows, dressed in a negligée and reading a magazine—probably *M'lle New York*. He is passive, she is active. The gender of the servant has also changed. This time around she is a maid, and she seems altogether at ease when tossing a knowing smile back in the direction of mademoiselle.

As opposed to the censorious policies of the establishment literary magazines, *M'lle New York* suggests that the daughters and their servants are all grown up, with no reason to hide from the *flagrante delicto* of the night before. Indeed, here and elsewhere, the bibelot is all about reproducing the clandestine sensations of the city streets long familiar to any good reader of Baudelaire and French yellow novels, making them available to both sons and daughters. If the literary scene in America was considered to be both aesthetically and morally unsophisticated, Thompson and Powers were offering *M'lle New York*'s namesake as the figurehead for a sexual revolution.

Much of this provocation happens visually, and in a style picked up di-

Tom Powers, illustration for inaugural issue of *M'lle New York*, August 1, 1895

Tom Powers, illustration for the second number of *M'lle New York*, September 1, 1895

rectly by magazines like *Vogue*, so it is important to take some time to understand the bibelot's iconography of desire. Illustrations make their way onto most of *M'lle New York*'s pages, where they move aggressively from the margins into the columns of text.[23] The print columns and type size were, themselves, irregular, so the visual effect is often startling. Text flows around images, images intrude on and divide text. The decorations run not just down the side margins of the page but down the center as well. In the article where Thompson complains about Howells's priggishness and snobbishness—he

While in England and America there is very little literary activity, in the unregarded corners of the earth new writers are coming to the front. Who has concerned himself with Italian letters in late years? And yet there are D'Annunzio and Negri. Spain, Holland, Sweden have felt the new impulse in literature and now there has come out of insignificant Portugal a writer whose work must be taken into serious consideration.

Portugal?

When one has said Camoens one has said almost all. Some of us have read Joao de Deus, a poet who has written wonderful, perfect lyrics. But Joao de Deus is old now. Last March his countrymen celebrated the sixty-fifth anniversary of his birth. His writing days are over. The man of the day in that disregarded little country is Eugenio de Castro. His latest volume has achieved an extraordinary success. Before that he was chiefly known by "Interlunio," which appeared, I believe, in 1891. Far more ambitious is the new work, "Belkiss, Queen of Sheba, of Axum, and of Hymiar" (Francisco Franca Amada, Coimbra). It is a dramatic poem in prose, if one may use an awkward phrase. It is written in a style which suggests the Flaubert of "Salambo"—plastic, vibrant, marvellously colored. There is occasional extravagance, and at times the volubility of youth is given full rein, but when all is said there remains a work of high power, distinction, and exquisite lyric quality.

A word of wisdom from Mr. Apthorp: "'Art, the noblest blossom of every age,' is always aristocratic. Democratic art is a contradiction in terms."

In de Castro's drama, Belkiss, the young queen of Sheba, loves Solomon, whom she considers the wisest and mightiest of kings, though she has never seen him. She proclaims aloud her love for him. Hadrad, the dethroned king of Edom, is a pretender to her hand. He assures her that Solomon is unworthy of her love.

"You are his enemy," the young queen replies, "Solomon is powerful, just, and tender."

"Ay, so strong that he has had to call on Egypt to aid him in conquering Guezer; so just that he has usurped the rights of his brother Adonijah; so tender that he left the Queen Vaphres to die of desertion and despair."

"It does not matter," the queen answers, "in spite of all I love him and shall be his."

However, the words of Hadrad have impressed the young girl. And in addition Zophesamin, the old priest and savant, who has instructed her since her childhood, urges her to put no confidence in the Jewish king. But in the insomnolent nights she dreams of the kisses of Solomon—of Solomon, who loves women as she loves precious stones. And Belkiss follows her destiny.

Her love was a form of humility, a ravished and ecstatic mode of genuflexion.

The Admiral of Solomon's fleet bears her tidings of Solomon's glory, his wisdom and beauty. Omens and the outcry of the court—nothing will stay her, and she sets out for Jerusalem. There her fate is accomplished. She is one among the splendid women whom Solomon loves as she loves precious stones. In the last act of this truly remarkable drama she has returned to the palace of Sheba. Youth is dead and dreams are dead; there is only knowledge of good and evil.

My objection to William Dean Howells is based not so much upon his intellectual priggishness as upon his moral snobbishness. I do not wish to rage against him as though he were the beast of the Apocalypse, but he and Gilder (the Misses Gilder) and that ilk are the chief defect of American literature. While Mr. Howells merits one's habitual indignation, Mr. Gilder is undoubtedly the worse of the two. I have never known a man so uniformly nul.

In Germany the notable event in letters is the organization of the Pan Society. Founded in Berlin a few months ago, its aim is, by according an equal care to all forms of art, to prepare the way for a multiple and organic artistic life. All formulae and doctrines are abandoned at the outset. Individuality at any cost—the antithesis of Richepin's chameleonic theory—is the end to be attained. This, by the way, is the note of young Germany, in politics as in letters, in art as in the conduct of life. Nietzsche has laid frantic emphasis on it; Langbehn, the mysterious and sterile author of "Rembrandt, Educator," about which there was so much pother five years ago, twanged the same string; Karl Kuechenmeister, the first of German critics in this day, discusses the question with admirable force in "Der Kampf um die Persoenlichkeit. You suggest that it is only a step from individualism to nihilism. Unquestionably. I once heard Prince Krapotkine define nihilism as "absolute individualism—the negation, in the name of individual liberty, of all obligations imposed on the individual by society, the family, and religion."

The trend of modern thought toward individualism is not without significance.

The Pan society has issued a review, which is undoubtedly the masterpiece of periodical literature. Two numbers have already appeared. It is published partly in German and partly in French. Among the foreign contributors are Whistler, Garborg, and Vallaton.

Illustration accompanying a denunciation of William Dean Howells as "the chief defect in American literature" in *M'lle New York*, August 23, 1895

also calls Howells "the chief defect in American literature"—the sentences are interrupted by a decorative ribbon descending seductively from the middle of the page down to a rowdy cupid on all fours in the lower margin. The image itself suggests the sexuality that Howells would not recognize. Readers' eyes are invited to slide down from the ribbon to a quip about Nietzsche and "the trend of modern thought toward individualism," and farther down to a blurb for the publication in Berlin of a German ephemeral bibelot *Pan* (see chapter 2). But they are also tempted to move from the text to illustrations adorning other parts of the page, where women in décolleté sit atop the text on the top left and to its side in the middle right margin. It may be that the women represent those depicted in a prose poem that is under discussion, a work by the new Portuguese poet Eugenio de Castro written in the style of Flaubert's *Salambo*. "Her love," we read, "was a form of humility, a ravished and ecstatic mode of genuflection." But the images do not register as illustrations of the text. Rather, they provide a visual juxtaposition that sets the mood, and that mood is salacious, erotic, and excessive—meant not to protect its readers from sexuality but to expose them to it.

The thing that makes early numbers of *Vogue* so curious today is that they not only share *M'lle New York*'s angry denunciation of American society's moral hypocrisy on the question of sexuality but that they also do so by visually linking that political position to the French avant-garde. *Vogue*, which predated the bibelot movement by several years, began operations under a very different set of assumptions than those set out by Thompson. As stated by its publisher in the first number, December 17, 1892, "[t]he definite object is the establishment of a dignified authentic journal of society, fashion and the ceremonial side of life." Nevertheless, one also finds in *Vogue* provocative editorials and works of fiction paired with floridly Decadent illustrations by two of America's best-known illustrators in the Beardsleyesque style, Louis Rhead and Will Bradley. Like the images decorating the margins of Thompson's *M'lle New York*, those in Redding's *Vogue* feel not only modern but also dangerous, especially when accompanying editorials making a feminist case against romanticizing marriage, promoting suffrage, and arguing that women should have careers—or when showing up alongside an erotic short story by Kate Chopin.

Redding, not surprisingly, was more interested than Thompson in the damaging effect of the idealization of women on women themselves; and there is no convincing way to make the argument that *Vogue*, which from the start was written for elite bourgeois society, was going to follow Thompson all the way down into the gutters of Montmartre. And yet, confining ourselves to the period in which the two magazines were appearing on newsstands, potentially side by side, we find a great deal of continuity between them visually. For instance, a *Vogue* editorial on September 12, 1895, combines text and image to warn that women are fooling themselves if they think that marrying will protect them from the world of worry and care, the image signaling that sex is also an appropriate subject in the discussion. First a sample of the text:

> Leaving out of account the not inconsiderable number of wives who are compelled to protect themselves and their children from their husbands, the experiences that marriage brings to most women are in reality very terrible. With maternity comes not only physical anguish, but care and anxiety that know no respite. . . . If maidens, young and elderly, would only force themselves to face the prosaic facts that husbands at the best are only comrades and breadwinners, not knightly "protectors"; and that matrimony is a state of reciprocal service, certain suffering and hazard, not a sheltered, restful haven for wives, they would spare themselves much postmarital disillusionment and misery.

At first, the image that accompanies the editorial might seem incongruous with such bold and practical advice. Orientalist oil lamp stands, each of them topped with bare-breasted sphinxes holding smoldering pots, flank the editorial in left and right margins. Smoke pours from them—dreamily, suggestively, erotically—over the top of the page, with the "V" of *Vogue* floating in the middle. The rest of the magazine's masthead is spelled out in globes on either side of the spiraling lamp stands, and their clawlike pedestals rest along a decorative bottom margin as if on some kind of carved, granite slab. The dreamy Orientalism of the image contrasts with the directness of the text, which gives a matter of fact explanation of the domestic and sexual obligations of the marriage contract, and the "reciprocity of one kind and another" expected of wives. But their juxtaposition adds an emotive twist to the editorial, the reality of expectations about sex in marriage opening upon the titillating iconography, which is suggestive of the pleasures of sex itself.

One finds in *Vogue* from this period any number of illustrations like this one that would have been entirely at home in *M'lle New York*, images of aesthetic transgression that visually transport the editorial and fictional content of both magazines. The *Vogue* masthead on the cover for the next week, September 19, 1895, reprises one of *M'lle New York*'s favorite aesthetic arts images, a woman taking shape in sinuous waves of mist emitting from a genie's lamp. It compares directly to images in the August 1895 *M'lle New York*, where one finds illustrations of a woman emerging from a wine bottle and the tip of a cigarette. A *Vogue* editorial the following year, May 21, 1896, which contrasts women's obligation to follow fashion to the mistaken idea that men are indifferent to it, is punctuated on one page with another image

Genie in a vase, *Vogue* cover, September 19, 1895

Genie in a wine bottle, *M'lle New York*, August 1895

of women emerging from cigarette smoke, "Fancies that Begin and End in Smoke," and on the next with an eroticized illustration of a young woman in deep décolleté with her head thrown back and darkened, belladonna eyes—a come-hither look that would have been at home in the margins of Thompson's bibelot.

And surely most striking of all are *Vogue*'s illustrations by Louis Rhead and Will Bradley, which were carried out in the style widely recognized at the time as that of Aubrey Beardsley. In the January 31, 1895, edition, the one featuring the cover of "Le Chat Noir" (see plate 1), Rhead provided a most astonishing image of an androgynous warrior in a mazelike sea of vines and flowers, the image accompanying a world-weary essay that advised readers to "[a]ccept the fact that the world is selfish, and do not expect it to scale altitudes of good behavior." In the April 11, 1895, edition, he provides another illustration of an androgynous figure, this time wearing an intricately designed robe that trails along the lower margin of the page. He or she carries a staff of lilies that sweeps from the left margin into the column of text—an editorial that begins, ironically given the image, "'Being a lady' is the goal of every woman's ambitions," which argues against the false airs women from poor backgrounds take when they enter into society. Yet another highly stylized figure by Rhead rules angelic over the editorial for June 27, 1895, which attacks the hypocrisy of the antisuffragists, whose "cause is a losing one, and despite their protests, some fine day they will find themselves no longer political bond women, classed with criminals and idiots, but free, the political peers of their brother voters."

Like these images by Rhead, Bradley's illustrations for *Vogue* during this same period, often featuring his stylized orchids, with dark masses balanced harmoniously against mazes of tendrils, are recognizable as being "Beardsleyesque." Although somewhat more subtle than *M'lle New York*'s, they, too, demand a transport to the scene of French and British Decadence. Bradley's illustrations invariably accompany the editorial pages, for instance, one on November 8, 1894, chiding men for having their vanity bruised by women who are "too vociferously self-assertive," or another on November 14, 1895, explaining the prevalence of divorce by asserting that the "feeling that mutually attracts a man and a woman to one another wears out very soon after marriage. This being the case, why pretend that it is eternal?" The Japanese influence on Bradley is particularly clear in the image for this editorial, in which an Asian woman's face is suggested in outline at the top left margin, her body taking shape only as the negative space of the open air, all of this worked thematically onto the fabric of a Japanese screen. These are quite a bit milder than Beardsley's famous illustrations for *Salomé* (1894) and *Lysistrata* (1896), and an essay published in *Vogue* on February 20, 1896, "A Word about Posters" (reprinted from the *New York Times*), even tries to argue that Bradley was nothing like Beardsley, despite what people were saying about him: "[O]ne feels irresistibly drawn toward such a man as one feels irresistibly repelled from Beardsley."

"BEing a lady" is the goal of every woman's ambition—except those, of course, who are so fortunate as to have been born to that estate. Ideals change with the circumstances of the aspirant. The over-burdened, poorly paid girl of the tenement, who works in a factory or stands serving in shops for a weekly pittance, sighs for wealth, idleness, fine clothes and "gentlemen friends." The wife of the suddenly enriched speculator or Tammany politician, or miner, possessed of wealth which places costly raiment within her reach, and leisure that leaves her free to devote her energies to the cultivation of fine ladyism, finds, however, many lions in the way.

At every turn she is made to realize that she is a social "out," and that her want of ancestors is very damaging. Her personal idiosyncrasies, her infelicities of language, her gaucheries of behavior, her lack of repose, betray continually that she is one newly arrived at wealth—a fact she wishes to ignore.

Her guests, usually selected with a view to pushing herself on, are invariably her contemptuous critics who attend her balls for the supper, or accept theatre or opera invitations as free show opportunities. It is a game on both sides. The guests lend themselves for use as social ladders, taking their pay in sumptuous fare and costly amusement. When once the Society bee gets into the parvenu's bonnet she straightway flings away every scrap of dignity she may have possessed. Fawning frequently becomes her ideal of social intercourse.

Even those who have little sympathy with the ambition of the newly enriched one for social recognition, can not but pity her when she undergoes the ordeal of contact with the "ins." Assured of their position, they contrive in the subtlest manner possible to make the poor "out" realize her costume, physical and linguistic deficiencies. The victim not infrequently makes the mistake of trying to meet insolence with aggressive pretentiousness, her object being to hide her social newness by assuming an I'm-as-good-as-you-are air. She deceives no one, however.

There is room for a manual of behavior prepared in the interests of the nouveaux riches, where stress could be laid upon one or two points that are ignored by current works on etiquette. If the parvenu could be persuaded to be simple and unaffected and to give up pretending to be other than she is, her social pathway would be shorn of many disagreeable experiences and mortifying explanations. Her voice, her footstep, her carriage, her vulgar self-consciousness, her address, all emphatically testify that she is not a lady, and neither diamond tiaras nor lavish expenditure can obscure this humiliatiug truth. In breeding and culture, and in the indefinable charm which results from refined associations the parvenu will always be at a disadvantage, a fact she would show wisdom in acknowledging, at least to herself. In that event she would refrain from weaving silly inventions which mislead no one. For example, her Irish hod-carrier father can not be transformed into an English country squire by word of mouth, for his daughter's hands and speech and lineaments proclaim the nationality and the humble occupation of that ancestor. Lying for social effect and failing to convince is a stupid, as well as wicked proceeding.

Parvenu, give up pretending that you've always been a butterfly!

WE fancy this number will seem somewhat unique to the public at large. It is almost wholly devoted to fashions—fashions, however, that in their admirable presentation and varied subject, are intensely interesting in themselves and particularly to Vogue's readers. Two years ago (it is well to remind the public that Vogue has attained its present position as a standard of authority in little more than this period)—such an array of excellent designs could not have been procured. Vogue only has succeeded among countless unsuccessful attempts in establishing itself as a paper specially acceptable to gentlewomen, and in giving adequate treatment to the very diverse considerations that fall within the broad idea of Fashion. That its success has been wholly of its own making it cannot for a moment claim. Without friends it could have accomplished little or nothing—many cordial friends who enjoy a weekly that is without impertinence, always clean and never dull. That it has a creditable past few will deny; that it has a most alluring future may be inferred from the enthusiastic opinions some of its readers are good enough to convey by written communication or casual remark. For such approval Vogue has to make its most appreciative acknowledgments.

Though, as promised in advertisements, more than one hundred available designs are given in this number, very many of those procured for publication have of necessity been held for the next two or three issues. Still experience having demonstrated that to be once a reader of Vogue is to be one always, the remainder of this abundant provision of valuable and practical design will reach in due course those for whom it is intended.

Louis Rhead, illustration for "After a Few Years of Adult Life," *Vogue*, January 31, 1895

And yet, there is really no mistaking what associations the images provoke, especially given the editorials that Redding had been choosing to accompany them. The new, modern style of both Rhead and Bradley's images insist on the sensorial relay between *Vogue*'s arguments and its illustrations; and the political effect of that relay varies from that to be found in *M'lle New York* more in its amplitude than in its substance. They both evoked a spirit of revolt, the evolution of new sexual subjectivities for men and women alike.

It needs to be admitted that this comparison between the iconography of desire in *M'lle New York* and *Vogue* is troubled by one rather important thing, the overt misogyny of the former's editor, Vance Thompson. It was a misogyny that was so blatant as to make at least some of the magazine's other contributors, including the coeditor James Huneker, take to the page in opposition. Thompson opens the sixth number of the fortnightly, from the second half of October 1895, with a spirited polemic on the merits of misogynistic men in the face of strong women, declaring that "God alone has the right to be a misanthrope; for man there is only misogyny": "Kiss her and coddle her, feed her immature flesh and cover her undeveloped bony structure with gay and riant robes, but have done with the foolish, flattering lie. She is beginning to take it seriously." Huneker gives a reply in the very next number, at the start of November 1895, with an article titled "Gynolatry" in which he writes that, "No, man is not woman's superior, mentally, physically, or morally; he merely happens to be born with harder muscles. He has terrorized her from the start. It has been might against right. And yet, with all this, woman remains sovereign of all she surveys."[24] But it is also significant that Thompson's misogyny is not the garden variety to which we are accustomed. It is quite different from that of Teddy Roosevelt, who famously decried "overcivilized man" in his call for a more strenuous life of modern war and big game hunting, a position not out of line with the literary prurience of the Atlantic group monthlies that exalted maidenhood and motherhood above all else.[25] Thompson is after other game. The tone of his writing is consistently self-mockingly brash and blasphemous. His syllogism, if God is a misanthrope then man ought to be a misogynist, coupled with his particular attention to the New Woman, suggests that what he wanted was to be flagrantly disruptive of dull and outmoded fixities in sexual, religious, and cultural life. Whether or not he was successful is, of course, another story.

What is certain is that there was continuity between *Vogue* and *M'lle New York* in their iconography of desire, as well as in their editorial screeds against moral hypocrisy, which suggests that they were reaching out to an audience that shared a common language. And in this respect, Chopin is an exceptionally useful bridge. After all, she would shortly be publishing in another New York bibelot, the *Criterion*, alongside a number of authors who were also contributors to *M'lle New York*. It seems fair to argue, for example, that Chopin's stories in *Vogue* are rather like James Huneker's first signed contribution to *M'lle New York*, an erotic short story from August 23, 1895, "Venus Victrix," later collected in *Melomaniacs* (1902). His biographer Arnold T. Schwab calls the piece "a Remy de Gourmont idea handled in the manner of Jules Laforgue," and as noted by another critic, it was printed alongside an untranslated poem by Laforgue. Huneker writes in his memoirs that he had been imitating Maupassant at the time, as too was Chopin.[26] Huneker's tale builds around the theme of the persecution of Christians and the cult of Venus in the time of Diocletian. A massive crowd of Romans had become bored with the spectacle of Christians dying before the lions with little fanfare, but they "surged with pleasure" when a young woman, a "slim figure, clad in clinging garments of pure white" is guided into the circus to worship the statue of Venus. She refuses to prostrate herself before the idol of the goddess, whom the story names the "foe of virginity," and so her persecutors lead in a Christian boy, "a goodly youth to look at—slender, lithe, olive-skinned with black curls clustering over a broad brow, and eyeballs blood-streaked." As a challenge to their Christian vows of chastity, the two are stripped, bound together, and urged by the statue of Venus and their tormentors to "love and worship her and forget their pale God." As one might suspect, the "subtile cruelty of the torture" seized not only Rome's fancy but also that of the two young souls, who lose their fight against the urges of the flesh. That evening, "the Venus was carried about Rome and great homage was accorded her" while the two young people, returned to their homes, weeping unceasingly before their discovery of the knowledge of "the power of music and its conquering evil."

The most obvious corollary in Chopin's *Vogue* stories is "An Egyptian Cigarette," written in 1897 and published on April 19, 1900. While similar to Huneker and Laforgue, the piece is somewhat unusual for Chopin to the extent that its empurpled prose recalls the highly wrought style of an earlier era. In it, a young woman is coaxed by an architect friend of hers, who was recently returned from "the Orient," to his smoking den with a special box of cigarettes, a gift given to him "in Cairo by a species of fakir."[27] With the shimmer of moonlight rustling over her, she deeply inhales the smoke of one of the cigarettes and slips off into an erotic dream, similar to the "mesmerist excursion" that had marked female sexual fantasy in popular literature at least since the 1840s.[28] Chopin's heroine imagines herself far removed from the drudgery of domestic space, alone in a blistering desert, where an abusive Arab lover had left her, without either the kiss or the fierce anger to which she had become addicted. She despairs, weeps bitter tears, and relishes her bruises. And then, still in the fog of the dream after waking, she longs to know what other dreams await her, "a vision of celestial piece; a dream of hopes fulfilled; a taste of rapture, such as had not entered into my mind to conceive."[29] The twist at the end of the story comes in the unwelcomed return of her architect friend, a banal and milquetoast substitute for the dark hero of her Arabesque dreams.

"An Egyptian Cigarette" has always been considered something of an exceptional case in Chopin's oeuvre, more purple and florid than her other stories. That said, while it is atypical in its stylization of masochism in the dream sequence, it is like many of her other stories in its desultory and ironic take on the dissatisfaction women are likely to find in entertaining dreams of desire. The play of desire and disappointment is quintessential Chopin, even if, stylistically, most of her other *Vogue* stories have a more Maupassantian snap to them. This snap, I want to argue, is more representative of the shift toward self-assured, public female figures of twentieth-century popular women's fiction whom we will consider shortly.

To get a feel for this style, we can turn to two of Chopin's *Vogue* stories that were reprinted in *St. Louis Life*—the magazine that became the bibelot, the *Criterion*, in 1897. In the sharply plotted "Two Summers and Two Souls," published in *Vogue* on August 8, 1895, a young woman falls in love with one of her suitors just as he is falling out of love with her. The story has three parts, spread over a single page of the magazine. At the start of the tale, he proposes and pursues her with an intense slew of love letters; she acquiesces only a year later, after he had lost interest in her; the story concludes with him honoring the original proposal, even though it felt like he was going "unflinchingly to meet the business obligation that he knew would leave him bankrupt."[30] Like many of her other stories, this one's lively cynicism is aimed directly at bourgeois domestic platitudes about matrimonial purity and disembodied love.

The second story, "The Unexpected," published in *Vogue* on September 19, 1895, is a similarly plot-driven tale exploring the inconstancy of sexual desire and its implications for courtship and marriage. A young man leaves his fiancée for a business trip, falls deathly ill, and returns a fortnight later disfigured and on the verge of death. Out of a sense of duty, he wants to push forward the marriage so that his fiancée will be provided for in case he dies, but she is repulsed by the idea.

> This was not the man who had gone away from her; the man she loved and had promised to marry. What hideous transformation had he undergone, or what devilish transformation was she undergoing in contemplating him? His skin was waxy and hectic, red upon the cheek-bones. His eyes were sunken; his features pinched and prominent; and his clothing hung loosely upon his wasted frame. The lips with which he had kissed her so hungrily, and with which he was kissing her now, were dry and parched, and his breath was feverish and tainted.[31]

As previously, the story's most striking aspect is a blatant cynicism toward the moral compass of bourgeois marriage, and in particular to the enshrinement of disembodied sexuality as an ideal. Not sensing her reluctance, the young man presses her to marry him. But his physical transformation is too much for the young woman to bear, and the story closes with her whispering "never" to herself, "not for all his thousands! Never, never! Not for millions!"[32] Chopin's frankness proves incredibly refreshing, especially in light of the more typically sentimental and moralistic fiction being published in the elite literary monthlies.

These two stories from *Vogue* share a great deal with Chopin's writing in the bibelots. Consider, for instance, two fugitive pieces, "A Scrap and a Sketch," published in the short-lived little magazine, *Moods*. The "scrap," since collected under the title "The Night Came Slowly," is a prose poem of fewer than three hundred words, which contrasts a highly wrought, erotic reverie of abandonment "to the soothing and penetrating charm of the night" with its interruption by a "detestable" bible salesman with "red cheeks and bold eyes and coarse manner and speech."[33] The "sketch," now known as "Juanita," is clearly modeled on Maupassant; it concerns the erotic coming of age of Juanita, the plump daughter of Missouri shopkeepers, who, like Maupassant's "*boule de suif*," was "not so unattractive to men as her appearance might indicate."[34] It is telling that just before writing these pieces for *Moods*, Chopin had corrected the proofs of a standard local color tale for the *Atlantic*, "Tante Cat'rinette," her first for that prestigious magazine. Emily Toth suggests that Chopin had probably been frustrated by the conventionality of that story, a "faithful slave" narrative similar to those made famous by the likes of Joel Chandler Harris.[35] In it, "Tante Cat'rinette" had been freed by her master for having successfully nursed his ill daughter back to health; when, as a grown woman, the daughter takes sick, Tante Cat'rinette nurses her again and goes even further, selling her home and giving all her savings to the daughter and her husband. Directly upon finishing the proofs, Chopin turned to translating, in her own words, some "delicious comedies" by Aristophanes and a particularly Decadent tale by Maupassant called "*Un cas de divorce*."[36] As Chopin renders it, Maupassant's story concerns a young husband's perverse obsession with hothouse flowers; he rejects his attractive, young wife in favor of their sweet perfumes, their "tiny bodies [which] throw the swooning soul into a paradise of visions and ideal voluptuousness."[37] The contrast between the bibelot stories and the one in the *Atlantic* is extreme.

Moods carried its own prestige as one of the more frequently commented upon bibelots published in the United States during the period. It came pack-

A∴SCRAP∴AND∴
A∴SKETCH∴

By Kate Chopin.

I AM losing my interest in human beings; in the significance of their lives and their actions. Some one has said it is better to study one man than ten books. I want neither books nor men; they make me suffer. Can one of them talk to me like the night—the Summer night? Like the stars or the caressing wind?

The night came slowly, softly, as I lay out there under the maple tree. It came creeping, creeping stealthily from out of the valley thinking I did not notice. And the outlines of trees and foliage nearby blended in one black mass and the night came stealing out from them, too, and from the east and west, until the only light in the sky, filtering through the maple leaves and a star looking down through every cranny.

John Sloan, illustration for Kate Chopin's "A Scrap and a Sketch," *Moods*, vol. 2, 1895

aged in a wrapper featuring drawings by John Sloan—the pre-Ashcan School Sloan, making his way professionally with magazine and newspaper illustrations squarely in the mold of the French aesthetic arts. The volume in which Chopin's stories appear shows a woman in jade green coming out from amongst the trees following, unsurprisingly, a white butterfly (see plate 7).[38] Sloan, during this period, was well known in the bibelot circuit. He did prints for the most famous of the bibelots, the *Chap-Book*, as well as for others including the *Echo*, the *Lotus*, and the *Fly Leaf*. One gets to Chopin's "scrap" by looking past another of Sloan's designs, which borders the text on two sides. Like the cover, this one also features a young woman who is dressed in the style of Art Nouveau sitting in a field, imposed upon by the dark shadow of a tree. *Mood*'s masthead carries the subhead *A Journal Intime*, which, of course, corresponds well to the intimate character of Chopin's scrap. But the Franglais of the subtitle also evokes Paris, which was, in aesthetic terms, at the journal's center of gravity; and, with the help of a crude nontranslation, it marks the bibelot as a journal "in time," as in time's stream. The paper is thick and fine-grained, the printing set thoughtfully on the page, the volume handsomely decorated with illustrations that, yet once again, reach out into the text.

And that brings us to Chopin's two stories for the *Criterion*, which had been moved by that time to New York and was being edited by Dumay. Published under the pseudonym La Tour, these two stories push sexual desire in a new direction, treating in turn perfidy and lesbian desire. "Miss McEnders," published on March 6, 1897, is another Maupassantian skewering of the haute-bourgeoisie, in which a morally self-righteous debutante discovers not only that her fiancé had had an affair with her seamstress, who is the unwed mother of a young child, but that her father made his money from bootlegging whiskey and illicit business deals. "The Falling in Love of Fedora," published on February 20, 1897, is an even more unusual and risqué tale that ends with a lesbian kiss.[39] In the story, the thirty-year-old Fedora has grown largely uninterested in "male beings," who had failed to measure up to her expectations, but then one of her sister's male friends catches her fancy. As she gazes up into his face, Fedora suddenly realizes "that he was a man—in voice, in attitude, in bearing, in every sense—a man."[40] There ensues a brief but intense infatuation on the part of Fedora, who, after a couple paragraphs of fierce longing, finds an excuse to be the one to pick up the young man's sister at the train station. Fedora recognizes a "suggestive resemblance of the girl to her brother," and, while driving her home in the buggy, "presse[s] a long, penetrating kiss upon her mouth." The girl "appeared astonished, and not too well pleased," but Fedora "with seemingly unruffled composure, gathered the reins, and for the rest of the way stared steadily ahead of her between the horses' ears."[41]

Critical opinion on "The Falling in Love of Fedora" has evolved over the years from seeing the kiss as an expression of a classically repressed spinster to a provocation for a queer reading of the "varieties of desire and sexualities" in Chopin's work as a whole.[42] My own proclivity, as you might suspect, is to choose the latter of these two options, which makes perfect sense from within the literary network of ephemeral bibelots. Readers of the *Criterion*, one can be sure, would have particularly enjoyed Chopin's open-ended flirtation with the possibility that Fedora tended toward Sapphic associations. As we saw earlier (in the introduction), the *Criterion* provided the relays needed to understand it as such. Dumay had raided the contribution of many of the earlier bibelots and was publishing, among others, Burgess, Thompson, and Huneker on the pages of the journal alongside "La Tour." The journal's new literary critic, Percival Pollard, was even publicizing a literary group in Hartford, Connecticut, calling itself the Black Cats, which had arranged a program of readings for the coming season including Georges du Maurier, Walt Whitman, James Lane Allen, Ambrose Bierce, Henrik Ibsen, and Bjornstjerne Bjornsen.[43] These are all familiar names in fin-de-siècle international aesthetics, but they are not ones we would typically associate with Chopin, and that is a mistake. Making the connection brings the shared world of *M'lle New York* and *Vogue* into view, where the frank discussion of sex and iconography of desire combined in surprising ways with consumer fashions and ideas about both feminism and faddishness.

The Butterfly Sex

Besides Chopin, what role was played by women writers and artists in the bibelot fad? It is well known that women founded and edited many of the little magazines shaping the Modernism of the early twentieth century. *Poetry* was established by Harriet Monroe in 1911, and the *Little Review* by Margaret Anderson in 1914. Marianne Moore became the editor of the *Dial* in 1925, and Victoria Ocampo the publisher of *Sur* in Buenos Aires in 1931. In 1933, Martha Foley and her husband Whit Burnett became the editors of *Story*, famous for being the first to publish Norman Mailer, Tennessee Williams, Carson McCullers, John Cheever, Richard Wright, and J. D. Salinger. In 1938, Dorothy Norman started *Twice a Year*. It might stand to reason that women would have had a less significant presence in the bibelots of the 1890s, not only because there would have been fewer opportunities, but also because the journals were in large measure produced and printed by college men like Stone. The situation, however, is significantly more complicated. While it is true that most of the magazines were edited, written, and printed by men, the exceptions have significant implications for how we read both the real and symbolic function of women in the magazines.

The two writers I focus on here, Juliet Wilbor Tompkins and Carolyn Wells, both wrote for the *Lark* at the beginning of their literary careers and then went on to publish hundreds of pieces of poetry and short fiction with the popular mass-market magazines, and also scores of well-received novels with major publishing houses. I would argue that they were the overlooked inheritors of the ephemeral bibelots' counter-Realist, satirical, rebellious, libidinous, free-flowing, and Modernist sexual sensibilities. They were not producing highly wrought fiction, but neither were they rejecting commercialism like the high Modernists. Instead, they shared Chopin's stylistic sensibilities and similarly moved the portrayal of female sexuality away from the context of domestic sentimentality and into the public arena of middlebrow literary taste, or what Nina Miller has called "popular Modernism."[44] They were among the first to poke fun at sex for the mass-market magazines, and to figure women on the giving and not just the receiving end of sexual advances. Like Chopin, they were interested in fiction that featured sharp-witted, sophisticated, and sentimentally unattached female characters. And they were stylistically interested in the associative aesthetic relations that typified the ephemeral bibelots—a relational aesthetic represented by the light, flirtatious style of their stories about young women and sexual desire.

Carolyn Wells published prolifically—more than 170 books over the course of her life. If her involvement with the bibelots was faddish, the style she developed there had the staying power that comes with commercial success. In the early years of the 1900s, she became widely known for her children's stories, nonsense lyrics, and especially, for developing a formula for writing detective novels. She published the earliest manual for writing in that genre, *The Technique of the Mystery Story*, in 1913, and she authored several long-running series of detective novels, the most important of which focused the scholarly, Holmes-like detective, Fleming Stone. Wells had been just as prolific in her work for the ephemeral bibelots in the 1890s. In her memoir, *The Rest of My Life*, she writes of having published in the *Lotus*, the *Savoy*, the *Fly Leaf*, *Whims*, *John-a-Dreams*, the *Bauble*, *Miss Blue-Stocking*, *Noon*, *Shadow*, and the *Cornhill Booklet*; and I might add that she also wrote for the *Chap-Book*, *Bradley His Book*, *Chips*, the *Philistine*, and the *Echo*. She was even, fleetingly, a bibelot editor of a volume called the *Daily Tatler* that was published by none other than Stone and Kimball for a fortnight in 1896. She described it as having been devised to address "the lack of really original sin in the imitative periodicals of the day"; the editorial position was attractive to her because of the "impossibility of the thing"—the impossibility of the "instantaneous process."[45]

Her career was covered in some detail by the *New York Times*, which linked it in interesting ways to that of Gelett Burgess. In January 1907, a column written for the *Times* by Otis Norman ran interviews with Wells and Burgess in subsequent weeks. Wells, giving what was billed as a "veracious and intimate account of a popular author's method," is said to believe in play, "in all different kinds of play, for all work is play to her." Without it, she would not be able to turn out so many "jingles, verses, and short stories and books for the last eight years with her power of production constantly increasing."[46] Two weeks later, it was Burgess's turn, and he brings up his friend as an exemplar of an original and exciting thinker. Drawing a distinction between the Bromides, who "think by syndicate," and the Sulphites, who always do the unexpected, Burgess is quoted as saying, "There are only seven female Sulphites in existence. Carolyn Wells is a Sulphite of the Sulphites. You never know what she's going to think, do, or say."[47] When she was in her fifties, the *Times* covered her first marriage on April 3, 1918, to the widower Hadwin Houghton, an heir of the Houghton Mifflin publishing house, and her move from her parents' home in New Jersey to the Hotel d'Artistes in New York, where she lived until her death. She is described dressed "in blue chiffon brocade in blue velvet over blue metal cloth, tipped by a large black lace hat and carrying clusters of la France roses."[48] The newspaper also noted her joint production with Burgess of a new play, *The Purple Cow*, which ran at the National Theater in New York in 1924.[49] It ran her obituary on March 27, 1942, as well as a perfect afterword to her colorful life a few weeks later. During her funeral, a thief broke into her apartment, stealing her ornamental jewelry but leaving behind her important Walt Whitman collection. "Burglar a Low-Brow," read the *New York Times* headline on April 17, 1942.

Wells complained that Thomas Beer must have been "color blind" when describing the 1890s as "the mauve decade," when in her mind "it allowed of no colors save olive or old gold, combined with peacock blue." She thought that Richard Le Gallienne was also wrong when he had called the era "romantic . . . because their representative writers and artists emphasized the modern determination to escape from the deadening thraldom of materialism and outworn conventions." Wells preferred to think of it as the decade of "shirtwaists and humor."[50] Her own writing was essentially humoristic and commercial, taking its energy from the wit and ingenuity of women playing the game. It was in this sense, I think, that she was perfectly at home in the *Lark*, which imagined itself engaged in a flirtation that stopped well short of full-blown Decadence—and that, in fact, blew it sky high. It dissociated sexual play from moral decay. It delighted, instead, in the middle-ground attachment, the playful flit and flutter of the game of correspondence, which is the fantasy of bohemian, aesthetic, and commercial sexual relations more familiar to us today, from the received history of modern love in the 1920s familiar to readers of *The Great Gatsby*.

Flirtation is the key relation coming from Wells's involvement with the *Lark*. She describes the start of her association with Gelett Burgess and the *Lark* as an epistolary adventure between two not-quite lovers. Having placed some stories in *Life*, *Puck*, and *Judge*, Wells says that she wrote to Burgess in the hopes of having something published in the pages of his new bibelot, which suggested "the medium of a limitless and illimitable imagination."[51] In his rejection letter, which she quotes, Burgess curiously explained that the *Lark* would have "no women contributors," a sentiment he also expressed in the draft of his never-published autobiography. Spurred on by the rejection, Wells pursued Burgess in a game of correspondence, sending him hundreds of letters.

She recalls that their correspondence served as her initiation into a "field of literature hitherto unknown to me," which she classed alongside Lewis Carroll, Edward Lear, and W. S. Gilbert.[52] Burgess later suggested that the epistolary whiplash he received from her established the bibelot's imaginative and romantic energy. Wells was his muse, whom he referred to in his *Lark* writings as H. R. H. the Princess Perilla ("perilla" being a minty, Asian spice); and Perilla was, in turn, one of the types for his imaginary Vivette (the other being a Parisian woman with whom he had an affair as a young man: see chapter 1). Burgess wrote fondly of Perilla in the *Lark*, describing her letters as a mode of epistolary love-making, a literary titillation, which he then fictionalized in his stories about Vivette and the Romance Association. "Such texts! Such epigram! Such versatility!":

> For it is true, Perilla has proved it,—the rational end of a letter is to excite—to create a sensation, pleasant if one may, shocking if one must, and in this book there is no page that falls short of the requirement. She has returned my envelopes (which were carelessly sealed) to all appearance unopened. She has mailed forty letters in a bunch, to rouse my lagging spirits. She has dedicated me to countless "farewell letters." She has bided me choose between the two sides of her character, and ordered me to return "A" or "B," confident enough that I would open both. What indeed has she not done, to bait my interest with personalities audacious beyond description? She has masqueraded in a thousand sailing fancies, giving me a thousand views of her character, but whichever facet is turned to me, there is ever the flash of the diamond, revealing the same Perilla, through innumerable disguises.[53]

The *Lark*, recall, claimed to have "demolished Decadence and picked Hope out of the dust-heap," but we are, here, not so many miles away from the indulgence of the morning kiss with *M'lle New York*.[54] The particular literary character of their epistolary attachment is largely unsentimental, devoid of tragedy or sympathy, and with no trace of nineteenth-century rules of sexual decorum. The literary jousting delights in masquerade, disguise, and flirtation; it is as multifaceted as the storefront window but leading neither to possession nor even emotional engagement. The attachment is both superficial and fleeting, and it is so multitudinous as to defy containment.

It may come as a surprise to learn that the sociologist Georg Simmel drew attention to flirtation at about the same time, writing in 1900 that it was "an intermediate state between having and not-having," the "variable interplay between consent and refusal," the "oscillation between affirmation and denial of genuineness."[55] It might as well have been Henry James writing on relations: flirtation is all middle, pleasure with no end in sight and no plan for completion, pure provisionality, leading nowhere, culminating in nothing. It was the butterfly passion. No wonder Freud found the idea, which he associated explicitly with America, so shallow and empty. He complained that with flirtation, there was nothing at stake, no serious consequences, and no willingness to actually engage in the more serious mode of love to be found in Europe.[56] Flirting suggested a new kind of sociality between the sexes, one in which one entered into love as a game. As Burgess put it in a 1905 article titled "Feminine Modernity" for the magazine *Sunset*, the intellectually emancipated woman "plays the game of love with her cards laid on the table, and wins as handily as in the old days when she was forced to use trickery and deception with the opposite sex." (Remarkably, his article was followed by a short story by Tompkins, who is discussed next, titled "The Almonds of Heaven.")[57]

The point is that Wells's adventure in the *Lark* suggests a course for her professional literary career in the early twentieth century, a key element of which was to link sexual frankness with the fashionable consumption of art. Her writing here and in other bibelots marks an aesthetic and sexual subjectivity in step with consumer capitalism, even while being marginally resistant to it. Ultimately, Burgess published three of Wells's pieces in the second volume of the *Lark*, making her one of only three other authors not on the original editorial team to be included in the magazine on multiple occasions, the others being Yone Noguchi and Tompkins. Her offerings were light and inconsequential, of a piece with her letters and the magazine itself. The first was a parodic celebration of palmistry, "The Science of Solistry," which concluded with an overload of puns about how with "the aid of these foot-lights the foundation will be laid for a correct understanding of the subject and the careful pedant will soon learn to unriddle the secrets of the sole." In another, she gave a medieval rendering of "The Purple Cow," twenty lines long in iambic pentameter with rhymed couplets. The third was a romantic tale about an enchanted violin that Burgess playfully critiqued in the magazine's headers, suggesting editorially that it was "a problem in Arabic fiction / solved a bit too hurriedly."[58] There is nothing of great moment in these pieces, but then, they can only be taken as part of the breeziness of the project as a whole—a project in which her epistolary persona, as Perilla or Vivette, can be felt on almost every page. Wells seems to have been made for just this kind of impossible project, and for an impossible movement like that of the bibelots. "It was all in the magic Nineties," she wrote, "and everybody was clever and quick of understanding."[59]

The other woman writer for the *Lark* was Juliet Wilbor Tompkins, whose contributions to the bibelot were even more directly flirtatious. Tompkins grew up in San Francisco, where she and her family were friends with Frank Norris and was published alongside Norris and Burgess in the *Wave*. Between 1896 and 1907, she was a regular contributor of short fiction to *Munsey's*, in which she placed nearly fifty short stories, and for a time also served as its associate editor. She moved to New York sometime around the turn of the century, where she was thrown into the company of Hamlin Garland, and in 1903 married Emory Pottle, then editor of the *Criterion*.[60] Continuing to use her maiden name, she published a total of fourteen novels and a half-dozen short plays, many featuring strong and independent heroines, and was featured in *Good Housekeeping*, the *Saturday Evening Post*, *Woman's Home Companion*, the *Ladies' Home Journal*, and *Collier's*. Her contributions to the latter magazine in the 1920s have been characterized by Tom Pendergast as being "far racier than anything the magazine had previously published."[61] But the very same might be said of her stories in the *Lark* and *Munsey's* in the 1890s, and looking at them can help clarify the Maupassantian style and feminist substance of what I have been describing as a literature of flirtation.

As with Wells, Tompkins's career reveals the connections between the new, the aesthetic, the commercial, and the feminist that took similar shape in the bibelots and the new class of popular magazines. She published three pieces in the second volume of the *Lark*. "Un Bon Quart d'Heure" is a touching reflection on watching a little girl playing with her doll and a black cat on the stoop of an adjoining building, which the author glimpses from her writing desk through an antique pane of glass. "An Interlude" is a story told almost entirely as a dialogue that takes shape between acts at the theater, where a bold young woman reveals to her male friend that he is in love with her. But it is "The Test of the Open Air" that is particularly audacious and surprising—a story openly about female sexual desire, told from the perspective of a young woman, that is entirely worthy of comparison to some of Chopin's best works on the subject. More daring than most anything else in the *Lark*, the quick-paced, first-person account of a sexual adventure is even more impressive when remembering that its author was not, herself, married when it appeared in the *Lark*'s final issue.

In essence, "The Test of the Open Air" is a sex scene, in the first person, for Burgess's character Vivette. The "test" in question is whether the fantasy of sexual freedom held out by the bohemia of the bibelots extended to a butterfly like her. The story is about the afternoon when the narrator went on a date with a man about whom she knew next to nothing. The young woman who narrates the story, who is unnamed but clearly stands in for Vivette, has been told only two things about the man she is to meet: he is an author and he makes terrible first impressions. In this, she is not deceived, and yet, persisting after a very unsatisfactory introduction, they set off on a hike that turns into an erotic adventure on the shores of the Pacific. They climb down foggy cliffs, arriving on a windswept beach, where "[a] sudden knowledge of the life primeval flashed from his eyes into mine":

> "Come," he said, holding out his hand, and then we were flying like gulls along the beach. Our reckless feet dared the clutch of the waves, and scattered the foam wreaths till they fled like white rabbits across the sand. We lifted our faces to the wind, and let it carry our laughter where it would. When the grey rocks cried a halt, sun and sea were our world; and Pan, our God, was not dead.
>
> He seized me by the shoulders.
>
> "I have found you. You are one of us," he exulted; I knew what was coming, but I did not turn away.

There follows the all-telling, fin-de-siècle ellipses. It is "the test of the open air"—a test that, of course, is not described but marked in the text by a series of dashes, a skipped line, and the start of a new paragraph. The tale then resumes after they have hiked back up the cliff, when the male lover tells the Vivette-like heroine to go back to her "Philistines . . . for fear of spoiling it." Having none of it, she rebuts him with plucky confidence.

> "You would n't condemn Vivette to that," I protested over my shoulder.
>
> "The ten minutes are safely over, and the ten years not begun," he said. "Run for your life!"

And then they separate. Despite the sex, or kiss, or whatever it was, the story has the modern feel of a flirtation with no lasting commitment and no consequences. There is sentiment—he told her it had been "too perfect"—but no sentimentality. Like Burgess's Vivette, who exits the *Lark* later in the same number by floating away in a hot-air balloon, Tompkins's lover parts with no strings attached. Hers had been merely an adventurous test, open-ended, fresh, flirtatious, and utterly unexpected in an American magazine.

Since nothing was ever signed in the *Lark*, readers would not have known who had written "The Test of the Open Air," or any of the preceding pieces, until getting the bound set, which included a table of contents with attributions. And yet, the story's choice of narrative perspective is, itself, significant for giving readers some direction about how to understand its unconventional, Vivette-like heroine without being shocked or offended. Not only is the first-person narrator a clever and sharp-witted young person, but she also has a remarkable sense of freedom, independence, and daring. When climbing down the cliff toward the sea, she appreciates the fact that her companion did not seem to think she needed his assistance. They make their way over a trail that is "broken, and treacherous with spray, but he sprang down without hand or eye for my progress." When she eventually joins him on the beach, he is writing poetry in the sand, and she seems to appreciate the symbolism represented by the fact that his lines are soon washed away in the surf. Everything about this story is transient and ephemeral.

Moreover, their happily concluded "test," which had been prompted by a mutual decision to "go back to the primer" and "be simply a man and a woman," was, we are also told, the sum of the successful avoidance of a meeting "degraded to a Sunday afternoon and a cup of tea." For anyone familiar with the essays of Tompkins's friend, Frank Norris, her heroine here would seem to be taking a cue directly from his criticism of the prudishness and banality of Howellsian Realism—except that Tompkins's heroine is actually setting the terms of the critique, not following them. It was not until several years later that Norris would publish "A Plea for Romantic Fiction," in which he damned Realism by calling it "the drama of a broken teacup, the tragedy of a walk down the block, the excitement of an afternoon call, the adventure of an invitation to dinner."[62] He may as well have been talking exactly about what the narrator of "The Test of the Open Air" had been trying to avoid; she, in effect, set in feminist terms those he would later use to justify a more virile and manly mode of Naturalist storytelling.

"The Tale of the Open Air" becomes even more striking when compared to an appropriately titled story of queer desire Tompkins published in *Munsey's* the very next year, in June 1897, "A Butterfly Lover." Again, what is signaled here is the linkage between bibelots and mass-market magazines, sexual experimentation and commercialization. In this story, a man in what we would now call a committed gay relationship worries, along with his lover, that he may have accidentally gotten himself engaged to a young woman he was flirting with at a dinner party. Not only does the story feature the unprecedented and utterly nonchalant treatment of two men living together lovingly, but it also is striking for its redirection of a familiar trope about the "butterfly sex" toward young bachelors. *Munsey's* pitched the story as being "[t]he series of awkward predicaments into which Jerome Latimer was precipitated by his amatory recklessness—A story of man's weakness and woman's wit." It begins "long past midnight" when Jerome opens the laboratory door of his friend, Dr. Will Perry, without knocking—"There was only one person in the world who opened that door without knocking, and for him no greeting was necessary." Jerome enters, concerned that one of the many young women he has been making love to, to whom he had given a French nickname, Mignonette, may have taken him seriously and confused his "high art flirtation" for an actual proposal.[63] The doctor is similarly worried and offers Jerome no consolation, saying that he would be honor-bound to respect the proposal if she had understood it as such. Jerome spends the night and wakes in the same bed as the doctor the next morning, at which point they put in motion an elaborate strategy for discovering what the young woman thinks had happened.

We learn several pages later that Mignonette and her group of friends had been leading Jerome on from the start. They were the ones in control and let the boys off easy. The story ends with Jerome and his lover happily together again in the intimate quiet of the doctor's laboratory, where "two cheerful faces came together at the door and went in for a smoke."

> "Poppy says she won't marry me," he [Jerome] began, and there was another pause before he added, "but she says she'll be engaged to me, just to keep the other girls away."
>
> The two men laughed, and hunched themselves down in ungainly comfort.
>
> "What will Violet White say?" asked Will.
>
> Jerome laughed.
>
> "What a guy they made of me!" he said. "They showed splendid team work. I suppose you know all about everything?"
>
> "Yes, pretty much. She told me her side tonight."
>
> "Oh, that's where you were. I must get another name for that girl. 'Mignonette' is altogether too artless and innocent. How would 'Foxglove' do?"
>
> "Leave it to me. I'll find you one," said Will [the doctor].
>
> Jerome stared.
>
> "Perhaps you would prefer Mrs. William Perry," he suggested.
>
> Will only laughed.[64]

The ending's allusive suggestion that Will might change Mignonette's name by marrying her may have provided just enough ambiguity about Will and Jerome's relation to get the story into print. But it should be clear that the butterflies in this story are the two bachelors themselves, the incorrigible flirt and his more serious doctor friend. The women made "a guy" of them both.

I was originally attracted to "A Butterfly Lover" for the way it reminded me of a *Vogue* cover for December 1894, which featured a young woman with her arms stretched behind her head like wings and hair streaming upward like hellfire, a swarm of *bachelor* butterflies being roasted by her beauty. The illustration by Albert Blashfield, "Dressing for the Ball: A Débutante's Reverie," matches up with Tompkins's character Mignonette: in both instances, the young women's control over their own sexuality, which has been objectified for the marriage market, allows them to exert a certain power over their suitors, who, in a delicious transference, become the ephemerals, the butterflies. It is as if to say that flirtation of this sort is more than just the young woman's game, it is her weapon, and like the classic femme fatale, she asserts the power to emasculate the impish men buzzing around in her mind. In Tompkins's story, it is true that the butterfly lovers seem to have managed a life for themselves that Mignonette and her friends are unlikely ever to realize. Tompkins makes no effort to paper over the fact that Jerome and his doctor friend are privileged in that respect. And yet

Albert Blashfield, "Dressing for the Ball—The Débutante's Reverie," cover for *Vogue*, December 13, 1894

Mignonette's flirtation is also a revelation. She is able to string her butterflies along, keeping them dancing on pins and needles, until revealing herself as being much more aware and in control of the rules than any of them.

None of Tompkins's later work quite lives up to the billing of either "The Test of the Open Air" or "A Butterfly Lover," although a number of them are fairly surprising on the question of homosexuality, and they all seem to push a model of strong women in charge of their own sexuality. So, for instance, she publishes another clever short story in *Munsey's* in 1896, "My Mother's

Diary," in which the heroine clandestinely reads about her mother's rejection of a proposal that turns out to have been from someone other than her father. The most popular of her novels, *Dr. Ellen*, was published in 1908, one of a series in which Tompkins explores the courtship decisions made by independent-minded heroines. This one focuses on the developing relationship of an unmarried woman, a doctor, who is struggling to keep alive her budding medical practice in a country town in the Sierras, and an attentive and brilliant architect from San Francisco. Dr. Ellen had decided to live in the country to take care of her younger sister, who has tuberculosis and needed the dry air. She is courted not only by the architect, who is there on vacation, but also by a woman who lives next door, a very successful farmer who is manfully useful with horses and farming tools, and who clearly pines after the good doctor. In the end, Dr. Ellen ends up with the architect, but her relationship with the local farmer woman is treated only with tenderness.

From the Bibelots to Anita Loos

To conclude, then, consider this anecdote about the bestselling novel of the 1920s, Anita Loos's *Gentlemen Prefer Blondes*. It leads us back to H. L. Mencken, whom we first encountered as one of the few reliable guides to the faddishness of the ephemeral bibelots of the 1890s (see the introduction). Anyone who has read Loos's novel, and not just seen the movie starring Marilyn Monroe and Jane Russell, will recognize the similarities between it and what I have been describing as the stylistic and thematic flirtatiousness of the writing of Wells and Tompkins in and out of the bibelots. All of this work forges the connection between the frank treatment of sexual desire and commercial success in both the marriage market and the literary marketplace, and that meant that serious Modernism was bound not to take it seriously at all. Loos credits the fact that her friend Mencken was an outrageous flirt as an inspiration for the novel, but the story I want to draw attention to concerns something Mencken told her about where to have it published. She writes in a preface to a later edition that he had advised her to send it to *Harper's Bazaar*, which is rather like telling Chopin to send her work to *Vogue* or Tompkins to give "A Butterfly Lover" to *Munsey's*.[65] Loos explains that Mencken had just left the *Smart Set*, which would have published her novel, for the *American Mercury*, for which he thought it was not right. At *Harper's Bazaar*, however, "it'll be lost among the ads and won't offend anybody."[66] One can imagine the exact same advice being given to Tompkins as she looked for somewhere to place her more risqué stories, and that perhaps she settled on *Munsey's* for that reason. Is this why Chopin's work ended up in *Vogue* instead of the *Chap-Book*?

The story told by cultural historians about "modern love" has, by now, a well-established set of coordinates, including most frequently Edna St. Vincent Millay's place at the imaginative heart of bohemian Greenwich Village in the teens, the nouveau-Decadent little magazines like *Rogue* and *Bruno's Bohemia*, Dorothy Parker and the Algonquin Roundtable, and Loos's best-selling novels and Hollywood comedies.[67] The bibelots of the 1890s appear to have played little role in the twentieth century's revival of Decadence, which is perhaps why few attempts have been made to reckon with the mass of popular women's writing from the prior decades, when our bibelotistes were most actively making their way into the popular Modernist press.[68] The only critical attention ever given to Tompkins in the last fifty years, as far as I know, comes in a chapter in the Marxist cultural history by Richard Ohmann, *Selling Culture*, which explains the ideology of corporate capitalism developed in mass-market magazines during this period. He reproduces and develops a compelling reading of her story, "On the Way North," published in *Munsey's* in October 1895. Needless to say, it is a much more conventional tale than the ones I have been discussing, a courtship story that reaches a predictably happy conclusion on a runaway train, which Ohmann convincingly uses to argue that the "formulas of mass culture work as smoothly as they do in part precisely because they reduce complex historical needs and conflicts to comfortable ideology."[69]

What I have been drawing attention to are the exceptions, not the norms; and these exceptions suggest the advent of possibilities for modern sexual subjectivities that are generally attributed to a later period. Of course, it is a truism of histories of this kind that precedents are almost always there for the taking. Fanny Fern, the highly paid humorist of the 1850s comes most immediately to mind as a precedent to Tompkins and Wells. Nonetheless, my suggestion, concentrating on the 1890s, is to move beyond the frame represented by Howells and the Atlantic group of literary monthlies to that of the bibelots and mass-market women's magazines, in which we discover a series of relations by which to associate aesthetic and sexual modernity under the sign of the fad. These relations are not only new in kind but new in quality as well, remarkable for the practiced evanescence of their swift plotting, their thematic resistance to settling down in traditional family relations, their ease with merely flitting and flirting. Given the presence of Wells and Tompkins, it is clearly the case that Burgess's initial ideas about "no women" in the *Lark* gave way to another strategy altogether. But what is even more striking is that the aesthetic élan of the contributions by women writers to his bibelot, their flirtatious celebration of the unsentimental attachments, anticipated a significant transformation of sexual sensibilities in the twentieth century, and the emerging mass market for sexually sophisticated print culture. The "butterfly lovers" of Chopin, Wells, and Tompkins may be obscure, but their emergence into print is the event horizon for change in Modernist sexual subjectivities.

5 The Edginess of Stephen Crane at the End of the Relational Era

> Evidently he [Crane] takes himself seriously, in spite of what seems occasional freakishness.
>
> John Curtis Underwood, "Review," 1899

> An impression needs to be constantly refreshed by new impressions in order that it may persist at all; it needs to take its place in a system of impressions.
>
> T. S. Eliot, "The Perfect Critic," 1920

So what happened to the bibelots?

They went the way of Stephen Crane's poetry. Here is the story.

Most of us come to Crane's poetry, *if* we come to it, by way of his novels and short stories, and it seems fair to say that we would probably not come to his poetry at all were it not for *The Red Badge of Courage* (or perhaps *Maggie*, or a short story, say, "The Open Boat"). Without his major works of fiction, Crane's poetry would probably be no more well known than that of the scores of other American poets from the 1880s and 1890s who, with the exception of Walt Whitman and Emily Dickinson, are mainly of interest only to specialists.

Some of the blame devolves upon Amy Lowell, who was the first major American poet and critic to have taken Crane's poetry seriously in the early twentieth century, editing and writing the introduction to the posthumous collection of his poetry in 1926, a little more than two decades after his death. Why blame Lowell? Because she confirmed a pattern of obscuring the relation of Crane's poetry to the ephemeral bibelot movement of the 1890s that this book has been working to resurrect, and, in so doing, cut his poetic work off from a complex stream of aesthetic relations—relations without which it has a hard time making sense. On finding Crane's poetry in the *Philistine*, yet another enigmatic ephemeral bibelot, where much of it was published, one comes to realize that he was an integral part of a group movement refashioning the aesthetic public sphere in late nineteenth-century America, and that the obscurity of that movement, its marginalization, has to do with the active forgetting that went on in the 1910s and 1920s by the much more well-known Modernist little magazine movement and some of its key votaries.

Lowell, like many critics since then, sensed the modernity of Crane's poetry. Indeed, the central claim of her introduction is that in "[s]o short a time as twelve years after his death, a type of poetry extremely like his came into being."[1] Lowell, however, finds it important to insist upon that twelve-year gap, and upon the idea that Crane as a poet was essentially an original, a "man without a period . . . [who] sprang from practically nowhere." In order to do so, she works to rescue Crane from his literary associates from the 1890s, suggesting that he owed his "thirty-year neglect [as a poet] largely to his various publishers." In particular, she blames the Roycrofters, the artisanal community assembled by Elbert Hubbard in East Aurora, New York, in 1895 that published a bibelot called the *Philistine*. It is, Lowell wrote, "a thousand pities that poems such as these should appear under the aegis of the Roycrofters."[2]

Lowell was not the first to want to dissociate Crane from the Roycrofters, but she set a highly visible precedent that has been difficult to shake. In the 1950s, two influential works appeared that made basically the same point. In his biography of Crane, John Berryman repeatedly referred to the detrimental effect of publishing with Fra Elbertus, whom Berryman disdainfully wrote off as a "busy, banal former soap salesman who entered Harvard at 36, in January 1893, for a little."[3] While not nearly so dismissive, Daniel Hoffman followed suit in the first book-length study of Crane's poetry. Hoffman could countenance the idea that Crane associated with fin-de-siècle Decadents; published in Hubbard's *Philistine*; approved of the eroticized orchids on the cover of his first book of poetry, *The Black Riders*, and Will Bradley's illustrations for *War Is Kind*; entertained the *Yellow Book* crowd at his home in East Sussex in England; took a prostitute as his lover; and even let an occasional Decadent image slip into his verse. But on definitional grounds, Hoffman could not accept the idea of Crane as a product of his time. He was not a Decadent because his "perversity" was not self-willed but compulsive; and if Crane was to some extent a Symbolist, Hoffman argued that he got it not by way of the French tradition but rather from the Transcendentalist writing of Emerson, Thoreau, Hawthorne, Melville, Poe, and Whitman.[4]

This tendency has continued. In the 1980s, John Blair insisted that Crane's bohemianism was merely a pose.[5] In the most recent biography, Linda Davis acknowledges that Crane and Hubbard were friends but then writes that Crane's poetry in the *Philistine* was entirely out of character for the 1890s and that his "flashes of strange imagery" were such that "no one but Stephen Crane could have written" them.[6] Even Max Cavitch, in an insightful recent account of Crane's place in the historical development of free verse, makes his point without referencing either Hubbard or the ephemeral bibelots and by way of a poem never published during Crane's lifetime.[7]

No links, not the hub of a tiny public of 1890s proto-Modernists, and certainly not a direct relation to the major figures of twentieth-century poetry, Crane has been made to stand alone. Indeed, dissociating him from the little magazine movement of the 1890s has been the first move made by critics looking to establish the Modernist credentials of his lines of verse.

And yet, affectionately referred to as "Stevie," Crane was the epitome of a network hub to the bibelot movement, both as an author and point of reference. He was cited by at least seventeen other ephemeral bibelots in the United States. Gelett Burgess singled him out in the important locater-poem in *Le Petit Journal des Refusées*, a poem called "Our Clubbing List," where Crane shows up just after mentions of the *Philistine* and the *Bauble*, and just before the *Lotus* and *Chips*: "S is for Stevie Crane, infant precocious/ Who has written some lines that are simply ferocious" (see plate 2). Along the same lines, *Miss Blue Stocking* puts him in league with Maeterlinck, Beardsley, and Will Bradley, joking that Crane's "curiously mangled 'lines' . . . read better up-side down than right side up—if anything about them is better."[8] In the *Lotus*, Walter Blackburn Harte used Crane ironically as a point of reference in promoting Gelett Burgess; and a couple of months earlier, in the *Fly Leaf*, he had published two other articles gently mocking the incomprehensibility of Crane's lines, writing of *The Black Riders* that it is "an interesting *freak* of a quick fancy playing over life and thought and taking all that comes to the surface in all seriousness."[9]

More than any other of the bibelots, however, it was Hubbard's *Philistine* that both established and took advantage of Crane's freakishness, and more than any other it was Crane's relationship to this publication that most of his biographers and critics have worked to obscure.[10] Hubbard published a favorable review of *The Black Riders* in the first number of the *Philistine*; he hosted a much-discussed banquet on Crane's behalf just before *The Red Badge of Courage* earned its widespread popular acclaim; and he offered first publication to and republication of many of Crane's stories, sketches, and verses up to the time of his death. Indeed, Hubbard went so far as to brag in the January 1898 issue that arrangements had been made with Crane to supply lines for the back of every *Philistine* for a decade, which the editor would duly print even if Crane were to be shipwrecked or the magazine itself cancelled.

What I suspect is that our reading of Crane as the author of Naturalist fiction has colored our experience of his poetry to such an extent that we have a hard time seeing it as representative of anything other than, in Cavitch's words, "cosmic despair, devastating beyond irony."[11] That fits in with our own times—with our sense, perhaps, of the ongoing crisis in the study of the humanities and conflict in the world at large. At such moments, critics and scholars have little time for marginal things; better that they be substantive and of unavoidable significance. Much of Crane's Naturalist prose fits that description. Most of his poetry, however, does not, especially when it is contextualized by way of the ephemeral bibelots, which were often ironic but rarely given over to cosmic despair.

As I have been suggesting, the prevailing mood of the bibelots was whimsy: they were queer and countercultural, but quietly so, hardly attuned to the pressing issues of the day except for that glancing regard to the woman question and attempts to provide a more frank portrayal of sexuality (see chapter 4). The bibelots seem most similar today to something like *McSweeney's Quarterly Concern*, the magazine project started in 1988, during the Reagan era, by David Eggers and which now includes a literature and humor website, a monthly magazine, food and sports journals, a DVD magazine, and several book imprints. The online literary magazine *N+1* opined not too long ago that *McSweeney's* was a "briefly significant magazine" but that the "Eggersards" had come to represent a "regressive avant-garde," regressive because too dependent upon the ethical claims of childhood and too prone to a depleted absurdism that "attacked the avant-garde hope for any transcendence of present conditions." Eggers seemed briefly "to be our generation's Andre Breton," wrote the editors of *N+1*, but his "obsession with childhood as a way of life" has become "the substitute for transcendence in the Eggersard world."[12] The same could most certainly be said of Gelett Burgess, who after his involvement with the *Lark* and *Le Petit Journal des Refusées*, went on to be known for his books of manners for children featuring his famous "goops" (see chapter 1); so, too, with Hubbard's *Philistine*, which was more given to parody and silliness than serious commentary, even with regard to Crane, and which, in the early twentieth century, was diminished to little more than an organ for Hubbard's bromides on various literary, social, and political topics.

On this reading, the ephemeral bibelots of the 1890s were like the Modernist little magazines of the twentieth century, except for their lack of seriousness. Without the artistic manifestoes and oversized literary personalities, the bibelots may have been destined for little more than their marginal status in literary history. But as it turns out, they achieved something even less than that: almost complete obscurity. They were buried nameless in the potter's field alongside the idea that Modernist art might have had a foothold in nineteenth-century America.

In drawing this book to a close, I want to consider three different ways to explain the ephemeral bibelots' disappearance not only from accounts of Crane and his poetry but also from literary history more broadly. By implication, I want to suggest some of the ways that art movements stop moving and artistic fads come to an end. The first answer concerns the feeling of emptiness that is often associated with the dynamics of network aesthetics; the second, the friability of personal reputations and relations; and, the third, the transformation of print culture in response not only to changing aesthetic codes and demands but also to the partial assimilation of the bibelots' provocations.

All three explanations are interwoven, but we can pull them apart to better characterize the significance of the difference between the tiny public of bibelots in the 1890s and most of the Modernist little magazines of the following decades. The explanations are based on a common premise, namely, that any marginal art movement is going to face long odds when the time comes to renew ties to it by way of historical writing and archiving, especially when historical crises occur that have critics and scholars in a defensive crouch. Art itself seems to thrive in such moments, but scholarship often contracts in a search for the essence of meaningfulness, letting more whimsical ties fall to the side.

In the case at hand, American Modernism explicitly cut its ties to the play of Crane's poems on the pages of the bibelots. While something akin to the spirit of the bibelots made a brief appearance in Greenwich Village in the 1910s, most Modernist little magazines adopted a stature of gravitas and a connection to nationalist localism that was conceived of in opposition to the dandyish internationalism of the prior generation's avant-garde, the avant-garde represented by the ephemeral bibelots. The peripatetic art of the 1890s, the relational aesthetic that was always a group movement, gave way to a less mediated and individualistic art of contact. Black cats and butterflies gave way to skyscrapers and jazz. The lines of relation that James was so fond of tracing were transformed into representations of the thing itself. Instead of Lambert Strether strolling along a river in France remembering a painting he almost bought but did not, William Carlos Williams gave us a red wheelbarrow and John Dos Passos *Manhattan Transfer*, a novel of vignettes in which the connective tissue is left entirely to the readers' imagination. It was the end of the relational era, of the attempt to represent the ties that bind. The ephemeral bibelots had been champions of the new in the face of their era's prevailing Realism and Naturalism; by the time the Modernist little magazines came to the fore, after the political and social upheavals of the start of the century, ties both to the bibelot vogue and the relational aesthetic it represented had become those to be abandoned. Modernism buried the bibelots, and, in so doing, cut ties to what had been modern about American art in the preceding decades.

The Emptiness of Edginess

One real problem with the ephemeral bibelots is that it can seem like they don't add up: they can feel, as Lowell seemed to imply, quite simply empty, as if nothing were there. But what if that feeling of emptiness was the feeling, precisely, of what Gelett Burgess called "the vagaries of the 'end of the century' madness" that this book has been trying to elaborate and describe, the feeling of an art constructed from the ephemera of associations? Might not a feeling of emptiness—which rises, in the context of the bibelot vogue, to another of those "minor taste concepts" to which Sianne Ngai has directed our attention, for example, when speaking of the "cuteness" of Gertrude Stein—be just the point, especially when contrasted to the pretentions of Realism and Naturalism as practiced, at the time, in more elite journals like the *Atlantic Monthly* and the *Century Illustrated*?[13]

Burgess suggested as much when bringing the *Lark* to a close, wondering whether anyone would ever understand what the little revolution had been about:

> THE LARK . . . has never cared to explain its actions, or translate its song into the idiom of the hour. It has believed that there is a quality of humour as there is

> of music, whose essence is not describable, and it has ventured its essays in the hope that some would smile, though they knew not why. It has dealt in symbols recognizable by a certain caste, one whose numbers have been too few to be represented in the literature of the day. In this hope the LARK has been abundantly rewarded, for surely no periodical ever made warmer friends, though it may have made a greater number.[14]

This passing, unsubstantiated "quality of humour"—which touches us like music, its essence indescribable, transmitted by symbols, available only to a countercultural coterie—might well have struck an outsider like Lowell as empty, had she heard it at all. Burgess had been in no mood to explain it. But even Henry James, whom we previously put forward as a theorist of the period's haloed literary exchanges, where relating registers as an art unto itself, seems to have shared some wariness about the untranslatability of relations (see chapter 3). The drama of *The Ambassadors*, in this light, could be rewritten as that of asking what happens if even Lambert Strether fails to make out the meaning of the movement's reverberations. Strether ought to be most aptly attuned to indescribable essences of the kind Burgess describes, the *Lark*'s humorous song being, one supposes, something like the hilarity of an afternoon party at Gloriani's with Little Bilham and Miss Barrace. But what if even the Strethers of the world were left standing alone, not catching the quality of the music, with no warm company, and without knowing why? There was always the risk that a song like the *Lark*'s would fail to be translated into "the idiom of the hour."

Much of the edginess of Crane's poetry went hand in hand with this more ephemeral feeling of emptiness, as I will try to explain by way of two examples of poems published by the Roycrofters. It is difficult to do more than smile politely at these poems without access to their relations with the bibelot phenomenon; but with those ties reestablished, and even especially then, they still can feel empty in an elusive and unsettling way. Consider "I stood upon a High Place," which appeared on the back cover of the *Philistine* in March 1899 after having been published previously in 1895 in the collection *The Black Riders* (see plate 8):

> I stood upon a High Place,
> And saw, below, many Devils
> Running, leaping,
> And carousing in Sin.

One looked up, grinning,
And said, "Comrade! Brother!"

What I have in mind by edginess is not the common sense of having a sharp or biting edge, of being daring or provocative, as in an edgy wit. These lines have a modicum of edginess in that sense, but not a lot more. They offer a somewhat vituperative refashioning of the verse from the book of Romans (3:23) suggesting that we all are sinners—or, perhaps, that we are all Decadents. This reading makes some sense in the context of *The Black Riders*, which features a number of poems that are angry with an indifferent god. It has long been a truism of Crane criticism that his poems are instances of the "usual adolescent rebellion," in the words of Hoffman, wherein he declared "independence from his family [and established] his own identity . . . through his rejections of familial piety and respectability," a reading that gains weight when remembering that Crane, the youngest of fourteen children, had a Methodist minister for both father and grandfather.[15] More recently, George Monteiro has suggested that another object of irony in "I stood upon a High Place" is probably the temperance movement, a number of Crane's works taking up the evils of drink, and there is no mistaking the fact that in the *Philistine*'s rendering of the poem, the devil is a lush.[16]

These are both plausible readings, but my suggestion that we call it edginess has more in common with network visualizations, where an edge is another name for the line linking people or ideas together. An edge in this more technical sense could be the link between individuals in a social network, as in the friendship between Hubbard and Crane. It could also be the link between the *Philistine* and *Le Petit Journal des Refusées* established by their mutual citation of Crane, "Stevie Crane" thus being an edge to the extent that his name links together all the disparate ephemeral bibelots. In poetic terms, an edge could also be the link between signifier and signified, as well as between a citation and its source. Edges are like Deleuze and Guattari's rhizomes; they are conjunctive and transitive, distributed and strung-along in the flow and movement of experience.[17] Edges are a structural element of all artistic forms, to the extent that no forms stand on their own, but certain forms depend on edges more than others. Parody, for example. We have parodies *of* other things; parodies always link back to previous forms, even if the intent is to damage them with humor and leave them behind.

Back in the 1890s, much of Crane's poetry was edgy in this technical sense, and "I stood upon a High Place" particularly so once resituated in the *Philistine*. It is a poem that points, in a remarkable number of directions, toward the broader citational assemblage of what was taken to be modern about art at the time. We often say that Modernism is characterized by talk about itself, privileging metadiscourse about art systems over representations of the real world. If so, then the publication of Crane's lines in the *Philistine* is exemplary of how, when, and where that discourse took shape.

The most significant edge in "I stood upon a High Place" comes in the last line, "Comrade! Brother!" which is a repurposing of the last line of Charles Baudelaire's famous invocation in *Les Fleurs du Mal* (1857), "Hypocrite lecteur,—mon semblable,—mon frère!" What is of interest is that this particular line has been of some significance to the received history of Modernist poetry of the 1920s. A little more than two decades later, T. S. Eliot made the same move, most famously as the concluding line of the first section of *The Waste Land* in 1922, but also as the concluding line of an essay he had published called "The Lesson of Baudelaire" in the Modernist little magazine the *Tyro* the year before. Eliot's use of the citation is frequently trotted out when rehearsing the story that he got his Baudelaire, and thus his French Symbolism, when he discovered Arthur Symons's book on Symbolist poetry in the Harvard library in 1908.[18] This may well be true, but Symons's book had been published in 1899, and it took up essays he had published in the *Yellow Book* and the *Savoy*, leading British ephemeral bibelots, between 1894 and 1896.[19] Moreover, Symbolism was discussed frequently in the bibelots, for instance, in Vance Thompson's essay, "The Technique of the Symbolists," in *M'lle New York* in November 1895. Somehow this decade-long gap, which leaps over America and the 1890s altogether, rarely gets mentioned. Eliot's claim, however, is altogether in line with Amy Lowell's argument that Crane's poetry sprang from nowhere, and that poetry like Crane's emerged only twelve years after his death, about the same time that Eliot's own first lines begin to appear in print.

So what happens if, in a mood of Stretherian receptiveness to relations, we read Crane's poem in the *Philistine* as citing Baudelaire? Hoffman has argued explicitly against it, suggesting that even if "Comrade! Brother!" reminds us of Baudelaire, Crane does not yet resemble him in poetic strategy. Hoffman thinks that will come later, "as Crane develops his own means to express attitudes and states of feeling far more complex than the theme of these early poems."[20] But we might nonetheless consider the possibility that Hoffman missed the ironic barb of the poem, or was uninterested in the creative misreading of it in the *Philistine* by Hubbard and the illustrator W. W. Denslow, the original illustrator of Frank Baum's *The Wizard of Oz*, a most freakish novel first published the very next year.

In that case, I might suggest that the point of Crane's poem in the *Philistine* only becomes clear if the line is read not as if it resembled Baudelaire, but as if it addressed him, or some poet like him, quite directly. In both Baudelaire and Eliot, the famous last line addresses readers, accusing them, that is to say us, of hypocrisy. Eliot even adds the "you" that is implied by Baudelaire. In Crane's poem, however, the line would appear to address not readers but the author of the lines. It is the poet who is standing on a high place looking down on a bunch of devils when one looks up and calls him out, directly, "Comrade! Brother!" It is an exchange between them, and we're on the outside taking their measure. If the poet is a devil, a comrade, then the devils are probably poets, too. And if that is the case, then those other devils below, the running and leaping ones "carousing in Sin," may well be the swarm of Baudelairian poets one finds, if so inclined, coursing around in the American bibelots. As portrayed in the *Philistine*, Crane is not addressing a general audience but rather a coterie public of fin-de-siècle devils, the kind who might smile at the whimsy of the reference without knowing exactly why.

Because let us not forget that picking out poetic devils from the American bibelots is like picking cherries from a pie, as any reader of the *Philistine* would surely have known. By way of illustration, consider the particularly edgy example we have already looked at from a bibelot Crane, as a former resident of the Art Students League building in New York, had to have read, *M'lle New York*, January 1896: the devil and his lover perched on the black cat's tail (see the prologue). The image links directly back to *Le Chat Noir*, the French cabaret in Montmartre, where the bibelot vogue took shape, outside of which hung the sign on which this same cat perched on the sliver of the moon. Below the image runs an excerpt from a poem about Pierrot Lunaire by Jules Laforgue, the French Symbolist poet who is said to have been the most significant French influence on Eliot. For our story, the poem is important because Eliot takes up the Pierrot theme in, you guessed it, 1910, when he began work on an unpublished manuscript called the "Suite Clownesque" and on his first major publication "The Love Song of J. Alfred Prufrock."[21] Arthur Schoenberg, incidentally, composed his *Pierrot Lunaire* in 1912. But back in 1896, the same is appearing in *M'lle New York*. Pierrot Lunaire, as you may recall, is the classic French figure of the devil's clown, and he is also the subject of one of the best-known French lullabies, "Au Clair de la Lune" (Au Clair de la lune, mon ami Pierrot, Prete-moî ta plume, pour écrire un mot). The Laforgue excerpted in the American bibelot is a blasphemous and macabre parody of the lullaby. In the lullaby, the poet's candle goes out, and here it is his brain: "Ma cervelle est morte,/Que le Christ l'emporte!"—"My brain is dead/let Christ carry it away." This interplay is an example of the kind of *fumiste* deflation that *M'lle New York*, the *Philistine*, and other American bibelots traded in all the time, a kind of proto-Dadaist sending up in smoke of the mind-numbing artificiality of bourgeois existence. Munch's *The Scream*, which we have had occasion to discuss before (see chapter 2), is on the facing page.

All this may seem rather too far afield from Crane's lines to make a difference, but such connections are precisely the kind that bibelot editors seem to have had in mind when imagining their magazines' relational field. The lines may seem empty, but they are edgy too. Hubbard would have known Pierrot intimately, as, too, would have Denslow and Crane. And if that is the case, then one might add one more connection, this time from the *Philistine* itself, coming in an image attributed to someone named Plug Hazen-Plug and titled "The Bluff" from August 1895. There is no devil here, but the humor is in the same key. The image is a remarkable and seemingly anachronistic example of Non-Objectivist, geometrical abstraction. Indeed, it is the kind of thing quite a bit more familiar to us in work appearing two decades later, for instance, Kazimir Malevich's *Black Square* (1915). However, as plugged-in bibelotists, we might recognize "The Bluff," in its historical time and place, as a parody of an image by Frank Hazenplug, a well-known illustrator who designed book covers for Stone and Kimball, titled "The Blind," which had been published two months earlier in the *Chap-Book* from June 1, 1895. Alongside Crane's lines, these line drawings are clearly a *fumiste* play on and humorous misreading of the artist's name and intentions. It is as if the bibelot is asking the reader to engage in a game of blind man's bluff, perhaps as a way of calling Hazenplug's bluff in the *Chap-Book*. But then, is it not also asking us to call Crane's? Or is Crane calling the *Philistine*'s?

What this brief example suggests is that just at the time Crane was coming into his own as an artist, and at just the time his work came to serve as a point of reference knitting together an expanding vogue for the ephemeral bibelots, his lines were amenable to association with stylistic proclivities of a particularly Parisian kind. Whether he meant them that way or not, Crane's lines linked together a coterie of bibelotists who found themselves, by way

Frank Hazenplug, "The Blind," in the *Chap-Book* 3:2, June 1, 1895

Plug Hazen-Plug, "The Bluff," the *Philistine* 1:3, August 1895

of Crane, in direct company with the leading figures of French Symbolism. And yet, today, reestablishing these ties may still be of little consolation. Substantively, curiously, problematically, reading Crane's lines as if they were reaching out in these other directions is still just as likely to feel empty as edgy. To name-drop Symbolism helps, but, in the end, any lines that depend so heavily on wispy allusions can't help but feel light on their own. Their "essence is not describable," in Burgess's terms, not only because they evoke an extravagant string of relations, but because they evoke them in a way that no two readers are likely to share. Indeed, it seems unlikely that anyone else reading Crane in the bibelots, then or now, would follow down the same path I have suggested here on their own.

To take another example, consider what happens to these lines from *The Black Riders* when we find them reprinted in a souvenir edition of the *Roycroft Quarterly*, which was brought out by Hubbard in May 1896 after a notorious banquet he had thrown on Crane's behalf the preceding December.

> I saw a man pursuing the horizon;
> Round and round they sped.

I was disturbed at this;
I accosted the man.
"It is futile" I said,
"You can never—"

"You lie," he cried,
And ran on.

As before, these lines announce the themes of futility and despair for which Crane's verse is known. But, especially when placed alongside the cover of the pamphlet, they read like parables of poetic allusion. The first English edition of Nietzsche's *Zarathustra* also appeared in 1896, and it complains of poets who "lie too much."[22] Crane's poem shows what happens when they do: they and their readers are left chasing an ever-receding horizon, running after relations that end nowhere. Because, notice, the first-person narrator of Crane's poem, who ought to be a stabilizing presence, is implicated in the man's hopeless chase. How else to explain the pluralization of the pronoun in the second line, "Round and round *they* sped" (my emphasis)? The "they" implies both the man and the horizon, but that makes the perspective all wrong, at least for anyone with their feet on the ground. The horizon should not be spinning with the man. Eventually, he should "catch it," or at the very least fade into it. Here, however, it seems that the narrator is also spinning on the pinwheel. No wonder he's "disturbed at this." He can't even finish his line, "You can never—." The man keeps running after the moving horizon, the poet after them, and, god save us readers, for the poetic edge never reaches its target but only arcs and keeps on going.

Crane is unlikely to have influenced the design of the souvenir volume in which the lines were reprinted, but the cover illustration suggests that the Roycrofters understood his poem in this way: it sends readers chasing after horizons. The illustration alludes to the book version of Crane's poems by having his "black riders of sin" mounted on polka-dotted hobbyhorses, which is another *fumiste* parody of two forerunners of the ephemeral bibelots. The *Hobby Horse* (1884-1894) was an Arts and Crafts journal founded by followers of William Morris, and the black riders' chivalric appearance is most likely an allusion to the *Knight Errant* (1892-1893), a Boston journal undertaken in Morris's style. Both of these magazines cultivated the "*moyen age*" in the terms peculiar to the late nineteenth century's handicraft aesthetic. In this, they were like *Le Chat Noir*, which had dedicated itself to reviving the sensibility of Louis XIII, and in which Emile Goudeau had believed

Souvenir number of the *Roycroft Quarterly*, celebrating Stephen Crane, May 1896

himself capable at long last of becoming a "*gentilhomme*."[23] The *Knight Errant* went so far as to position itself against mainstream literary criticism with a medievalist mock-manifesto against Realism: "to war against the Paynims of realism in art, to assail the dragon of materialism, and the fierce dragon of mammonism, to ride for the succour of forlorn hopes and the restoration of forgotten ideals."[24] Contributors included the Canadian Bliss Carman, whose 1893 book of poems, *Low Tide on the Grand Pré*, would certainly have been connected by most readers to *The Black Riders* (the *Clack Book*, for instance, featured a parody mocking the two, "A Karmenokranian Idyl" by Bliss Krayne), and who served as associate editor of the *Chap-Book* for a few of its early numbers.[25] Also contributing was Louise Imogen Guiney, America's most renowned female poet of the fin de siècle, who proclaimed herself the "literary 'godmother'" of both the *Knight Errant* and the *Chap-*

Book.[26] Not incidentally, Guiney had been the first to recommend publication of *The Black Riders* to Copeland and Day.[27]

Crane quite purposively insisted on calling his verse not "poems" but "lines."[28] As with the man pursuing the horizon, lines also go on and on, page after page—much like James's sentences and Fuller's serpentine skirts, and also like Hubbard's allusions. "Lines" suggest the kind of nonending horizon of relations that were indicative of the moment and movement of the ephemeral bibelots. The point may be counterintuitive given that Crane's lines add up to some utterly short poems—only six and eight lines in the ones considered here. However, one can assume that bibelotists would have appreciated the open-endedness of Crane's verse given their predilection for relational run-ons, the denial of substantives, and the meaningful meaninglessness of ever receding horizons. In the world of the bibelots, Crane's lines were impressively edgy little things. The risk, of course, is that if the lines can feel edgy, they can also feel empty. And so Lowell and others, who were no longer amused either by the Roycrofters or Burgess, having long lost the ear for their "quality of humour," attempted to rescue Crane from the abyss of such emptiness by finding him some more substantive, and more properly Modernist, literary companions.

Public and Private Relations

Crane's biographers have, with near unanimity, excoriated the event for which the Roycrofter souvenir volume was produced, an elaborate dinner celebration of the young author whose work Elbert Hubbard had claimed for the *Philistine*, arguing that it was nothing but a gaudy publicity stunt.[29] If inclined to admire Hubbard, as a PBS documentary did in 2009, one could suggest he was "an American original," a nonconformist who challenged public norms on both artistic and personal levels.[30] The consensus line, however, follows Frank Luther Mott, who argued that it "would be possible to place a higher value on Hubbard's writings . . . if one could believe in the man's sincerity."[31] Hubbard was unconventional in his marital relations, irascible and disloyal to innumerable friends and relations, flamboyant and opportunistic in artistic affairs, and politically idiosyncratic, both a socialist and a jingoistic supporter of American business. By the 1910s, Hubbard had become so thoroughly discredited in artistic circles that the effort to save Crane from him makes sense. But what about before then? To what extent could the divisiveness of one of the bibelot movements' central figures shortly after his relationship with Crane have contributed to the dissolution of the bibelots' tiny public?

The story that Hubbard took advantage of his friendship with Crane for the purpose of personal enrichment, which has been a truism of Craniana since Lowell's time, was certainly fed by his notoriously bad relations with other writers. He split on acrimonious terms with the first two editors of the *Philistine*, Harry Taber and Walter Blackburn Harte, both of whom claimed with increasing vehemence over the years to have been misled as to the nature of their partnership, and in particular as to proprietary stakes in the bibelot.[32] He similarly alienated Rudyard Kipling and George Bernard Shaw with unauthorized and bowdlerized Roycrofter editions of their work.[33] What is worse, after most of the other bibelots had folded, Hubbard's *Philistine* became a wild success. The transformation was due to the immense popularity of a nationalistic paean to American initiative and hard work, "A Message to Garcia," originally printed without a title in 1899 on the back pages of the *Philistine*. Picked up and reprinted in pamphlet form, the essay was widely distributed to railroad passengers and employees, selling more than forty million copies in thirty-seven languages. It was released as a film in 1936 and featured on Glenn Beck's show in 2013.

Within ten years of the founding of the Roycroft community, Hubbard's reputation went from that of a bohemian socialist publisher of an avant-garde magazine to a self-promoting publisher of a vanity journal with impressive circulation numbers, consistently near 100,000, hardly the stuff of the avant-garde. The *Philistine* may have ushered in what MacLeod identifies as the second wave of the bibelot movement, the periodicals of protest, but Hubbard's positions were wildly inconsistent. He promoted free love, women's suffrage, and socialism, but he was also a probusiness sycophant known for spouting middlebrow platitudes about hard work and entrepreneurialism.[34] It seems obvious, in retrospect, that even if he hadn't been killed in 1915 when voyaging on the RMS *Lusitania*, there was no way Hubbard's literary reputation could have survived that transformation. For our purposes, however, the point is simply that the major turn in Hubbard's reputation occurred after his engagement with Crane's verse, and the shadow that his tarnished image has cast over it was largely retrospective. The relation of Crane's lines to the bibelots has been unfairly sullied by the reputation Hubbard earned, for the most part, after both Crane and the bibelot vogue were long dead.

In the 1890s, Hubbard fit right in with those involved with the bibelots.

It is likely that he had met Herbert Stone and Ingalls Kimball at Harvard in the fall of 1893, the semester before they started the *Chap-Book*. After his one semester there, Hubbard traveled to England and Ireland, where the Arts and Crafts press of William Morris inspired him to found the Roycroft community, devoted to the ideal of artisanal production. With Taber and William Mackintosh, he began publication of the *Philistine*, which is easily identifiable as one of the ephemerals, in the summer of 1895. Four by six inches in size, it was printed in something like Jenson type, the cover in black and red on brown butcher's wrapping paper. Like many other bibelots, the *Philistine* positioned itself as "a periodical of protest," reserving a particular animus for Edward Bok, editor of the *Ladies' Home Journal*, and Richard Watson Gilder of the *Century*. Hubbard never tired of mocking the *Misses Home Journal*, or the *Loidy's Own*, or "Mr. Sok's journal of deportment and advertising."[35] Of Gilder, Hubbard wrote that he "dishes up monthly beautifully printed articles which nobody cares about, but which everybody buys, because *The Century* looks well on the library table."[36]

As was typical for ephemeral bibelots, Hubbard's editorials kept regular tabs on its peers. He never missed an opportunity to take a jab at the *Chap-Book*, which he consistently referred to as the *Chip-Munk* and used to arrange the cartography of the vogue. His tone is well represented by a May 1896 article about a new bibelot called the *Fad*: " 'If I owned Hell and Texas, I'd rent Texas and live in Hell,' once said Phil Sheridan. But now comes the *Fad*, of the *Chip-Munk* brood, printed on green paper at San Antonio, and claims that Texas has more real, sure enough Culture than all New England. This is only truism—Rodents!"[37] A December 1895 number wondered how much it cost to get out an edition of *M'lle New York*, musing that "about three pipefuls [of opium] would be ample to do the business."[38] In April 1897, the magazine was following William Marion Reedy's *St. Louis Mirror*, with which Kate Chopin had been involved, and in May 1897 it welcomed the *Clack Book* as well, noting that "[t]he sympathy of my valuable friend the *Clack Book* is welcome."[39] Still going strong as other bibelotists began to quit the field, Hubbard delighted to note the passing of the *Bauble* and the *Lark*: "De *Lark* trowed up de Sponge on April First; an' de *Bauble*, dat allus was a Fool Ting, have done de same."[40] In September of 1898, after he had outlasted the *Chap-Book*, Hubbard beamed, "Will the Philistines please observe that although the 'Chap-Book' is dead, very dead, thro fatty degeneration of the cerebrum, I have not once said 'I gloat, I gloat!' "[41]

The *Philistine* was deeply entangled in the aesthetic public sphere. It published at least one poem by Gelett Burgess, "Karma," and another by Burgess's disciple Yone Noguchi. Indeed, although it never came to pass, Hubbard had wanted to have a second banquet modeled on the one for Crane to honor Noguchi.[42] An early number of the *Philistine* carried an ad for the *Lark*, referring to it as the *Shark*. Moreover, the directionality of these friendly barbs went both ways. There was a magazine called the *Anti-Philistine* published in London, and a parody in Chicago called the *Bilioustine*, which published two numbers in 1901. Bert Leston Taylor published a satirical column for the *Chicago Tribune* and *Puck* based on Hubbard called "Line-o'-Type." The Chicago version of the column came out on fine paper and issued out of Evanston, masquerading as East Aurora.[43] This is the kind of *fumiste* banter and exchange that, as we have seen, was stylistically the most obvious link between the ephemeral bibelots, and around which new links took shape.

It is precisely this network of relations from which Crane's biographers and contemporary admirers have worked to separate him, and no other single event has played a more significant symbolic role in this effort than the dinner banquet thrown by the Philistine Society on Crane's behalf, the occasion for the *Roycroft Quarterly* souvenir volume. The dinner highlights the breach between two possible publics, the aesthetic public of the bibelots and the Modernist literary establishment that later came to rescue Crane from it either by situating him more resolutely with the Realists or claiming that he was, sui generis, a Modernist, Lowell's "man without a period." On the one hand is Hubbard, who first met Crane in New York in 1894 and began publishing his lines in the *Philistine* almost immediately. On the other are the more established figures of the American literary establishment, foremost among them Hamlin Garland, whom Crane had met in 1891 and to whom he dedicated *The Black Riders* in 1895, when it was first published. It takes some time to unravel this story, but I want to take it here because of all it reveals about the values attached critically to loose associations of the kind that made Crane's verse so edgy, for a time, during the bibelot craze.

How the dinner is recounted hinges on choosing sides, and Crane's biographers have always chosen Garland's. Sorrentino argues that Crane "found his teacher" in Garland.[44] The two became friends the year Crane dropped out of Syracuse University and began working as a journalist in Avon-by-the-Sea, New Jersey. Garland was a champion of Crane's first novel, *Maggie, A Girl of the Streets*, and he introduced the younger author's work to Howells. Garland was receptive of Crane's poems and tried unsuccessfully to place them with Henry Mills Alden, then editor of *Harper's Monthly*. As told and retold in the biographies, the gist of this tale is that among the many relations Crane developed in these early years of the 1890s, there was something particularly important about the one he had with Garland, who gave Crane the artistic direction and encouragement he had sorely been lacking. Howells's and Garland's approval is said to have cleared the way for the dramatic expansion of his reputation with the publication of *The Red Badge of Courage* in 1895, giving him access to the mass public of the major monthly literary magazines.

Howells never published in an ephemeral bibelot, and Garland limited himself to the *Chap-Book*, which, as we have seen, had a circumspect relation to the bibelot movement. Neither of them attended the banquet. Instead, in 1894, as the bibelot vogue was getting under way, Garland published a book of essays, *Crumbling Idols*, which makes the case for American Realism by arguing that writers should quit imitating Europe and concentrate on local color instead. Garland wanted fiction to have "such quality of texture and back-ground that it could not have been written . . . by any one else than a native."[45] Howells had earlier made similar pleas in his monthly essays in *Harper's* for the direct observation of life and the abandonment of imitative styles of representation, his notion of the democratizing of literature meaning that authors and artists be considered "not in proportion to any other author or artist, but in his relation to the human nature, known to us all, which it is his privilege, his high duty, to interpret."[46] Arguments such as these could not have been further from the Montmartre-oriented aesthetic of *fumisme* shaping the context for the reception of Crane's lines in the *Philistine* and in the collected volumes. The relational aesthetic was anything but dutiful, direct, or native.

The dinner had been difficult to organize. Letters between Crane and his closest friends document the young author's shy reluctance to attend; only twenty-four years old, he was both flattered and confused by the attention.[47] But he should have felt at home among the guests. Taber described them as people "more or less interested in that curious movement of the mid-nineties which found a certain expression in the making of small magazines and the development of such men as Crane, Percival Pollard, Walter Blackburn Harte and a few other protestants."[48] Firsthand accounts of the proceedings were mixed. The most negative report of the evening came from Claude Bragdon, a close friend of Burgess and an illustrator, designer, and architect known to some in the bibelot movement as "the Beardsley of America," who sat next to Crane at the dinner. He called it "a distressing memory—like the sight of a young ox led to the slaughter" and at one point got up to leave in protest.[49] But Bragdon was not a close friend of Crane's and, somewhat surprisingly, seems just as likely to have mistaken the tone of the evening's clowning, which was in keeping with the ironic banter of the little magazines. Crane's Delta Upsilon fraternity brother Frank Noxon described the evening differently. He wrote that Crane was seated before a crowd of "freaks or near-freaks," fellow travelers who "in the best clown and gridiron manner . . . guyed and ragged [Crane and each other] from start to finish." He was "having the time of his life."[50] Noxon writes that when Bragdon got up to leave, he was blocked by Crane's closest friend, Willis Brook Hawkins, who assured him that Crane felt "more complimented by the spirit of this meeting than he would have been by all the solemn eulogies that could be pronounced."[51]

Nothing here really suggests any reason to suspect that the dinner would have led Crane to believe himself "the dupe of his own vainglorious notions," as Stallman contrives it, unless we understand being associated with and beloved by bibelotists to be, itself, a problem.[52] Sorrentino may well be right to conclude that Crane was made uncomfortable. A "shy bohemian rebel who restrained his emotions," Crane revealed himself, in the months after the dinner, as by turns "despondent," "full of self pity," and "maudlin."[53] However, his friendship with Hubbard appears to have survived. Immediately after the dinner, Crane went to visit Hubbard's family in East Aurora and bought a little brown horse from him named Peanuts. Two years later, he wrote one of many friendly letters, addressed to "My dear Hubbard," in which he apologizes for a lapsed correspondence. It "is a dangerous thing to forget to communicate with one's friends. . . . I am glad you wrote to me because I have been believing myself an ass in your respect and now I have an opportunity to say so." In the same letter, it becomes clear that their literary collaboration had continued as well, as Crane goes on to write that he had sent "a thing to the *Bookman* with instructions in a circuitous way, that if they could not use ($) it, they should forward it to the *Philistine*."[54] The next year, in a note ribbing Hubbard for the success of "A Message to Garcia," Crane wraps up by writing that "[w]hen I think of you I rejoice that there is one man in the world who can keep up a small independent monthly without either dying, going broke, or becoming an ass."[55] In 1900, when Cora Crane wrote Hubbard to announce Crane's death, she expressed regret that Hubbard had not been able to complete a planned trip to see them in London. "Stephen talked so often to me of you," she wrote, "and your photo was always in his study."[56]

Given such friendliness, the decision to portray the banquet in a negative light reflects the critical decision that I have been describing to lay claim to Crane as either a Realist or a Modernist, but not a bibelotist. It reflects a choice between two kinds of publics. One took Crane fastidiously as a serious author, while the other took him as a serious freak. One read Crane for substantives, while the other read him for relations. There is little doubt where Hubbard stood. He responded to contemporary critics of the banquet in the *Philistine* in February 1896 with the quip that "I don't think it's necessary to defend Mr. Crane against the Serious Critic, but one thing may be said in his favor by way of contrast: he knows a joke at sight." This may be self-serving, but it signals, I think, a larger split between the aesthetic public of the little magazines and that of both the elite and the popular press. Hubbard had previously revealed his position in a letter to Crane written sometime in late July 1895, describing the difficulty he had actually figuring out what Crane's lines meant:

> I do not confess to an unqualified liking for your work. When you hand me the book I am grown suddenly blind. It rather appeals to my nerves than to my reason—it gives me a thrill. Your work is of a kind so charged with electricity that it cannot be handled. It is all live wire. It eludes all ordinary criticism and it escapes before one can apply his Harvard Rhetorical Test. What is left? I'll tell you, we can stand off and hoot—if we have columns to fill we can fill them with plain hoot. Your lines show too much individuality to pass by and so we laugh and work the feeble joke. Thank God for the feeble joke! It fills many an awkward pause.[57]

Part of what Hubbard says here is pure business: he has columns to fill, so why not Crane's verse? But he, like the other bibelotists, took their joking seriously. In emphasizing the effect, not the substance, of Crane's lines, the way they produce "a thrill," "all live wire," and allow others to "work the feeble joke," Hubbard reveals that he is reading in a transitive not substantive mode. It is the edginess of emptiness: he reads with nerves not reason, a poetry that is charged not handled, and for a lark not permanent renown.

There is perhaps no more telling register of the split between Hubbard and the "serious critic" than the last pages of the souvenir volume from the dinner with which we began, which includes regrets sent by invitees from around the country who were unable to attend the festivities. Assembled under the title "Fate Frowned Upon Them and They Could Not Come," each of the entries is flippant and witty but for two, those sent by Howells and Garland. Bliss Carman writes that "[i]t would do me great pleasure to sit at feast with Mr. Crane and the bold and worthy Philistines, but I cannot find East Aurora in my Railroad Guide." Ambrose Bierce jokes that "[w]ere it not for the miles which separate us, I would be with you and lick a plate so clean that it would not have to be washed for a month." Hayden Carruth gives a parody of "I saw a man chasing the horizon," a twenty-line poem beginning, "I saw a Man reading an invitation, / Anon he chortled like a bull-frog." The concluding entry of the bunch even finishes with a reference to Burgess's "The Purple Cow," which had gone viral seven months earlier with its publication in the first number of the *Lark*, when a Col. John L. Burleigh writes, jokingly of course, that he had been with Crane at Antietam: "When a Rebel General remonstrated with him, Steve, in a red fury, gave him a kick like a purple cow when all at once—but the story is too long to tell now." As it turns out, Burleigh was a New York lawyer who hailed originally from Ann Arbor, Michigan, suggesting some of the extent to which the bibelot vogue was traveling.

Howells's and Garland's contributions strike a completely different tone: they are both insufferably pretentious and dull, entirely missing the mark of the souvenir volume as a whole. Howells pats himself on the back while praising Crane, "I am very glad to know that my prophecies are being realized and that Mr. Crane is receiving recognition at a time in life when he can most enjoy it." Garland's note feels similarly self-righteous: "I take a very special interest in Mr. Crane, as I was one of the very first to know about Maggie and the Red Badge." One could not get further from the freakish good cheer of the other contributors.

And so, while it may be true that Crane dedicated *The Black Riders* to Garland, it seems even more telling to insist that it was published on Guiney's recommendation by Copeland and Day, the fine arts press that also brought out an edition of Oscar Wilde's *Salomé* illustrated by Aubrey Beardsley and *Vivette*, Gelett Burgess's novel drawn from stories first published in the *Lark*.[58] It also seems worth insisting that Crane was probably not at all offended by the parodying and ribbing he received in the bibelots at large. Hubbard kept it up well after the banquet, as for instance in the *Philistine* for February 1899, where he published a parody of Crane, "I saw a man tugging at his Boot Straps," with another illustration by Denslow:

I saw a man tugging at his Boot Straps
"It is futile," I said,
"You can never lift yourself that way."
"You lie!" he cried,
And tugged on.

You lie, indeed! Crane's lines come to life when brought into association with these works in ways that they do not when placed alongside *Crumbling Idols*. But you can't judge what you can't see, and most serious critics have chosen not to see Hubbard. His early erasure from the scene took yet another hub out of play, yet another tie to the ephemeral bibelots vogue gone.

Against the American Grain

There is at least one recent account linking Crane to the bibelot movement, a work of fiction. In 2007, Edmund White published *Hotel de Dream*, a novel that imagines Crane, on his deathbed, struggling to complete a story about a boy prostitute, which he is rumored to have begun shortly after *Maggie*. The story was reportedly to have been called "Flowers of Asphalt," after a collection of French poetry, *Fleurs de Bitume*, by none other than Emile Goudeau—founder of the Hydropathes (see chapter 1). The anecdote White draws on for the novel comes from a letter written by Crane's friend, James Gibbons Huneker, author of the decadent short story "Venus Victrix" discussed in the previous chapter, who had become an associate editor of *M'lle New York* after its fifth issue, in October 1895. There are some doubts about the letter, which was in the papers of Crane's notoriously unreliable first biographer, Thomas Beer, but we do know Crane and Huneker to have been friends at the time. Huneker describes having pointed out the handsome young boy, painted and looking "like a Rossetti angel—big violet eyes—probably full of belladonna—Crane was disgusted. Thought he'd vomit. Then he got interested."[59] Following the pattern we saw earlier, the novel has Huneker blaming Garland for upending the boy-whore novel that might have come from the meeting. In White's rendering, Garland, "with all his Wisconsin gravity," had destroyed the pages out of envy. Crane thinks to himself that Garland had "never written anything so raw and new, so *modern*, and urban. No, he has his rolling periods and his yarns about his father playing the defeated pioneer farmer in the Dakotas, but he couldn't have written my pages."[60]

As we have seen, the story most frequently told has been that his association with Hubbard, not to mention Huneker and the other bohemians of the bibelot movement, effectively quashed Crane's reputation as a poet until Lowell came to the rescue. Obviously, the argument I have been making sides with White. Hubbard's banquet can be read as the catalyst that set off a lopsided contest between competing publics for the right to claim Crane as one of their own. This contest was very much still alive at the time of his death in 1900: was Crane to be seen as part of a dominant literary culture in which Realism and Naturalism held sway, or as part of a subcultural youth movement that had been interested in a new, freakish art of revolt? By the time Lowell came to his verse, the question appears to have been largely moot; the bibelot vogue had been forgotten and Crane's place in it reduced to a footnote about his unfortunate association with the Roycrofters. By that time, Crane's verse may well have seemed so distinctive, so utterly unlike anything else they knew, that it could be nothing else but Modernist. And one has to admit that their argument is perfectly in line with the origination myth upon which Modernism has long fed, which depends on hard breaks like this one. An account of Crane's poetry that has lost almost all ties to the bibelot fad reinforces the well-trod notion that "on or about December 1910, human character changed."[61] The uniqueness of his verse was the exception to prove the rule.

Following this hard line of demarcation, I want to turn, for a third explanation of the end of the bibelot vogue, to a brief consideration of the Modernist little magazines of the early twentieth century. Upon final examination, I would argue that the ephemeral bibelots were, indeed, far afield from most of the magazines associated with Lowell that have held perennial sway in the history of Modernism. It may not be entirely fair to blame Lowell for short-circuiting our ties to the interaction of Crane's lines and the ephemeral bibelots because a slew of other Modernists made a similar choice when they turned quite completely against the bibelots' relational aesthetic. It wasn't just a rejection of Hubbard. The main line of Modernist little magazines of the 1910s, '20s, and '30s had little time for either the internationalism or the whimsy of the bibelots' relational aesthetic, which they would likely have written off as being humdrum, aimless, and at loose ends. Instead, what one finds, both in most Anglo-American Modernist magazines and those being published around the world, is a distinctly localizing trend. A localist aesthetic replaces the relational aesthetic. There is a distinct shift in the tenor of most of the period's keywords, away from relations and toward direct contact, the particularity of place, the integrity of aesthetic experience, organic unity, the native seed, and cultural nationalism, terms one would have been more likely to associate with Howells and Garland, and especially the latter, than with the ephemeral bibelots. Strange to say, but Garland, on this account, becomes more Modernist than bibelotists like Burgess, Huneker, Hubbard, and the others.

Before pursuing this point, though, it makes sense to consider a major qualification. There could be a temptation to make a connection between the bibelot vogue and the early twentieth century by way of reasserting the place of Decadence in the constitution of Modernism, as numerous literary historians have begun to do.[62] In many respects, this connection would seem intuitively correct as a way to pull the bibelot vogue forward into the twentieth century. Despite the explicit claim of one of its contributors that the *Lark* had "demolished Decadence and picked Hope out of the dust-heap," the edgy emptiness I have been describing finds something of a match in what Kristin Mahoney has described as a political mode of offbeat, bohemian aestheticism.[63] She has argued that the writers in the 1910s adopted a stance of detachment, to be found stylistically in camp, parody, and perversity, which they held onto as "an antidote to the chauvinism of wartime and the despair of the interwar period."[64] Here, one sees something like the same bohemian gestures of what we have seen in the *Lark*, *M'lle New York*, and the *Philistine*, not to mention in Kate Chopin's stories for *Vogue*, including a disregard of aesthetic hierarchies, social and sexual rebellion, spirited parodies, puns, and off-color humor. But what one does not find is any direct citation of the earlier American bibelots or bibelotists, not even of those who were still actively publishing.

The American version of Modernist Decadence took shape in Greenwich Village in the 1910s, and a number of magazines emerged to promote it. The absence in them of the bibelotists from the 1890s is absolutely striking. For example, the literary historian Stephen Rogers has recently drawn attention to the magazines started by the Eastern European immigrant Guido Bruno, who was something of a Hubbardian figure in terms of the very mixed reception he received historically. He had a "reputation as a huckster" for his promotion of the Village's bohemianism to the bourgeoisie, and seems to have wanted to combine the taste for this style with the attack it implied on prevailing attitudes toward sexuality.[65] Bruno published fine art editions of Alfred Kreymborg's *Edna: A Girl of the Street* (1915) and Djuna Barnes's *The Book of Repulsive Women* (1915), which, as described by Rogers, "were attacks on the prevailing reluctance to deal openly with sexual content in literature by flouting conventional morality."[66] Of course, *Vogue* or *M'lle New York* had done exactly the same thing, but while the aestheticized style of their protest persists, there is no mention of either of them as precedents. Along the same lines, we can find Crane making an appearance in *Bruno's Weekly* on September 2, 1916, in an article by Alfred Ernest Keet, "Stephen Crane: A New York Poet." However, lines to the bibelots have been severed. There is no mention of the *Philistine* or Crane's association with the previous generation's bibelot vogue, and he is celebrated, instead, as a Realist indebted to Garland. The article concludes, strangely but predictably, by quoting Edith Wyatt on Crane's "genius for direct expression" and the "penetrating ascertainments of American life" to be found in his "static lines of verse."[67] These descriptors may help us understand Crane in relation to Imagism, with which Wyatt compares him favorably, but they are far from the relational terms of his appearance in the *Philistine*.

The Greenwich Village little magazine most like a bibelot from the 1890s, both in its political and stylistic inclinations, was certainly *Rogue*. Deborah Longworth has argued that *Rogue* "defies the canonized history of poetic modernism and the primary narrative of an Anglo-American formalism originating from the development of the Imagist school of poets."[68] The magazine has long been associated with Dada, and Longworth's contribution is to situate it as a counterweight to the formal principles emerging out of Chicago with *Poetry*. It also reads like a latter-day *Lark*, from its celebration of puffs from other magazines to its abuse of William Dean Howells. For instance, on April 1, 1915, its second number opens with a humorous list of notices about itself that could have been taken straight from the fifth number of Burgess's bibelot (as described in chapter 2), and the second of the puffs even comes from *Vogue*:

> Dear Rogue:
> We accuse you of appropriating all the letters of our name but one. You know our copyright laws are very strict. Perhaps, though, we should be glad you left us a V.

In spirit, *Vogue*'s puff could have been lifted directly from the *Lark*'s "*Avis au lecteur*" from September 1895, although *Rogue* got a larger range of more popular magazines to play along. These included *Harper's Weekly*, the *Smart Set*, and the *Ladies' Home Journal*. Along the same lines, the sideways jab at Howells comes on the editorial page calling itself "The Editor's Difficult Chair," not to be confused with the "Editor's Easy Chair" column Howells wrote for *Harper's Monthly* from 1899 to 1909. *Rogue* even offers a parody

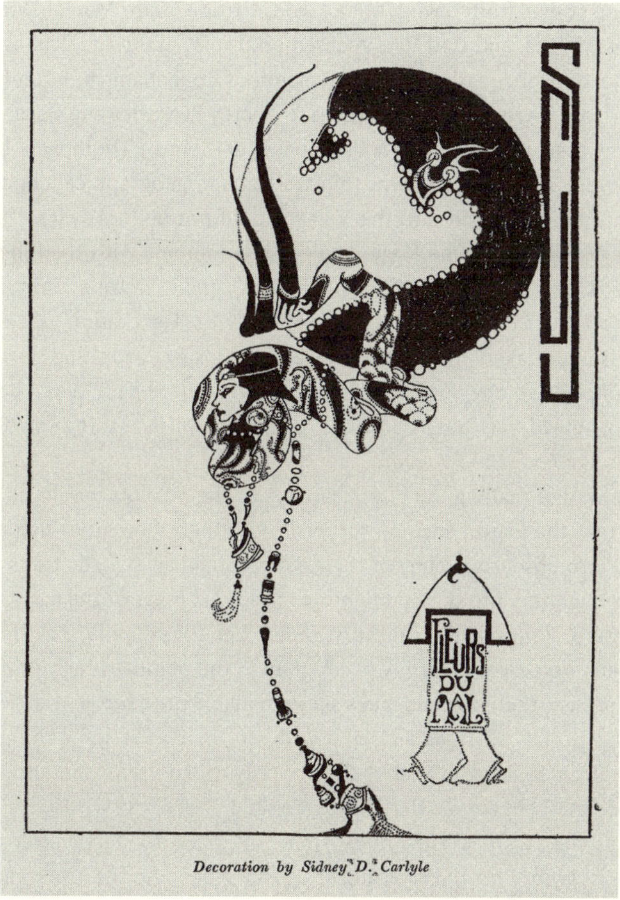

Sidney Carlyle, "Les Fleurs du Mal," *Rogue* 2:3, October 1915

of the Pierrot sketches in the same number. "Filling a Page: A Pantomime with Words" renders Pierrot and his harlequin lover, Columbine, in written dialogue, not images, consisting of unsettling nonsequiturs: Columbine: "I have orange slippers." Pierrot: "In the green grass?"

The question remains, however, whether the bohemianism of Greenwich Village in the 1910s represented a revival of the bibelot spirit of the 1890s or its further descent into oblivion. To be dizzyingly sure, *Rogue*'s main contributors entered the pantheon of Modernism in ways that the bibelotists never did, James, Chopin, and Crane notwithstanding. The curiosity of the magazine comes from having Mina Loy, Gertrude Stein, Marcel Duchamp, Wallace Stevens, and Carl Van Vechten on display alongside, and as representative of, a peculiarly bourgeois version of bohemianism. But why, one wonders, are there so many references to Aubrey Beardsley and Oscar Wilde, and none at all to *M'lle New York*'s Huneker and Vance Thompson, both of whom were still alive, and whose historical and geographical connection to avant-garde magazines in the Village could not be more clear? Instead of *M'lle New York*, "Dame Rogue" spices her columns with the "chocolate charmed Oscar Wilde [and] his dainty heroes"; and in October 1915, following a short piece by Van Vechten, Sidney Carlyle's "Decoration" of *Les Fleurs du Mal* is undertaken in the phallic style of Beardsley decorating *Lysistrata*.[69] But again, why so obviously Beardsley and not Louis Rhead? Was it because, by then, Rhead was busy contributing articles on fly fishing for outdoor journals like *Forest and Stream*?

One way of reading the disappearance of the bibelots would be simply to say that they succeeded all too well. Although their titles had already slipped into obscurity, many of their more bohemian stylistic traits appear to have migrated into the middlebrow modernist press of the early twentieth century, alongside their authors. Remember, for example, that Tompkins and Wells were by then firmly established in the popular press. And if that were the case, then it would make sense to take a cue from Harriet Monroe, who was no fan of *Rogue* and who said very much the same thing about Crane's lines. Writing in *Poetry*, she not only called them "sententious and platitudinous" but argued that they were stale, "full of the wisdom of yesteryear." As she put it, Crane's lines "somehow cease to startle after twenty years—so swiftly do the radicalisms of today become the commonplaces of tomorrow."[70] Even Longworth admits that *Rogue*'s obscurity today may be due to its "lightweight and frivolous tone, and to what appeared to be the tired 1890s imagery and effete aestheticism of much of the writing it contained."[71]

But another way to understand this transformation without quite so fully diminishing the 1890s is to read it as the end of the relational era. In other words, we could take Monroe to heart and agree that the commonplaces of today were the radicalisms of yesterday. And in that case, the appearance of Wilde and Beardsley in *Rogue* really does feel dated. Their prominence as points of reference in Greenwich Village comes not because they are shocking, but because they are icons of shock. A reference to them is not edgy, but rather too full. Their bohemian style remained, but the feeling had certainly changed. The whimsy no longer depended on the edginess of connections, and there was no grasping after allusion. If the avant-garde of the black cat era had been to some extent produced by the frisson of relations that jumped the tracks, from the edges bridging structural holes—from black cats going walking around much of America and South America, from Montmartre to the *Clack Book* in Lansing, Michigan—that whole circulatory ethos had become conventionally circumscribed by the imaginary boundaries of the lower west side of Manhattan. Wilde and Beardsley had been commoditized, made recognizable as permanent fixtures of bohemianism that could be put into circulation without the need for allusions. The *Lark*, by contrast, had been forgotten, except for the purple cow; and by that time, even the purple cow had become a thing unto itself. Williams College, recall, adopted it for a mascot sometime around 1907.

As for the main cohort of Modernist little magazines, they took off in another direction that further circumscribed the bibelots' historical mobility. The internationalism of the 1890s avant-garde in America gave way to the localism of the avant-garde worldwide. This move has long been understood in the American context in relation to the emergence of a public sphere newly attuned to cultural pluralism, and to magazines responding to the particularity of ethnic, national, and racial identities.[72] Two recent books on the Modernist little magazines of the 1920s and 1930s argue that this move in the United States found an echo abroad. Eric White and Eric Bulson both address what might be understood as the translocal paradox of modernism. Twentieth-century Modernism is known for its internationalism; however, with regard to its little magazines, what was shared internationally was an ideological commitment to the development of indigenous avant-gardes.

Like the ephemeral bibelots, Modernist little magazines took shape from a matrix of transnational and national print cultures, which explains the continuity of their design vernacular. Bulson points out, for instance, the worldwide uniformity of their typographical experimentation and the widespread use of a grid format developed in the early Dada magazines. In this respect, they are not at all unlike the bibelots, which also developed shared print conventions (see chapter 2). What is different, however, is the emergence of the localist aesthetic. Both studies suggest how little magazines manipulated an array of early twentieth-century cultural elements with an eye to cultivating what White terms "an outwardly indigenous avant-garde."[73] For Bulson, "disconnection" best describes the Modernist little magazine network, the magazines being a place for the absorption of Western models with an eye toward the production of "an indigenous literature." The little magazines, Bulson writes, "derived their force from production at a specific address within the borders of a specific nation, using the world post as a convenient transport system that could connect individuals, leaving traces along the way."[74]

Examples of this transformation abound. White, for instance, discusses the involvement of William Carlos Williams with the American little magazines *Contact* and *Pagany: A Native Quarterly*—the difference from the ephemeral bibelots already being self-evident in their titles. With both of these, Williams worked to develop a materialist poetics of place that emphasized the haptic immediacy of experience, the reconnection with certitude. *Contact* promoted "native work in verse, fiction, criticism or whatever is written . . . to maintain a place" and sought to collect work representing "intelligent, informed contact with the locality."[75] In *Pagany*, that poetics starts low to the ground; Williams suggested to his friend Richard Johns, the magazine's founder, that he would have to "fasten to the native shale or sandstone" and work up from there.[76]

It is a dramatic change in emphasis that has long been understood to be a defining feature of early twentieth-century American art. When the Dadaists Marcel Duchamp and Francis Picabia move to New York, they teach the Americans to make Modern art out of skyscrapers and consumer goods. Robert Frost, Willa Cather, Sherwood Anderson, and Sinclair Lewis turn to small towns and Main Street, USA, for inspiration. In 1917, Alfred Stieglitz closes his eclectic gallery 291 and forms his close-knit second circle of American artists, all of whom stop traveling abroad. In 1925, he puts together a new blockbuster exhibition called *Seven Americans* of pictures described in the catalogue as being "an integral part of their makers."[77] The "lost generation" ends up in Paris, but nothing could be more American than the expatriate community they chronicle there. And John Dewey starts adapting philosophical Pragmatism to the cause of recovering the immediacy and vitality of aesthetic experience. For instance, in an article titled "Americanism and Localism," published in 1920 in the Modernist little magazine the *Dial*, he suggested, famously, that "the locality is the only universal."[78]

What could be further from the way Crane's lines were treated in the bibelots? The very notion of art being "integral" to its makers, and all the more American because of it, would have been anathema to the bibelotists of the 1890s. It runs counter both to the internationalist lines of association upon which the reception of Crane depended and to the notion of externality and correspondence upon which the aesthetic took shape. With reference to the late nineteenth century, the transformation marks the ultimate ascendance of Garland over Hubbard. It is not the stuff of bibelotic revolt but rather of the conservatism of local color writers like Mary Wilkens Freeman, Bret Harte, and Mark Twain, all of whom Dewey eulogizes in his article on localism. The relational aesthetic of the bibelots, which depended not on an integrated but a dispersed sense of self and art, of relations that multiply and never end, could not have been further afield.

Moreover, this transformation is not simply an Anglo-American story. Bulson makes the case that the same turn inward can be seen developing elsewhere at the same time. He focuses on two magazines in the mid-1920s, *Mavo* out of Tokyo and *Kallol* out of Calcutta, in order to show editors making an argument very similar to Dewey's that "locality is the only universal." In each of these cases, the magazines use the world form of the little magazine to explore and elaborate the particularity of their own situation, while conversely using the indigeneity of their own practice to construct a relation to the international cultural field. The little magazine is a world form, but one shaped from the dynamic entailed by the circulation of ideas through local, national, and international contexts.

The Indian little magazine *Kallol* is of particular interest because, as Bulson explains, its editors largely defined their project against the work and perceived politics of Rabindranath Tagore, whom I extolled earlier for his 1890s Bengali-language ephemeral bibelot *Sadhana* (see the introduction). Their disavowal of Tagore bears a remarkable resemblance to the American Modernists' rejection of Hubbard and promotion of Crane as an original. Tagore's bibelot, which he started like so many other editors after a trip to Paris, was part of what appears to have been a flourishing periodical culture in Calcutta in the 1890s and early 1900s, where at least a dozen magazines in the literature, satire, and illustration genre were published.[79] Bulson argues that the editors of *Kallol* turned against Tagore, whom they chided for an unchecked Anglophilia—otherwise interpretable in terms of the relational aesthetic—in order to express their "desire less to look outward from India than to look inward." They still published Modernist authors from abroad, including Norway, Japan, and Russia; but they did not publish authors from the colonial center of England, and they turned away from Tagore's cosmopolitanism in order "to descend into the dirt to search for the great truths that may be hidden there."[80]

What we might read into their decision is something akin to the argument between Lowell and Hubbard, or to the decisions made by Williams represented by his turn to "native" soil in *Pagany*, especially if one is careful to add on the colonial history of India after the Great War. That history is obviously not unrelated to the newfound status of New York at the same time. It certainly seems reasonable to make *Pagany* a third member of Bulson's group, part of a worldwide development of little magazines invested in cultivating their own national and cultural differences. The turn of the little magazines of the 1920s and '30s to local contexts was broadly orchestrated by world systems. And at the same time, it was very much like Lowell's rendering of Crane. The localism of the 1920s and 1930s was a lot less edgy, but it was no less relatable to the aesthetic ideals of its moment than the bibelots had been to theirs.

From a network perspective, Bulson's point is similar to the one I made when considering how cultural elements shared by the ephemeral bibelots circulated even when physical copies of the magazines did not (see chapter 2). As with the ephemeral bibelots, the "world form" of the little magazine network developed around significant structural holes, some of which were actively cultivated for aesthetic and political effect. As such, the story Bulson tells is as much one of what he calls "dead links" and "dark matter" as it is of active connections.[81] He is absolutely right to point out the regional particularity of print cultures that were "[d]ecommercialized, decentralized, decapitalized, disconnected."[82] As we saw before, it is around the brokerage of such impediments that interesting things happen, and that was true in the little magazines of both the 1890s and 1920s.

The lesson I would draw, however, is that while network dynamics shape ways of producing art and reading it, roughly equivalent structures can lead to radically different ends. The two movements had notably different ways of explaining very similar structural holes. It isn't that the network structure changed significantly between the moment of the ephemeral bibelots and that of the Modernist little magazines; rather, what changed were the contexts and meanings attached to negotiating that structure. In the bibelots, the relational aesthetic reflects and reproduces the fractured sense of self resulting from consumer culture, changing sexual and religious mores, and the bohemian subcultures of cosmopolitan European cities; whereas for Modernist networks, the localism addresses the pervading sense of disconnection from the organic unity of everyday life resulting from still more consumerism, the Great War, and colonialism. The bibelots made an art of loose and wispy connections, whereas the Modernist little magazines did the same with the gaps. The bibelots tended to find work that bridged structural holes innovative and full of interest, whereas the Modernist little magazines found it more innovative to blow up the bridges. War can do that.

Conclusion

The ephemeral bibelotists who settled on Crane's verse as a point of reference did so in ways that are remarkably distinct from those who took up his case as an early exemplar of Modernism. For Edith Wyatt, writing appreciatively of Crane in the *New Republic* in September 1915, his verse was a forebear to modern poetry because of its directness: his "poems seem to me to evince a far deeper and better conception than the Imagists' of direct expression in poetry."[83] But for Jonathan Penn, writing somewhat less appreciatively but more to the point in the *Lotus* in October 1896, Crane's genius came not from its directness but from its triggering of small world associations. For Penn, Crane's verse linked to Loie Fuller, since it was like "the latest whirlwind dance of another sensation, that has been cleverly 'boomed,'" and to the poster fad, since it took full advantage of a modern movement identified as "'poster' literature," his "chromatic effects—a sort of 'poster' commentary."[84] It also linked to the French *petites revues* because of its "lunacy." His genius exploited a "strong vein of illogic," cultivating "the power of the ludicrous and irrelevant in immediately arresting attention" and giving full swing to "any startling bait of lunacy" (185). Crane was a "sincere lunatic" (186); his writing "is lunacy revealing the irony of sanity, and its goblin atmosphere admirably suits the literary epicure who has enough catholicity to thoroughly enjoy the surprises of folly" (185). Given Penn's own location in the bibelot movement—he had already written another article about Crane for the *Fly Leaf* that included one of the first parodies of Crane's style—there seems little doubt that he was referencing the French "lunatic" *revues—La Lune*, *L'Eclipse*, *La Lune Rousse*, *La Petite Lune*—that led, in the hands of Emile Goudeau, to the literary and artistic relations "*les Incohérents*" and "*les Hydropathes*" (see the introduction). And the "goblin atmosphere"? Penn could not have known it, but we know that in Germany, *Pan*, in the same year and month, used the same word to describe the American little magazine fad, calling it a "kind of Goblin-literature."[85]

My point in this chapter should not be taken to be that Lowell and Wyatt were wrong and that Crane's verse was not direct. Rather, in the context of the bibelots, it was direct in a most circuitous way. Penn got it right when he suggested that Crane stopped working to overcome the "vague illogic in his mental constitution": he "realized . . . the immense sensational value of the bizarre in this epoch of literary cocktails" (185). Crane's verse is much more interesting—livelier, less pretentious—when put back into conversation with the self-proclaimed "freaks" writing in these little magazines. It makes the lunacy of this string of connections come to life and gives a cumulative sense of velocity, perhaps even ferocity, to his lines.

A useful anecdote to illustrate the point is that even Louise Imogen Guiney had admitted to feeling that Crane was "extravagantly young" and that he "takes himself too seriously."[86] My specific argument about Crane has been that he was, indeed, very young and that we have taken him far too seriously. The enigma of Crane's poetic style made it ripe for the associative art one sees in the *Philistine*, and the successive Crane parodies give us one way to register what was new and modern about the aesthetic public sphere. He is exceptionally recognizable from within the movement, a suitable poster-child for what Harte described that same year in the *Fly Leaf* as a group that "does not look to the future . . . with any affected fin de siècle weariness or ennui, but with the hopefulness and stirring courage of youth."[87] Crane makes an exceptionally interesting freak, at least as a poet, and the reason is that his lines make so many connections to the *fumiste* excess of the relational aesthetic developed by the bibelot movement.

But reading his lines for their edginess demands a different kind of reading than we are used to, a different kind of relating to reading. Reading is nothing but relating: relating with a text, relating it to other things we know, including other texts. Network theorists tend to talk about strength of ties and modularity coefficients, indicating whether ties are strong or weak, and whether groups are tightly or loosely connected. But in artistic relations like the ones we have been discussing in the bibelots, they have even more qualitative characteristics, like textures, speeds, sounds, and colors. They can feel rough or slick, pocked or smooth, solid or ethereal, red or blue or green. They also have a multiplier effect in which the feeling of a work's symbolic depth, or lack thereof, is a reflection of the number and range of its relations. The relations can feel near or far, local or distant, native or foreign, rich or empty, deep or shallow, common or arcane. Relations can seem to have speed, being fast or slow, easy or belabored, ephemeral or enduring.

And they need to be renewed. If a work of art is said to have stood the test of time, what we really mean is that it has been carried along with renewed ties. Cut the ties, lose track of the associations, discount their variety, and they will fall by the side. Take out the hubs and they lose their connections to the present. And so, as you have seen with my own attempt to bring the bibelots back to our present, certain strategies can be deployed to open up lines of association. Name-dropping helps, and so one finds here Chekhov and Tagore, Mallarmé and Laforgue, the James brothers, Chopin, Hubbard, and Crane. Linkage to known history goes some way as well, and thus I have tried to situate the movement in relation to the rejection of Realism and the embrace of the spirit of Montmartre. Another line of connection might come by way of theoretical problems in literary criticism and methods of reading, or in the story of how artistic movements move, how they go viral and fade. These are not topics, merely. They are invitations to link to the world of the ephemeral bibelots, to have them become of renewed interest, to draw more and more relations into their stream, to make them edgy once again.

For William James, there was a substantive mode to match the transitive, a resting place for every bird in flight. The substantive was less interesting to him because more natural to our normal way of thinking, which as he put it "tends at all times towards some other substantive part than the one from which it has just been dislodged."[88] For readers, every flight of fancy takes off from the substantive words on the page. And yet I suspect that most people who truly enjoy reading fiction and poetry are Jamesians at heart and tend to get restless when we settle on words and fix their meaning. Words are precarious resting places. If they have any aesthetic bearing on our lives, they cannot really be said to sit still at all. To take them up, or take them in, is always a kind of relating. One line follows the next, with us readers perched in the middle, scurrying both forward and backward, as we read along. Is there really any way to end this game?

So what have I been suggesting? Artistic movements come and go—and with marginal ones like that of the ephemeral bibelots, they mostly go. A sense of crisis, such as that developing for the bibelots from the perceived fixity of Realist aesthetics or the drab portrayal of sexual desire, or for the Modernist little magazines from the geopolitical realignments of war, may seem to free up marginal art movements, allowing them to develop elaborate and frequently intense network ties. But by the same token, it is easy to lose track of these marginal movements, and not only because they are marginal to history. They are also marginal to the way we tell it, as we have seen, for instance, when considering the difficulty of delineating the significance of individual authors and artists in group movements. They can be buffeted by personal reputations. They prefer relations to resting places, a situation that makes it more difficult to pin them down and can make them feel empty or shallow. Archivists and collectors are left in the lurch, without objects to put in the archives. And when the next crisis hits, our ties to marginal movements can lose out to our sense of having little or no time for the nonessential. Our vision of the past constricts, at such moments, around what we take to be subjects of more vital and long-lasting importance.

All of these factors contributed to the ephemerality of the bibelot vogue, which was never meant to be a substantive thing in the first place. Perhaps this book will speed the development of a new set of relations, new lines on which to descend from the familiar aesthetic nodes of Realism and Modernism to the forgotten extremities of international experimentation and freakishness in the 1890s. And yet, it is admittedly hard to get a hold on a movement that insists upon being grasped by the edges, especially when those edges are sharp—when they keep running, leaping, and carousing in Sin.

Notes

Prologue

1. After the election of Donald Trump, I published a version of this introduction online, "The Original Pussyhat?" that suggests that the image resonates with the "pussyhats" of the protest movements in 2016–17, http://politicsslashletters.org/the-original-pussyhat/.

2. For information about Le Chat Noir cabaret, see Auriol, *Le Chat Noir Guide*; Goudeau, *Dix Ans de Bohème*; Fields, *George Auriol* and *Le Chat Noir*; Velter, *Les Poètes du Chat Noir*; Cate and Shaw, eds., *The Spirit of Montmartre*; Weisberg, ed., *Montmartre and the Making of Mass Culture*; and Brigstocke, *The Life of the City*.

3. For anyone familiar with my book *Before Cultures*, it will be clear that I was looking at *Vogue* shortly after writing the chapter "Howellsian Chic: The Local Color of Cosmopolitanism."

4. Dennis Cate quotes Willette for this story: "Since the print run of the journal was only eleven hundred copies, *Le Chat Noir* was not available at all newsstands, and asking, 'Madame, do you have *Le Chat Noir* [a black pussy]?' often earned you a slap when the dealer was a brunette." See Cate, "The Spirit of Montmartre," 37. Unless noted otherwise, emphasis in quotations is in the original.

5. From *Les Fleurs Du Mal*, "Le Chat":

Viens, mon beau chat, sur mon coeur amoureux;
Retiens les griffes de ta patte,
Et laisse-moi plonger dans tex beaux yeux,
Mêlés de metal et d'agate.

Lorsque mes doigts caressent à loisir
Ta tête et ton dos élastique,
Et qu ma main s'enivre du plaisir
De palper ton corps électrique,

Je vois ma femme en esprit; son regard,

Comme le tien, aimable bête
Profond et froid, coupe et fend comme un dard,

Et, des pieds jusques à la tête,
Un air subtil, un dangereux parfum
Nagent autour de son corps brun.

6. The caricatures are identified by Cate in "The Spirit of Montmartre," 68.

7. For information on this image, which was published in a very limited edition portfolio of four illustrations of Poe's stories by Aubrey Beardsley, see Gullans and Espey, "More Addenda," 360–362.

8. Stone, "The Poster and the Cat," 53–54. Others he cites include one by Penfield where a cat "sits erect on the brilliant red sofa jealously eyeing her mistress, whose attention is wholly absorbed by her 'Harper's,'" one by Powers for the bibelot *M'lle New York* of "a scrawny creature that I am sure is a 'low-down' cat and lives in Hester Street," and another for the *New York World* (a daily newspaper) of a "nightmare of a cat . . . [with] eyes as large as the proverbial saucer, and a tail that would make a feather boa feel insignificant."

9. The black cat with Maggie Cline is an illustration of Huneker, "A Brunhilda of the Bowery"; the black cat as devil's perch accompanies Thompson, "The Bishop and the Lord." The bibelot is not paginated. The black cat was a favorite of the ephemeral bibelots. They show up in *Chips*, the *Yellow Book*, *Ye Quaint Magazine*, and several more times in the *Chap-Book*, which on one occasion, the edition of April 15, 1898, uses an image by Steinlen himself. Probably the most delightful instance comes on the outrageous pages of *Le Petit Journal des Refusées*, where the black cats are even more than usual of the prototypically saucerlike eye variety of Montmartre. For these and other cats, readers are encouraged to visit https://sites.rutgers.edu/bibelots.

10. See Toth, *Kate Chopin: A Life of the Author*; and Knights, Introduction to *The Awakening and Other Stories*, especially xvi–xvii.

11. The story is most fully told by Nancy Glazener, whose book on the production and reception of the Realist movement in what she calls the "*Atlantic* group" of elite, bourgeois monthlies remains definitive. See Glazener, *Reading for Realism*. For other influential accounts, see also Kaplan, *Social Construction*; Broadhead, *Cultures of Letters*; Ohmann, *Selling Culture*; and Noonan, *Reading the Century Illustrated*.

Whether or not it was truly the case, Howellsian Realism was pitched as having been prudish and conservative by Modernist critics of the early twentieth century, and as the elite monthlies were replaced by less expensive magazines with greater mass appeal, the aesthetic and intellectual avant-garde defined itself against Howellsian Realism. When Sinclair Lewis gave his Nobel Prize speech in 1930, he was still complaining of Howells as "a pious old maid": "So strongly did Howells feel this genteel, this New Humanistic philosophy that he was able vastly to influence his contemporaries, down even to 1914 and the turmoil of the Great War." Glazener argues that the challenge to the status of Realism was paralleled by the declining cultural significance of the elite monthlies.

12. The reference is to Cady, *The Light of Common Day*.

Introduction

1. For a thorough historical survey of the social and print-cultural contexts for the American little magazines, as well as for the most complete bibliography of them to date, see MacLeod, *American Little Magazines of the Fin de Siècle*. MacLeod and I have shared our enthusiasm for the ephemeral bibelots for many years, and I am grateful for her book's painstaking bibliographical and contextual work. In the work at hand, I focus in a more concentrated fashion on the aesthetic register evoked by the bibelots' international network of allusions and associations. I am also very interested in making a theoretical claim about how the dynamics of circulation represented by the international fad for the ephemeral bibelots not only shape art movements but opinions about them, a claim that is historically portable. It is for this reason that I argue, for example, that telling a story about why the bibelots were forgotten is as interesting as telling one about their lasting significance (see especially in chapter 5).

For other overviews of these publications, see MacLeod, "The Fine Art of Cheap Print"; MacLeod, *American Little Magazines of the 1890s*; Evans, "'Ephemeral Bibelots' in the 1890s"; Drucker, "Bohemian by Design"; Drucker, "*Le Petit Journal des Refusées*: A Graphical Reading"; and Evans, "Review Essay: Johanna Drucker."

2. Mott, *A History of American Magazines*; Hoffman, Allen, and Ulrich, eds., *The Little Magazine*; Ziff, *The American 1890s*.

3. Bulson, *Little Magazine, World Form*.

4. "The Extensions of Literary Activity," 1.

5. Durkin, "Chekhov and the Journals."

6. On Latin American reviews, see Hanneken, "Going Mundial"; Franco, *Geopolíticas de la cultura finisecular en Buenos Aires*; and Aching, *Politics of Spanish American Modernismo*.

7. William Radice, Introduction to *Selected Short Stories*, by Rabindranath Tagore, 2.

8. Baumbach, "Who Do They Think They Are?," 626.

9. Warner, "Publics and Counterpublics."

10. Burgess, "Memoir," n.p.

11. Glazener, *Reading for Realism*, 5; Mott, *A History of American Magazines*, 4:3. This class of magazines has played an outsized role in our understanding of US cultural history. See, for instance, Kaplan, *Social Construction*; Broadhead, *Cultures of Letters*; and Ohmann, *Selling Culture*. In a more recent book, Mark Noonan challenges the argument that the *Atlantic* group was monolithic in its promotion of Realism, in *Reading the Century Illustrated*.

12. See Schneirov, *The Dream of a New Social Order*; Johnson, "The Rise of the Negro Magazine"; McHenry, *Forgotten Readers*.

13. Mott, *A History of American Magazines*, 4:11.

14. It is perhaps worth noting that, while we agree on most things, MacLeod and I have rather different points of emphasis when defining the qualities of these magazines. To some extent, her ideas about what she calls "little magazineness" are more encompassing (5). In *American Little Magazines of the Fin de Siècle*, MacLeod attempts to schematize and contextualize the full range of small magazines from this period, whereas this book focuses on what she would call "aesthetic little magazines," a category she distinguishes from "periodicals of protest" and "hybrid magazines" (14). But, then, whereas MacLeod is primarily interested in North America, my argument depends on seeing the bibelots as maximally attentive to the dynamics of international circulation. This story, necessarily, begins at Le Chat Noir in Montmartre and extends throughout Europe, Asia, and the Americas, and that takes in not only the novels of Henry James but also the French-inspired illustrations of Will Bradley and the Parisian dances of Loie Fuller. Moreover, whereas much of MacLeod's study is given over to explaining the fin-de-siècle little magazines as part of an emerging commercial, professional, middlebrow print culture, my focus has been on the period's aesthetic register. I am interested in the period's art of association—a relational aesthetic that, as I will argue, is represented in the ephemeral bibelots but not unique to them; that is anti-Realist but also rejected by twentieth-century Modernists; and that is of vital importance not only to reading the bibelots but to reading some of our most beloved American writers from the period.

15. Bennett, *Poets in the Public Sphere*, 182.

16. Bourriaud, *Relational Aesthetics*, 61, 14. Bourriaud's theory has exerted a major critical influence and reaction, the most noteworthy critique coming from Claire Bishop in "Antagonism and Relational Aesthetics." As a literary scholar, I have found Amy J. Elias's "The Dialogical Avant-Garde," which offers a cohesive summary and bibliography, to be exceptionally useful for thinking about relational aesthetics in relation to literature.

17. The point I am making about relational aesthetics, here, is also entirely consonant with Matthew Potolsky's revisionary account of the Decadence, which he characterizes as a "mode of reception, rather than a discernable quality of things or people." Decadence was part of the currency of the ephemeral bibelots, and one sees in the bibelots the same international, antinationalist framework of Decadent writers who, in Potolsky's words, were "fascinated with the creation and destruction of communities" and who looked "decisively beyond the frame of any localized national coterie to new and radically international frameworks for sociocultural belonging." See Potolsky, *The Decadent Republic of Letters*, 6.

18. *The Bauble* 1:3 (September 1895): 35–36.

19. Tiffany, *Infidel Poetics*, 12.

20. Burgess, *Bayside Bohemia*, 13.

21. They share, that is to say, the fate of other materials held in library special collections and rare books. Most of my research was completed at the Zimmerli Museum at Rutgers University, which has an extensive collection of French print ephemera from the period, and in Special Collections at the Princeton University Library. See MacLeod, *American Little Magazines of the Fin de Siècle*, for a list of titles currently available on HathiTrust or from other online sources.

22. Barthes, *The Pleasure of the Text*, 8–10; Cleto, *Camp: Queer Aesthetics*, 3; Liu, *The Laws of Cool*, 177.

23. Drawing largely on Eve Kosofsky Sedgwick and Axel Nissen, Chris Looby recently made a similar argument about the nineteenth-century American short story in his introduction to the anthology, *"The Man Who Thought Himself a Woman,"* see especially vi–ix.

24. Felski, *The Gender of Modernity*, 91.

25. In the *Epi-Lark*, May 1897, 11.

26. See Glazener, *Reading for Realism*, 230.

27. Fleissner, *Women, Compulsion, Modernity*, 136.

28. Bulson, *Little Magazine, World Form*, 1.

29. The bibelot network was not unlike the hub and spoke model currently used by the airlines to plan their flight schedules: links to the peripheries pass through the hubs, which means that a few major magazines played an outsized role in the circulation of the elements through the network as a whole. Take down a hub and you take out the network. The same principle applies in epidemiology. See Barabási, *Linked*. For another popular account, see Gladwell, *The Tipping Point*. For a scholarly overview, see McLean, *Culture in Networks*.

30. From the title page of the *Fly Leaf*. For the career of Sui Sin Far in the *Fly Leaf*, see Chapman, ed., *Becoming Sui Sin Far*.

31. Faxon, *Ephemeral Bibelots*, 5.

32. In the Burgess Papers, Bancroft Library, University of California at Berkeley.

33. "Another Attack on Chicago," 4.

34. Unsigned Editorial—No title. *New York Times*, September 10, 1895, 4.

35. "Mais cette fille miraculeuse état trop belle pour vivre longtemps; aussi est-elle morte quelques jours après que j'eus fait sa connaissance, et c'est moi-même qui l'ai enterrée." From *Le Spleen de Paris* (1869).

36. Burgess, untitled editorial, *The Epi-Lark*, May 1897, 11.

37. The letter from Roosevelt to Burgess, dated from the White House on February 17, 1938, is in the Burgess Papers at the Bancroft Library.

38. Burgess, *Bayside Bohemia*, 26.

39. I offer these numbers with a few caveats. Deciding what counts is obviously

an issue, and existing bibliographical sources also sway the tally. Faxon's 1903 bibliography included just shy of three hundred titles; MacLeod's updated bibliography, which limits itself to North American titles, adds many more from various sources to arrive at 334 titles. For the later years, I have depended on the resources pulled together at the Modernist Journals Project, http://dl.lib.brown.edu/mjp/periodicals.html, which has collated a wide range of bibliographies and other scholarly works, most notably Hoffman, Allen, and Ulrich's *The Little Magazine* (1947). It should be noted that the latter work's bibliography includes nearly six hundred titles but covers both the North American and continental titles from 1891 to 1945. For comparison purposes, I selected the decade running 1912 to 1922, which includes seventy-nine North American titles. That said, we still cannot be sure if these early bibliographers of the Modernist little magazines undertook their task with the same curatorial eye of an antiquarian like Faxon, who, it should be noted, included some very rare numbers indeed.

40. Pollard also suggests that the novel be placed besides those of Balzac, Flaubert, or Gautier, "[s]o skillfully and so hardily does the book reveal the growth of animalism in a woman, that we feel as if we were attending a medical lecture." Pollard, *Their Day in Court*, 41.

41. Mencken, *Prejudices: First Series*, 76. These lines were first published in 1919. In *Newspaper Days*, published in 1941, Mencken briefly returns to the topic, describing the literary movement of the nineties as a "cosmic event":

> I remember haunting a newsdealer's shop in West Baltimore, hot to grab every new magazine as it came out, and first and last I must have waded through scores of them. The majority were idiotically eccentric: there was one, for example, in which the illustrations, printed separately, were pasted in, and another sold pretentiously for a cent. But my critical faculties were still embryonic, and I devoured the bad with the good. The *Chap-Book* and the *Lark* went through my mill, but so did many an arty monstrosity that lasted but one number. I recall, however, enjoying *M'lle New York* better than most, for there was in it a writer named James G. Huneker whose illuminating sophistication and colorful, rapid style gave me a special thrill. Years later I was to know him well and see much of him, but in 1895 he was as far out of my world as Betelgeuse.

See Mencken, *Newspaper Days*, 248.

42. It is one of the most difficult of the magazines of this period to find in the archives. It began its life in St. Louis in 1889, as *St. Louis Life*, as a fairly banal magazine of social life and current events with a regional circulation, and to my knowledge those copies are held only by the St. Louis Public Library. The name change and move to New York was made in 1897. Only the Center for Research Libraries holds a complete run of this later substantiation of the magazine, and it has not been archived online as of 2019. John Adcock provides the fullest account of the

magazine I have seen at his blog, https://john-adcock.blogspot.com/search?q=cri terion.

43. From the inaugural New York issue of the *Criterion* 16:401 (September 25, 1897): 1.

44. Pollard, "The Criterion Independent Theatre," 4.

45. "Comment and Criticism," 196.

46. Pollard, "As You Like It," 8–9.

47. Hughes, "James Huneker," 39.

48. Mott, *A History of American Magazines*, 4:65–66.

49. Beer, *The Mauve Decade*, 155.

50. For a convincing account, see the concluding chapter of Glazener's *Reading for Realism*.

51. Lowell, Introduction to *The Black Riders and Other Lines*, xxviii.

52. Pound, *ABC of Reading*, 29.

53. Drucker, Afterword to *Le Petit Journal des Refusées*, 36.

54. Mencken, *Prejudices, Third Series*, 334–335.

55. Ibid., 335.

Chapter One. Gelett Burgess and the Flight from Reality

1. The *San Francisco Chronicle*, for instance, likes to drum up Burgess every few years, most recently on November 12, 2016, in an article by Gary Kamiya, "Anarchic Bon Vivants." Another example is a volume edited by Alfred Jan, *A Gelett Burgess Sampler*. For more information on Burgess, see especially Hart's introduction to *Bayside Bohemia* by Gelett Burgess, v–x; Drucker, "Bohemian by Design"; Drucker, "*Le Petit Journal des Refusées*: A Graphical Reading"; and Evans "Review Essay: Johanna Drucker."

2. Burgess, *Goops and How to Be Them*, 3. By the early 1930s, the volume had gone through at least twenty-three editions. As far as I know, Gwyneth Paltrow's online shopping and lifestyle resource, goop.com, is thankfully unrelated. The *Paris Review* published a remembrance of the volume online by Sadie Stein, "Disgusting Lives," on March 11, 2014, https://www.theparisreview.org/blog/2014/03/11/disgusting-lives/.

3. Burgess, "Wild Men of Paris," 401.

4. See chapters by Cate and Grojnowski in Cate and Shaw, eds., *The Spirit of Montmartre*. Calvin Tomkins makes a related claim regarding the influence of Symbolism, and especially of Alfred Jarry's 1896 play *Ubu Roi* in *Duchamp: A Biography*, 66–71.

5. Shaw, "All or Nothing?," 128, 130.

6. Warner, *Publics and Counterpublics*; Fine, *Tiny Publics*.

7. Drucker, "Bohemian by Design," 40. See also Drucker, "*Le Petit Journal des Refusées*: A Graphical Reading." I have written previously of the *PJR* in "Review Essay: Johanna Drucker" and "Introduction to *Le Petit Journal*."

8. Unpublished materials cited in the following account are drawn from materials in the Burgess Papers held at the Bancroft Library, University of California at Berkeley.

9. Burgess, *The Romance of the Commonplace*, front matter.

10. From an unpublished autobiography held at the Bancroft Library, C-H 52 Pt. 1 Carton 3.

11. Burgess pulled from these notes for articles published after his death in a volume titled *Bayside Bohemia*.

12. One of the few critics to attend to Merrill in recent years is Edwin Cady, who cited him when looking to clear some space for William Dean Howells as a "modern" poet; see his introduction to *Pebbles, Monochromes, and Other Modern Poems*.

13. Merrill, "Oscar Wilde."

14. Ironically, *The Bibelot* (1895–1914) would not have considered itself an "ephemeral bibelot" at all, as suggested by the mission it set itself in its first volume: "THE BIBELOT does not profess to exploit the new forces and ferment of fin-de-siècle writers; it offers the less accessible 'things that perish never,'—lyrics (from Blake, Villon's ballades, Latin Student songs, —Literature once possessed not easily forgotten of men." Mosher, *The Bibelot*, 1.

15. Just the one to resuscitate for our joy and terror the bloodthirsty princess, the one to kiss the decapitated lips of John the Baptist. Merrill, "Oscar Wilde," 118.

16. See Garland, *Crumbling Idols*. It is somewhat ironic that Garland's argument for the development of an indigenous American literature was published by the same house bringing out the *Chap-Book*, which was one of the primary venues for the spread of European ideas about Modern art. But as I will explain in subsequent chapters, the *Chap-Book*, while the most well-known ephemeral bibelot, is not, itself, the most consistent representative of the coterie public I am describing here.

17. Cate, "The Spirit of Montmartre," 25. Carolyn Williams makes this point about parody in *Gilbert and Sullivan: Gender, Genre, Parody*.

18. Grojnowski, *Aux commencements du rire moderne*, 44.

19. Brigstocke, "Defiant Laughter," online.

20. Fragerolle, "coupe[r] le ciel de prud'homie sous lequel nous vivons," quoted in Cate and Shaw, eds., *Spirit of Montmartre*, 23.

21. Grojnowski, "Hydropathes and Company," 104. See also Schiau-Botea, "Performing," 41.

22. It seems highly unlikely, but there is a slim possibility that Burgess got the idea for "The Purple Cow" from Goudeau. Goudeau published a novel titled *La Vache Enragée* in 1885, and a decade later, the same year Burgess published his quatrain in the first number of the *Lark*, it became the central icon of one of the French avant-garde's more well-known carnivals. The enraged cow was memorialized by Henry de Toulouse-Lautrec in a famous poster (easily viewable online), also, tantalizingly, from 1895.

23. The following overview is indebted to Fineberg, *Innocent Eye*.

24. Baudelaire, "Painter of Modern Life," 8.

25. Ruskin, *The Elements of Drawing* (1857), in *The Works of John Ruskin*, 27.

26. The photograph is now held by the Fondazione Federico Zeri, in coordination with the University of Bologna, which has a remarkable online archive. Unlike Burgess, we can determine that the photograph was taken by Filipepi Alessandro, and that it is a portrait not of Mirandola but rather Cosimo the Elder, the first patron of the Medici family, http://bit.ly/11Kgpdv.

27. Stewart, *Nonsense: Aspects of Intertextuality*.

28. Burgess, *The Burgess Nonsense Book*, 7.

29. Wells, ed., *A Nonsense Anthology* dedication page. Wells, who is discussed at more length in chapter 4, went on to collect and edit *A Parody Anthology* (1904), *A Satire Anthology* (1905), *A Whimsey Anthology* (1906), and *A Vers de Société Anthology* (1907).

30. Burgess Papers, Bancroft Library, C-H 52 Pt. 1 Carton 3.

31. Burgess Papers, Bancroft Library, Box 3.

32. Drucker, "Bohemian by Design," 30.

33. Burgess, *Bayside Bohemia*, 26.

34. Drucker, "*Le Petit Journal des Refusées*: A Graphical Reading," 139.

35. Ibid., 148.

36. "Weird Costumes at Cubist Ball," 11.

37. See Agha, "Surrealism, or the Purple Cow," image on 61.

38. Norris, "An Opening for Novelists," 1113. One of the ironies of this essay is that Burgess was the editor of the *Wave* at the time, having just taken over the reins from Norris. It is not clear why he agreed to publish it.

39. Norris, *The Octopus*, 61. For more information, see also Graham, "Studio Art in *The Octopus*," and McElarath and Crisler, *Frank Norris: A Life*, 230–231.

40. See Graham, "Studio Art in *The Octopus*," 658. On Noguchi, see also Hakutani, "Yone Noguchi's Influence on Ezra Pound's Imagism," and Halverson, "Typical Tokio Smile."

41. Norris, *The Octopus*, 313, 314.

42. Correspondence from Burgess to Bragdon, December 15, 1898. Held by the Bancroft Library, Box 3.

43. Burgess to Bragdon, June 4, 1898. Burgess Papers, Bancroft Library, CH052, Box 3.

44. Burgess to Bragdon, July 1, 1898. Burgess Papers, Bancroft Library, CH052, Box 3.

45. See Burgess, "The Romance Association," 250, and "Correspondence: A Protest from Mr. Gelett Burgess," 315.

46. MacLeod suggests that the second wave was dominated by "periodicals of protest," which gave voice to a middle-class, professional social and political agenda,

as well as to a new mode of journalistic opinion writing. *American Little Magazines of the Fin de Siècle*, 15.

Chapter Two. What Travels? What Doesn't? The International Movement of Movements

1. See Cate and Shaw, eds., *Spirit of Montmartre*; Makela, *The Munich Secession*; Shedel, *Art and Society*; and Weir, *Decadent Culture*.

2. Casanova, *The World Republic of Letters*, 24, 29.

3. Warburg, "Amerikanische Chap-Books," 345. My thanks to Ariane Mühlethaler for bringing *Pan* to my attention and for providing the translation.

4. Casanova, *The World Republic of Letters*, 127.

5. Ibid., 126–27.

6. These critiques tend to focus on Casanova's investment in the symbolic economy of aesthetic value instead of the political economy of hegemony, and on Paris instead of the world elsewhere. Representative discussions include Prendergast, "The World Republic of Letters"; Damrosch, *What Is World Literature*; McGann, "Pseudodoxia Academica"; Ferguson, "Planetary Literary History"; and Hanneken, "Going Mundial."

7. On structural holes, see in particular the publications of Ronald Burt, starting with *Structural Holes*. Burt's model, discussed later in this chapter, is one of several developed by network sociology to describe a similar diffusion phenomenon. See, for contrasting examples, Granovetter, "The Strength of Weak Ties"; Watts, "A Simple Model of Global Cascades"; and Watts "The 'New' Science of Networks."

8. Coincidentally, at the same time as the worldwide cascade of interest in ephemeral bibelots, there was a growing interest in what the anthropologist Franz Boas called "The Occurrence of Similar Inventions in Areas Widely Apart" (485–486). The topic there was "primitive" folk art, but the curiosity about diffusion or parallel invention was alive and well for the avant-garde too. For a discussion, see my article "Where Was Boas during the Renaissance in Harlem?"

9. Burt, "Structural Holes and Good Ideas," 349.

10. Ibid.

11. Ibid.

12. Bergel, "The Chap-Book," 168.

13. Gourmont, *Les Petites Revues*, 2. Gourmont's bibliography has an American counterpart, Frederick Faxon's *Ephemeral Bibelots*.

14. To be altogether clear, a search on WorldCat now shows that *Le Chat Noir* is held by seventy-seven libraries in North America, which can be explained by a 1972 reprint edition and the publication of an online edition by the Beinecke at Yale, which university libraries, like the one at Cornell, list as a holding in their catalogue. It is also clear from bookplates that there were private collectors of the magazines, and

library holdings have expanded as their copies of the magazines get passed down over the years. Since what interests me is the historical circulation of the magazines, the *Union Catalogue* proves to be a better source.

15. Hutton, "Literary Notes," 1.

16. Latour, *Reassembling the Social*, 147.

17. Norris, "An Opening for Novelists," 1113. The essay was originally printed in the *Wave* on May 22, 1897.

18. Tiffany, *Infidel Poetics*, 12.

19. There is a massive sociological literature on citation networks. For a sample of foundational works, see Kessler, "Bibliographic Coupling between Scientific Papers"; Solla Price, "Networks of Scientific Papers"; and Crane, *Invisible Colleges*.

20. So and Long, for example, have taken precisely this approach in their work on Modernist literary networks, "Network Analysis and the Sociology of Modernism."

21. The idea here is similar to what Lucy Delap has called "periodical communities," in "The Freewoman, Periodical Communities." See also Delap's "Individualism and Introspection," especially 172–175, and Delap and DiCenzo, "Transatlantic Print Culture."

22. I am excluding from this account a magazine that MacLeod includes in her recent bibliography, the *Parisian* (1896–1901), which included nothing but translations from the French, for the reason that it does not function according to most of the other aesthetic rules I've been describing as characteristic of an ephemeral bibelot: it was longer, visually drier, and less plugged in editorially to the avant-garde cues of faddish ephemerals.

23. Mallarmé, "Arthur Rimbaud" and "Les loisirs de la poste."

24. "Notes," *The Chap-Book* 3:9 (September 1895): 353. What the *Chap-Book* did not know was that Thompson had plagiarized most of his writing on the Symbolists directly from French sources, in essence translating without acknowledgment. See Morrissette, "Vance Thompson's Plagiarism" for a preliminary and by no means complete account of Thompson's uncredited borrowing from French sources.

25. The form I am describing is part of the late nineteenth-century economy of "puffing," described by Laurel Blake, "whereby a network of friends assures that their books are noticed, in prominent places, and largely favourably, by an exchange of favours." In "Censorship, Puffing, 'Piracy,' Reprinting," 424.

26. "Flotsam and Jetsam," 7.

27. "Among the Fools," 13.

28. *The Bauble* 1:4 (December 1895): back cover.

29. My translation:

> She is quite a modest creature, *The Lark*; she does not bother herself with personalities; being a morning bird, she busies herself with worms [a play on "verse"]. Nonetheless, she does not go so far as to feign indifference to the laudatory Notes

from the cages down below where other birds live. *The Lark* is not ungrateful, and she thanks *The Critic* for the information about her circulation; *The Boston Journal*, which finds her a bit wild; *The Chap-Book*, which called her risqué [being a play on "un journal intime," a diary]; *The New York Times*, which saw in her a menace to the "modernité chicagoenne" [i.e., to the *Chap-Book*], and *The New York Tribune*, kind professor of larkeology, which names it a goose, undoubtedly because of her golden eggs.

30. Anton Chekhov's brother, Mikhail, whose memoir was translated into English and recently republished, confirms that *Sverchok* (*The Cricket*) had been "modeled on the French magazines of the day" by its editors Evgeny and Mikhail Verner, who had lived abroad for a long time. They also published *Around the World*, which introduced the Russian reading public to the writings of Louis Henri Boussenard, Robert Louis Stevenson, and Henry Rider Haggard, all of whom were frequently cited by the American bibelots. See M. Chekhov, *Anton Chekhov*, 83.

31. Published in *Oskolki* in January 1883. The excerpt is translated in Bartlett, *Chekhov: Scenes from a Life*, 133.

32. See M. Chekhov, *Anton Chekhov*, 79.

33. Harte, "Comment," 135.

34. Huneker, "The Ghost of a Turtle," n.p.

35. In fact, they exhibit many of the characteristics of "scale-free" networks described by Barabási, "Scale-Free Networks: A Decade and Beyond."

36. See "What Middletown Read."

37. *The Clack Book* 2:5 (March 1897): 183.

38. *The Clack Book* 3:1 (April 1897): n.p.

39. *The Philosopher* 1:1 (January 1897): 31.

40. *The Philosopher* 1:3 (April 1897): n.p.

Chapter Three. Relating in Henry James

1. Burgess, "Our Clubbing List"; Anonymous, "Fad Periodicals," 12. Notably, the *Critic* was not an ephemeral bibelot.

2. Giles Bergel makes the same point in a history of the magazine, noting that its "position in the history of the Modernist magazine can only be described as ambiguous." In Bergel, "The Chap-Book," 154.

3. In other words, he was a network hub. Anne Diebel makes essentially this point in reference to his appearance in the *Yellow Book*, suggesting that its editors "used not James's fiction but his personality to promote their magazine." See Diebel, "'The Dreary Duty,'" 46. For more on this theme, see Kate Hext, "Henry James's Impressionistic Satire," who argues that James satirizes the editors and audience of the *Yellow Book* in his writing for it.

4. Henry James to William James, May 28, 1894, in Edel, ed., *Henry James: Selected Letters*, 277. Diebel provides the fullest account of his thinking with regard to his continued association with the *Yellow Book*, especially around 49–50.

5. We know significantly more about his dealings with the *Yellow Book* than with its American counterpart, for instance, that he was both flattered by the attention of its editors when they approached him, personally, for a contribution to their new endeavor. In addition to Diebel and Hext, see Anesko, *"Friction with the Market"* and Freedman, *Professions of Taste*. As for the *Chap-Book*, the best source is Schlereth, *The Chap-Book: A Journal*. Authors complained frequently about not being paid by the *Chap-Book*, or even notified of the acceptance of their work; Stone had to put off paying American creditors in order to cover European authors, writing to the Chicago office that "[y]ou can deal with the people at home for they know us and know father but these creditors 3000 miles away don't know the family and don't like the slow pay" (Herbert Stone to Melville Ned, May 24, 1898, quoted in Schlereth, 12). For the anecdote about Stone stranding himself in England to pay James, see Schlereth 144, n. 50.

6. Pollard, *Their Day in Court*, 374.

7. Ibid., 375.

8. Kirsten MacLeod's overview of the *Chap-Book* provides a useful contextualization and comparison of the two magazines. See *The American Little Magazines of the Fin de Siècle*, especially 117–124.

9. The author is unidentified. "The Aesthetic Magazine," *Leslie's Weekly* 81, October 17, 1895, p. 246.

10. MacLeod, *The American Little Magazines of the Fin de Siècle*, 120.

11. Felski, *The Gender of Modernity*, 91.

12. Symons, "Stella Maris," 130.

13. Felski, *The Gender of Modernity*, 91.

14. "Notes," *The Chap-Book* 1:2 (June 1, 1894): 73.

15. La Rose, "The Yellow Book," 165.

16. "The Decadent's Progress," *The Chap-Book* 6 (March 15, 1897), 370.

17. The illustrations were described as such in an advertisement for the new *Chap-Book* appearing in *The Bibelot* 3:4 (April 1897): n.p.

18. *The Clack Book* 2:5 (February 1897): 179.

19. *The Red Letter* 1 (January 5, 1897): 132.

20. Schlereth, *The Chap-Book: A Journal*, 12–13.

21. For instance, in its second volume, the *Chap-Book* noted that "[i]t would be a source of some gratification if the discerning persons who write 'Literary Notes' for the newspapers would cease to assert that 'Chips,' and 'The Bibelot,' and 'Moods,' and the 'Little Journeys,' are like THE CHAP-BOOK. The assertion, no doubt kindly meant as incense to our nostrils, has ceased to please. But, of course, this was a protest too much. The 'Note' came towards the end of his magazine's first year in

print, and despite what it says, and the pleasure it takes in renouncing such company is not hard to discern." "Notes," *The Chap-Book* 2 (1894–1895): 446.

22. Cameron, *Thinking in Henry James*, 174. Future references will be cited parenthetically.

23. Phenomenological approaches to Henry James began in 1961 with Georges Poulet in *Les Métamorphoses du Cercle*. Richard Hocks, whose seminal work *Henry James and Pragmatistic Thought* took the history of consciousness as a central focus, makes an interesting connection between phenomenology and "relating" in his recent book on *The Ambassadors*. Considering the significance of "ambulatory relations" in William and Henry James, Hocks draws his own interests in line with Paul Armstrong's study of the "'ceaseless meaning-making' of consciousness, interpretation, and bewilderment" in *The Phenomenology of Henry James* and Susan Griffin's examination of the dramatic nature of perception in *The Historical Eye*. See Hocks, *"The Ambassadors": Consciousness, Culture, Poetry*. Future references to this text will be cited parenthetically. For an overview of phenomenological approaches to James at the moment of its apotheosis, see the two chapters on the subject that conclude John Carlos Rowe's *The Theoretical Dimensions of Henry James*. For a recent account along these lines to which my own thinking is indebted, see Bill Brown's account of the "object-relation" in "Now Advertising: Late James," 20.

24. By way of a prelude to the discussion to follow, consider the significance of the relation to William's 1904 description of consciousness in "Does Consciousness Exist?": "Consciousness connotes a kind of external relation, and does not denote a special stuff or way of being. *The peculiarity of our experiences, that they not only are, but are known, which their 'conscious' quality is invoked to explain, is better explained by their relations—these relations themselves being experiences—to one another*." In W. James, *Essays in Radical Empiricism*, 13. Emphasis in original.

25. Latour, *Reassembling the Social*, 5, 7. Future references will be cited parenthetically.

26. Latour spends the first 150 pages of *Reassembling the Social* explaining the trouble with "networks," describing five "sources of uncertainty" that, in effect, muddy the waters in order to make the idea of the relation less transparent. For his discussion of terminology, see 131–132. It is surely thanks in part to Latour's penchant for describing networks in literary terms like these that he has found such a receptive audience among the literary critics, just as Geertz found a similar audience for his theory of "culture" by describing it as a "text." Curiously, I find myself answering the same kinds of questions about the prominence of Latour in today's literary criticism to my friends in sociology that I did, back in the 1990s, when trying to explain the prominence of Geertz to friends in anthropology. The extent to which Latour is not present in the citational field of American sociological research into networks is therefore striking.

27. Henry James, *The Ambassadors*, in *The Novels and Tales of Henry James*, vol. 21,

182. The novel appears in volumes 21 and 22. Future references will be cited parenthetically.

28. The quote is from Bersani's *The Freudian Body*, and I come to it by way of its relation in David McWhirter's fine review essay "Bersani's James" in the recent special edition of the *Henry James Review* 32:3 (2011): 212, devoted to Bersani, in which the topic of the Jamesian relation makes a regular appearance.

29. Sedgwick, "The Beast in the Closet," and *Epistemology of the Closet*, 201; Pippin, *Henry James and Modern Moral Life*, 147.

30. Miller, "What Is a Kiss?," 744–745.

31. See Felski, "Context Stinks!," which offers a reading of what Latour might do for literary study. The move to rethink literary sociality is coming from many theoretical directions. I would include the call for "surface reading" by Stephen Best and Sharon Marcus in "Surface Reading: An Introduction"; for abstract models of literary history by Franco Moretti in *Graphs, Maps and Trees*; for "description" by Heather Love in "Close but not Deep: Literary Ethics and the Descriptive Turn"; and for the project rethinking periodization that led to a new organizational structure of the major divisions of the MLA in 2014.

32. Brooks, *Henry James Goes to Paris*, 51.

33. One of the best of these, in my opinion, is by So and Long, "Network Analysis and the Sociology of Modernism."

34. The *Chap-Book* began publication of *What Maisie Knew* on January 15, 1897, vol. 6, no. 5. As with many of his novels, James revised the novel for publication in the collected edition of his work, known as the New York Edition, published between 1907 and 1909. For ease of reference, I will provide both references parenthetically in future citations, while also noting significant textual variations. This first citation, then, is from the *Chap-Book* (hereafter cited in text as *CB*) 6:5 (January 15, 1897): 214; and in *The Novels and Tales of Henry James* (hereafter cited in text as *NYE*), vol. 11, 6.

35. Sianne Ngai suggests that the impossibility of such a project explains, in part, the "obsessive" character of Latour's narrative style, which she reads as emblematic of late capitalism. I very much agree with her argument that "[n]etwork for Latour is . . . an *aesthetic property of texts*, not what texts narrate or describe," as should become clear in what follows. See Ngai, "Network Aesthetics," 380.

36. Henry James, *Roderick Hudson*, vii.

37. Henry James, "The Lesson of Balzac," 139. Future references will be cited parenthetically. It is possible that the "trees of the forest" metaphor is a reference to a similar image in Baudelaire's poem "Correspondances," which I discuss a bit later in the essay.

38. Watts and Strogatz, "Collective Dynamics," 440.

39. Of note is that the word was spelled "connection" in the *Chap-Book* and was revised for later editions.

40. Richardson, *A Natural History of Pragmatism*, 146.

41. Grimstad, *Experience and Experimental Writing*, 94.

42. In Bergson, the question was how sensory perception related to memory; in Muybridge, it was how the mind jumped over the gap between snapshots to the sense of motion. See Crary, *Suspensions of Perception*.

43. Taupin, *L'Influence du symbolisme français sur la poésie Americaine*, 32.

44. A. Warburg, "Amerikanische Chap-Books." My thanks to Ariane Mühlethaler for the translation.

45. Hocks, *"The Ambassadors": Consciousness, Culture, Poetry*, 80. Levin, *The Poetics of Transition*, ix. Symbolism's investment in "Correspondances" took shape around Charles Baudelaire's 1857 poem of the same name.

46. This "stop-time" conception of the linguistic representation of movement is one characteristic of Imagist poetry, which has strong roots in the Symbolist tradition. Pound's long essay "Henry James" in the *Little Review* and Eliot's interest in James both indicate that they understood James's prose as anticipatory of their own avant-garde poetics.

47. From Mallarmé's "Divagations," English translation in Albright, *Traces of Light*, 41. The French reads as follows (in Mallarmé, *Divagations*, 173): "À savoir que la danseuse *n'est pas une femme qui danse*, pour ces motifs juxtaposés qu'elle *n'est pas une femme*, mais une métaphore résumant un des aspects élémentaires de notre forme, glaive, coupe, fleur, etc, et *qu'elle ne danse pas*, suggérant, par le prodige de raccourcis ou d'élans, avec une écriture corporelle ce qu'il faudrait des paragraphes en prose dialoguée autant que descriptive, pour exprimer, dans la rédaction: poème dégagé de tout appareil du scribe."

48. Albright, *Traces of Light*, 32, 26. Albright notes that it would be easy to dismiss Mallarmé's appraisal on feminist grounds, and Will Bradley's image of Fuller for the *Chap-Book* as well, for their erasure of the female body—in Bradley's prints, we see only her black boots poking out from the swirl of fabric—except for its suggestion of the metaphoric remains or traces of the "corporeal writing," the poem of movement disengaged from the apparatus of writing.

49. William James, *Writings, 1878–1899*, 159. Subsequent references will be cited parenthetically.

50. The poem can be found in Mallarmé, *Collected Poems and Other Verse*, 216–225. On the poem and Whistler, see Lloyd, *Mallarmé: The Poet and His Circle*, 139–40.

51. Hocks, *"The Ambassadors": Consciousness, Culture, Poetry*, 84.

52. Grimstad, *Experience and Experimental Writing*, 109.

53. At his most Latourean, Grimstad suggests that the epistemology of the subject-object relation ought to be reframed as the ontology of the relation. He does not cite Latour, but the language is similar to Latour's long-running critique of phenomenology. For example, Latour writes in the introduction to *Pandora's Hope: Essays on the Reality of Science Studies*: "Phenomenology deals only with the world-for-a-human

consciousness. It will teach us a lot about how we never distance ourselves from what we see, how we never gaze at a distant spectacle, how we are always immersed in the world's rich and lived texture, but alas, this knowledge will be of no use in accounting for how things really are, since we will never be able to escape from the narrow focus of human intentionality. Instead of exploring the ways we can shift from standpoint to standpoint we will always be fastened down into the human one" (9).

In the online version of the current "AIME" (An Inquiry into the Modes of Existence) project, Latour goes further by summarizing the difference between his own work and phenomenology as follows: "In this sense, aime inherits from and generalizes phenomenology and takes up its descriptive intuitions, of pure phenomena, the 'back to things' approach, but after having extirpated itself from the Subject-Object configuration which has imprisoned this tradition." This online version, which is free, and from which this quote is taken, contains more content than does the book. To sign up (and search for yourself), go to modesofexistence.org.

54. The first of these quotes is from a letter from Henry James to William James, November 23, 1905, quoted in Jehlen, "On How, to Become Knowledge," 48. Jehlen, who offers a wonderful discussion of this letter, changes the regular directionality of criticism: she looks at William's writing by way of Henry's ideas, finding William lacking not only in taste but also in understanding. The second of the quotes is from Henry James, "The Lesson of Balzac," 136.

55. See, for instance, Rowe, *The Theoretical Dimensions of Henry James*, 198, and Griffin, *The Historical Eye*, 52–54.

56. Joan Richardson offers a brilliant account of "relations-between-relations" such as these on the level of the Jamesian sentence in *A Natural History of Pragmatism*, 152.

57. For instance, in "Does Consciousness Exist?" he writes of the "complete parallelism in point of reality between the presently felt and the remotely thought," quoting Münsterberg to the effect that "both make up my real world." In *Essays in Radical Empiricism*, 10.

Chapter Four. Butterflies, Faddishness, and the Iconography of Desire

1. Murray, *A New English Dictionary on Historical Principles*, 1219.

2. See Michael Moon's discussion of the butterfly in relation to sexuality, bohemian camaraderie, and the utopian community founded by Charles Fourier, in "Solitude, Singularity, Seriality." Along the same lines, later period, see Benjamin Bagocius, "Queer Entomology: Virginia Woolf's Butterflies."

3. See Schmidgall, *Containing Multitudes*, 282. Wilde to Arthur L. Humphreys in 1895, rpt. in *The Complete Letters of Oscar Wilde*, 630.

4. *Vogue* frequently referred to young women as the "butterfly sex." See, for example, "Those Jesting Paragraphers Whose Lively Pens," *Vogue* 1:2 (December 24, 1892), 17; and the cover for 4:6 (August 9, 1894) is titled "A Summer Butterfly."

5. The image is from a short play, unattributed, "A Maiden Metamorphosis," published in *Vogue* on July 29, 1893. It follows a young woman from her first act, "The Ingénue," in which at age eighteen she chokes back the genuine shock of her first proposal from Jolly George Van Piper, a Harvard junior, "handsome, intensely susceptible," to her last, "The Dénouement," in which at age thirty-two she accepts a proposal from the same, who now has a German PhD and an inheritance worth thirty thousand a year (55). In between time, she rejects and then botches three other proposals, including one worth up to four million that comes to an end when she spills a drink into the millionaire's lap, and another with a British aristocrat cut short after she sent a pair of opera glasses tumbling "over the velvet box-rail . . . drop, bang!" This leaves readers to wonder about her acceptance of Jolly George when, more coyly this time, he finishes by renewing his proposal: Is theirs a first, true love come full circle and happily concluded? Or is she just desperate?

6. Fleissner, *Women, Compulsion, Modernity*, 124. Fleissner's prime example is the characterization of what happens to Verena Tarrant when she gets caught up, faddishly, with the Woman Movement in Henry James's novel *The Bostonians*.

7. Harris, *On Company Time*, 6. See also Hammill and Leick, "Modernism and the Quality Magazines," and Earle, "Pulp Magazines and the Popular Press."

8. The quote is from the header of the monthly column, "In Vanity Fair," from *Munsey's Magazine* 17:1 (April 1897): 154.

9. Chopin to Stone, January 2, 1896. In Toth and Seyersted, eds., *Kate Chopin's Private Papers*, 209. Scholars of Chopin are indebted to Toth's two biographies of the writer: *Kate Chopin: A Life of the Author* and *Unveiling Kate Chopin*.

10. The *Philistine* 4:5 (April 1897): 155. The *St. Louis Mirror* (also known as *Reedy's Mirror*) was a long-running review of literature and culture that promoted not only Chopin but, later, also the poets Sara Teasdale, Edgar Lee Masters, and Carl Sandburg. Emily Toth calls Reedy "the greatest promoter of Kate Chopin's writings . . . her most loyal colleague" (*Unveiling Kate Chopin*, 186).

11. For details, see Toth, who complains that Dumay's translation shifted the focus from the wife to the husband's friend who breaks the news to her. *Kate Chopin: A Life of the Author*, 284–285.

12. Ibid., 280.

13. "Latest Fads," *Munsey's Magazine* 16 (1896–1897): 252.

14. Bull, "The Modern Swordsman," 491–496; for a "summer butterfly," see the cover of *Vogue* for August 1894, an illustration by Will Bradley, discussed later in this chapter.

15. Burgess, "The Lark His Matin Peal Has Sung," no page numbers.

16. Ohmann, *Selling Culture*, 311.

17. Keyser, *Playing Smart*, 13. What Keyser describes would seem to qualify as a telling case of what Lauren Berlant would call "cruel optimism," in *Cruel Optimism*.

18. Ziff, *The American 1890s*, 144, 135.

19. Originally in *Harper's Monthly* for June 1889; rpt. in Howells, *Editor's Study*, 198.

20. From Thompson's editorials in *M'lle New York* for 1:1 (August 1, 1895) and 1:2 (August 13, 1895). It was an industry that persisted at least until 1930, when, in his Nobel Prize acceptance speech, Sinclair Lewis called Howells a "pious old maid." Lewis continued, "So strongly did Howells feel this genteel, this New Humanistic philosophy that he was able vastly to influence his contemporaries, down even to 1914 and the turmoil of the Great War," http://www.nobelprize.org/nobel_prizes /literature/laureates/1930/lewis-lecture.html.

21. Beam, *Style, Gender, and Fantasy*, 80.

22. It is notable that this number of *M'lle New York*, September 1, 1895, is not included in the only digital scan currently available, which was produced from the New York Public Library for Google Books; my source was a copy purchased by the Rutgers University Library. As I discuss elsewhere in this book, digital reproductions of the bibelots are far from comprehensive. A full run of *M'lle New York* is available at this book's companion website: https://sites.rutgers.edu/bibelots.

23. The reason may have to do with the magazine being associated with a printing company, not a publishing house. This situation was typical of the ephemeral bibelots. Each number of *M'lle New York* includes an ad for Fleming, Schiller and Carnrick, printers of high-class catalogues, books, brochures, circulars; Fleming is listed on each cover, just below a Vance Thompson ad alongside the magazine's other main illustrator, the aforementioned Powers.

24. In 1917, Thompson would seem to switch gears when he published a widely circulated, profeminist book, *Woman*. It begins with a mea culpa, "I, like every male of the species, thought it rather clever (in the spotted necktie, yellow-spat period of life) to crack mean and silly jokes about women," and goes on over eleven chapters to champion the "dawning of the Woman's Age" (viii, 3). Still, Huneker had no truck with the idea that Thompson had reformed. "A man may alter his views twenty times, as a snake sloughs its skin, but when he writes such words, words like the virile ring of crossed blades, then he is primarily a Caveman. Who knows whether as a sexagenarian he may not doff the garb of civilisation and emerge hairy, rugged, in a bearskin, and over his virile shoulders a mighty club! Beware Woman!" Huneker, *Steeplejack*, ii, 194.

25. See the discussion of Roosevelt's speech delivered in 1899, "The Strenuous Life," in Bederman, *Manliness and Civilization*. Most of the men involved with the bibelots would have positioned themselves in opposition to manliness of this kind.

26. Schwab, *James Gibbons Huneker*, 96; Moore, "*M'lle New York* and James Gibbons Huneker," 64; Huneker, *Steeplejack*, ii, 196.

27. Chopin, *Complete Novels and Stories*, 894.

28. See Beam, *Style, Gender, and Fantasy*, 81.

29. Chopin, *Complete Novels and Stories*, 897.

30. Ibid., 788.

31. Ibid., 790.

32. Ibid., 792.

33. Ibid., 772.

34. Ibid., 773.

35. Toth, *Unveiling Kate Chopin*; see discussion on pages 159–160.

36. The diary actually juxtaposes the Maupassant translation and the two stories printed in *Moods* on successive pages—and as such one can imagine the kind of spatial proximity that Chopin might have imagined them having. The diary is something of a "scrapbook" in that it does not contain the kind of personal entries one might expect but is rather more of a writing tablet. The two pieces for *Moods* do not have titles in the diary. "A Night Came Slowly" and "Juanita" were added in later. The diary is housed at the Missouri Historical Society; it is reprinted under the title "Impressions: Kate Chopin's 1894 Diary" in Toth and Seyersted, eds., *Kate Chopin's Private Papers*, 176–194.

37. Maupassant, "A Divorce Case," translated by Kate Chopin, 182.

38. Much of Sloan's work from this period has been collected by the Delaware Art Museum. Some of it can be found in Sloan, *American Art Nouveau*.

39. Most anthologies follow the Per Seyersted edition, which shortened the title to "Fedora" and incorporated changes made by Chopin in her account books.

40. In Chopin, *Complete Novels and Stories*, 798.

41. In ibid., 800.

42. For a review and argument of the latter position, see Bucher, "Perversely Reading Kate Chopin's 'Fedora,'" 375.

43. Pollard, "As You Like It," 8–9.

44. Miller, *Making Love Modern*, 88.

45. Wells, *The Rest of My Life*, 173–175.

46. Norman, "The Confessions of Carolyn Wells," 22.

47. Norman, "Gelett Burgess Talks Gravely of Literature," 22.

48. *New York Times*, April 3, 1918, 13. Burgess, who was four years younger than Wells, also married late in life, leading one to wonder if there was not a potential relationship between them. He wed the actress Estelle Loomis in June 1914.

49. "Gossip of the Rialto," *New York Times*, September 14, 1924, 170.

50. Wells, *The Rest of My Life*, 118, 119.

51. Ibid., 146.

52. Ibid., 147.

53. Gelett Burgess, "H. R. H., the Princess Perilla," *The Lark* 19, n.p.

54. From Bruce Porter's letter to Burgess in the *Epi-Lark*, 2.

55. Simmel, *On Women, Sexuality and Love*, 133, 135, 138.

56. See Phillips, *On Flirtation*, especially xx–xxii.

57. Burgess, "Feminine Modernity," 580–581. Burgess elaborates the same idea in many of his later pieces of popular humor, like *The Maxims of Noah, Derived from his Experience with Women both Before and After the Flood* (1911) and *Why Men Hate Women* (1927). These books are almost entirely composed of satirical witticisms about the battle of the sexes told from a condescendingly masculine, frequently misogynistic, but also self-ironizing point of view.

58. These pieces appear in numbers 14, 18, and 24 of the *Lark*.

59. Wells, *The Rest of My Life*, 174.

60. According to Keith Newlin, who edited the memoir of Garland's daughter, she was, for a time, Garland's serious girlfriend—so much so that the diary pages in which he described his relationship have been torn from the diary, whether by him, his daughter, or just as likely, his wife is hard to tell. Personal communication.

61. Pendergast, *Creating the Modern Man*, 151. He cites "The Fortunate Woman," published in *Collier's* in 1926. The story is about a divorced woman who, finding herself bored by her perfectly constructed but sexless life, decides for excitement to move to Arizona with her charming but ailing ex-husband. On Tompkins's life, see also the brief mention in Lord, *A Summer to Be*, 59–60.

62. Norris's essay was originally published as "A Plea for Romantic Fiction," *Boston Evening Transcript*, December 18, 1901, p. 14.

63. Tompkins, "A Butterfly Lover," 400.

64. Ibid., 408.

65. Sarah Churchwell enables us to make another connection from Loos to the bibelots by noting that both *Vogue* and *Harper's Bazaar* were part of a subset of the market known as "class fashion periodicals." See Churchwell, "'Lost Among the Ads,'" 142.

66. Loos, "The Biography of a Book," xli.

67. See, for instance, Miller, *Making Love Modern*; Keyser, *Playing Smart*; Eldred, *Literate Zeal*; and Longworth, "The Avant-Garde in the Village."

Of note is the fact that Millay was well known for her romantic involvement with women and was from Vassar (class of 1917)—as, for that matter, was Juliet Wilbor Tompkins. Recalling the fact gives a new turn on Mencken's discussion of his luncheon with Huneker, discussed in the introduction to this volume: perhaps they're actually discussing "whether a girl educated at Vassar could ever really learn to love [men]"? My thanks to Elizabeth Dean for this observation.

68. Indeed, to my knowledge, there is only one collection of writing by women for the popular press from the early twentieth century, Maureen Honey, ed., *Breaking the Ties that Bind*. Notably, the volume includes a story by Tompkins.

69. Ohmann, *Selling Culture*, 311. An earlier version of the chapter was published in 1988 as "History and Literary History: The Case of Mass Culture."

Chapter Five. The Edginess of Stephen Crane at the End of the Relational Era

1. Lowell, Introduction to *The Black Riders and Other Lines*, xxviii–xxix. Crane has increasingly been situated in relation to modernity in recent years. Among the more important recent treatments, see Fried, *Realism, Writing, Disfiguration*; Brown, *The Material Unconscious*; and Cavitch, "Stephen Crane's Refrain," 33–54.

2. Lowell, Introduction to *The Black Riders and Other Lines*, x, xxvi.

3. Berryman, *Stephen Crane*, 90. A recent PBS documentary on Hubbard (available for viewing online at: https://www.pbs.org/video/wned-tv-documentaries-elbert-hubbard-american-original/) does little to dispel the notion when it dubs him "the original hippie."

4. Hoffman, *The Poetry of Stephen Crane*, 225.

5. Blair, "The Posture of a Bohemian," see especially 219–220.

6. Davis, *Badge of Courage: The Life of Stephen Crane*, 138, 117.

7. The poem is "A man adrift on a slim spar." Cavitch, "Stephen Crane's Refrain."

8. "Notes," *Miss Blue Stocking* 1:5 (March 1, 1896): n.p.

9. Harte, "Comment," n.p.; Harte, "Bubble and Squeak," 28, my emphasis.

10. There have been very few exceptions to this rule. For three, see Dickason, "Stephen Crane and the Philistine"; Vanouse, "Hobby-Horses, Horseplay, and Stephen Crane's 'Black Riders'"; and a PhD dissertation by Cheek, "Stephen Crane and *The Philistine*."

11. Cavitch, "Stephen Crane's Refrain," 45.

12. The article can be found at http://nplusonemag.com/regressive-avant-garde.

13. See Ngai's *Our Aesthetic Categories: Zany, Cute, Interesting*; the chapter on Stein was previously published as "The Cuteness of the Avant-Garde."

14. There are neither page numbers nor titles in the *Epi-Lark*, the twenty-fifth number of the *Lark*, published May 1, 1897, although the entries are signed. Each page has its own running head. This passage appears under the heading "Nor Shall the Mounting Lark the Muse Detain."

15. Hoffman, "Many red devils upon the page."

16. See Monteiro, *Stephen Crane's Blue Badge of Courage*, 123.

17. For "rhizome," see Deleuze and Guattari, *A Thousand Plateaus: Capitalism and Schizophrenia*.

18. For example, in Gray, *T. S. Eliot's Intellectual and Poetic Development*.

19. Elisa Bizzotto has recently argued that Symons's "rejection of literary currents is in fact rooted in late-Victorian poetics" and, in particular, in Walter Pater. See "Re-crediting Arthur Symons," 33.

20. Hoffman, *The Poetry of Stephen Crane*, 80.

21. See accounts of the Pierrot theme in Eliot's poetry in Storey, *Pierrot: A Critical History of a Mask*; Habib, *The Early T. S. Eliot and Western Philosophy*; Chintz, *T. S. Eliot and the Cultural Divide*; and Maddrey, *The Making of T. S. Eliot*.

22. Nietzsche, *Thus Spake Zarathustra*, 179, 183.

23. In other words, the fad in Paris described by André Velter is comparable to what T. J. Jackson Lears described in the United States. See Velter, *Les Poètes du Chat Noir*; and Lears, *No Place of Grace*.

24. Cram, "The Quest," 1.

25. For more on "A Karmenokranian Idyl," see MacLeod, *American Little Magazines of the Fin de Siècle*, 201.

26. Schlereth, *The Chap-Book: A Journal*, 32.

27. On Guiney, see Colvert, "Fred Holland Day, Louise Imogen Guiney."

28. The story goes that he was disinclined to write "poems" because, as Christopher Benfey recently put it, he "thought the word 'poems' had a sissy ring to it." "The Library of America interviews Christopher Benfey about Stephen Crane." In a letter to Nellie Crouse sent on December 31, 1895, Crane proclaimed himself to be "very properly enraged at the word 'poet' which continually reminds of long hair and seems to me to be a most detestable form of insult." In *Correspondence*, 162, and quoted in Davis, *Badge of Courage: The Life of Stephen Crane*, 138.

29. Not all of Crane's biographers read the dinner in the same way. One exception is Jean Cazemajou, *Stephen Crane: Écrivain Journaliste*, who declines to take part in the opinion of a significant part of American critics, who argue that the banquet, in its excess, was a decisive turning point in Crane's life. He disagrees, in particular, with Stallman, who suggested that after the event Crane's vision of himself changed, and that he now saw himself as "the deluded hero, the dupe of his own vainglorious notions"—and would not be fooled again. (The quote is from Stallman and Gilkes, *Stephen Crane: Letters*, p. 73, n. 99; quoted in Cazemajou, 76). Another is Edwin Cady, whose 1980 biography, *Stephen Crane*, agrees that there "is no evidence that Crane was upset" (51).

30. This was the approach taken in the 2009 PBS documentary, *Elbert Hubbard: An American Original*.

31. Mott, *A History of American Magazines*, 4:643.

32. In *Stephen Crane: A Critical Bibliography*, Stallman includes three pieces from Taber documenting his dislike of Hubbard: a long article published in 1916 in the *Philadelphia Evening Ledger* following Hubbard's death on the RMS *Lusitania* that was based on an interview with Taber; a letter sent by Taber to Thomas Beer in 1923 after the appearance of his biography of Crane; and another letter sent by him to David Balch in 1941 after the publication of his *Elbert Hubbard: Genius of Roycroft*. The gist of these materials, which grow increasingly bitter over the years, is that Hubbard took advantage of whomever he could to advance his own interests. Paul McKenna, in a history of the Roycroft shop, writes that Hubbard's "ego dominated his natural friendliness and fairness and led to considerable bitterness among those who broke with him. His success because of and later without them may have fueled the anger but too often Elbert Hubbard was the cause of the breakup." McKenna, *A History and Bibliography of the Roycroft Printing Shop*, 9.

33. See McKenna for details. Kipling was upset that his verses were titled *The Dipsy Chanty* (1896) instead of "The Last Chantey," as they had been known when first published in the *Pall Mall Magazine* in June of 1893. McKenna does not note it, but Kipling had at first titled the work "The Dipsea Chantey"—that is, "deep sea"—making the title in the *Philistine* a bit less of a surprise. (Interestingly, when Kipling's verse appeared in the *Philistine* in December 1895, the bibelot included Taber's name on the masthead as its editor.) For his part, Shaw was incensed about a Roycroft edition of *On Going to Church*, in which "the wretch Hubbard" had Americanized the language into what Shaw called "feeble patent-medicine-advertisement English." Shaw characterized Roycroft as an inept, commercial imitation of Morris's Kelmscott Press, going into great detail about Hubbard's "ignorance" of good printing and concluding with a barb directed, seemingly from nowhere, at the *Chap-Book*: "America, having read a great deal about art, and not knowing anything about it, is being duped most frightfully by intense young people who are resolved to make Chicago flower with a fifteenth century luxuriance, and who will find one day that, as Wagner put it, they have grasped art and let their lives slip by them. So, no more Roycroft books." Rpt. in McKenna, *A History and Bibliography of the Roycroft Printing Shop*, 14–15.

34. MacLeod's discussion of Hubbard in *American Little Magazines of the Fin de Siècle* suggests that Hubbard was an important transitional figure, and that "A Message to Garcia" gave a second wind to the movement, ushering in a second wave of "periodicals of protest and hybrid magazines" (274). She provides an extended and nuanced analysis of the *Philistine*, noting in particular its importance to a chatty new style of journalistic writing developed in the early 1900s. Nonetheless, any such nuance was lost on modernists like Lowell, who felt it necessary to condemn Hubbard in order to champion Crane's poetry.

35. *The Philistine* 4:4 (March 1897): 118.

36. *The Philistine* 1:1 (June 1895): 17.

37. *The Philistine* 2:6 (May 1896): 198.

38. *The Philistine* 2:1 (December 1895): 29.

39. *The Philistine* 4:6 (May 1897): 181.

40. Ibid., 184.

41. *The Philistine* 7:4 (September 1898): 113.

42. *The Philistine* 3:6 (November 1986): 161, 171. "Where is Literature At?" *The Philistine* 1:2 (July 1895): 36.

43. See Mott, *A History of American Magazines*, 4:647.

44. Sorrentino, *Stephen Crane: A Life of Fire*, 87.

45. Garland, *Crumbling Idols*, 37. The fact that Garland's book was published by Stone and Kimball does give pause, but then, as described earlier, the *Chap-Book* had quite an ambiguous relationship with the bibelot vogue.

46. Howells, "Editor's Study," originally in *Harper's Monthly* 76 (December 1887): 154, reprinted in *Editors Study*, 111.

47. Crane's friend Willis Hawkins wrote that he was initially panic stricken and in "a blue funk" at the invitation but ultimately considered it all as "kindly-intended bosh . . . for he had repeatedly assured me that he had done nothing to warrant any part of this praise." In Sorrentino, ed., *Stephen Crane Remembered*, 168.

48. Harry Taber letter to Thomas Beer, December 19, 1923. In Stallman, *Stephen Crane: A Critical Bibliography*, 311.

49. For a discussion of Bragdon in the context of Burgess's struggles in the 1890s, see chapter 1. The quote regarding "the Beardsley of America" is in Bragdon, *Merely Players*, 69; the quote about "a distressing memory" is in the same volume, 68. Sorrentino draws from *Merely Players* for the pages by Bragdon, reprinted in *Stephen Crane Remembered*, 169–170.

50. Sorrentino, ed., *Stephen Crane Remembered*, 75.

51. Even Sorrentino describes Hawkins as Crane's "closest friend in 1895 and 1896." See *Stephen Crane Remembered*, 75.

52. In Stallman and Gilkes, eds., *Stephen Crane: Letters*, 73, n. 99.

53. Sorrentino, *Stephen Crane: A Life of Fire*, 183, 184.

54. Crane to Hubbard, October 29, 1987. Rpt. in Stallman, *Critical Bibliography*, 585.

55. Crane to Hubbard, May 1, 1899. In Stallman and Gilkes, *Stephen Crane: Letters*, 220.

56. Quoted in Stallman, *Stephen Crane: A Biography*, 525.

57. Crane, *Correspondence*, vol. 1, p. 115.

58. On Guiney, see Colvert "Fred Holland Day, Louise Imogen Guiney." My argument is somewhat tempered by the fact that Garland published in the *Chap-Book* and his *Crumbling Idols* was brought out in 1894 by Stone and Kimball, the bibelot's publishers. Although also a fine arts press, Stone and Kimball managed a more serious list, as suggested earlier in my discussion of James (chapter 3) and Chopin (chapter 4).

59. Edmund White reviews debates about the authenticity of the letter and reprints it in his novel, *Hotel de Dream* (New York: Harper Perennial, 2007), 224.

60. Ibid., 9.

61. From Virginia Woolf in her essay "Mr Bennett and Mrs Brown," requoted here, yet again, with apologies.

62. Among these, see Weir, *Decadent Culture*; Mahoney, *Literature and the Politics of Post-Victorian Decadence*; and Sherry, *Modernism and the Reinvention of Decadence*. For a definitive overview and bibliography of aestheticism as "the other side of the great divide," see the introduction to Coste, Delyfer, and Reynier, eds., *Reconnecting Aestheticism and Modernism* (quote from p. 2).

63. Bruce Porter, "My Dear Frank Burgess," n.p. It is important to remember that, even in the 1890s, Decadence was camp. When it appears in the bibelots, it is generally with many grains of salt. For example, see James G. Huneker's satirical sketch, "The Dream of a Decadent" in *M'lle New York* 1:3 (September 1895), in which a bored

astral spirit flies down to New York for a performance of *Alice in Wonderland*: he delights in the part about the Jabberwock, which was paired with music from Wagner's "Ride of the Valkyries."

64. Mahoney, *Literature and the Politics of Post-Victorian Decadence*, 5.

65. Rogers, "Bruno's Bohemia," 453.

66. Ibid., 456.

67. Keet, "Stephen Crane: New York Poet," 953. Keet is quoting from Edith Wyatt, "Stephen Crane," from the *New Republic* in 1915. Wyatt goes on to suggest that Crane is actually more direct in his treatment of the subject than the Imagists.

68. Longworth, "The Avant-Garde in the Village," 479.

69. Dame Rogue [pseud.], "Philosophic Fashions," 13.

70. Monroe, "Stephen Crane," originally in *Poetry*, June 1919, rpt. in Weatherford, ed., *Stephen Crane: The Critical Heritage*, 307.

71. Longworth, "The Avant-Garde in the Village," 472. Douglas Mao makes an argument along these lines when considering the Greenwich Village Decadent Donald Evans, suggesting that "if Evans and his poems faded from view, this was perhaps partly because the shocks he sought to distribute were so soon assimilated." See "The Naughtiness of the Avant-Garde," forthcoming.

72. See, for example, Mark S. Morrison's analysis of this subject in *The Public Face of Modernism*. Morrison's account builds on Walter Benn Michaels's *Our America: Nativism, Modernism, and Pluralism* and Michael North's *The Dialect of Modernism*.

73. White, *Transatlantic Avant-Gardes*, 20. See also White, "In the American Grain."

74. Bulson, *Little Magazine, World Form*, 50, 69, 72.

75. Williams in *Contact*, quoted in White, "In the American Grain," 250.

76. Williams, letter to Richard Johns, July 12, 1929. Quoted in White, "In the American Grain," 260.

77. Quoted by Wanda Corn in her exceptional account of this transformation, *The Great American Thing*, 18.

78. Dewey, "Americanism and Localism," 688.

79. See Abhijit Bhattacharya, *A guide to the Hitesranjan Sanyal Memorial Collection*. Sadly, I am limited in linguistic ability here, but of interest would be the following magazines: 32. Binapani; 45. Gan o Galpa; 57. Janhabi; 75. Nabajiban; 77. Nirmalya; 78. Pakshik Samalochak; 85. Pradip; 94. Sadhana; 97. Sahitya Kalpadrum; 98. Sahitya Ratnabhandar; 99. Sahitya Sanghita; 112. Shilpa Puspanjali.

80. Pramatha Chaudhuri, *Kallol* (1926), quoted in Bulson, *Little Magazine, World Form*, 70.

81. Bulson, *Little Magazine, World Form*, 73.

82. Ibid., 49.

83. Wyatt, rpt. in Weatherford, ed., *Stephen Crane: The Critical Heritage*, 304.

84. Penn, "A Humorous Study of Crane," in the *Lotus* 2 (October 1896); rpt. in

Weatherford, ed., *Stephen Crane: The Critical Heritage*, 184, 185. Future references will be cited parenthetically.

85. Warburg, "Amerikanische Chap-Books," 345. My thanks to Ariane Mühlethaler for providing the translation.

86. Colvert, "Fred Holland Day, Louise Imogen Guiney," 22. Guiney also did not like the idea of calling Crane's book *The Black Riders*, suggesting in its place a title that would have been visually well suited to today's network crowd. She thought it might be called *Sagittulae*, Latin for "little sharp arrows," which she may have thought of because Crane's little barbed poems had nasty edges that were wickedly piercing. I can also imagine her pointing the way to the edginess of relations, both those made by Crane and elicited by his lines.

87. Harte, "The Stir in Literature," 4.

88. James, *Psychology: Briefer Course*, 160.

Bibliography

"A Maiden Metamorphosis." *Vogue* 2:5 (July 1893): 55–61.

"Among the Fools." *The Bauble* 3:1 (October 1896): 13.

"Another Attack on Chicago." *New York Times*, May 16, 1895, 4.

"Comment and Criticism." *The Philosopher* 2:5 (1897): 196.

"Fad Periodicals." *The Critic: A Weekly Review of Literature and the Arts* 27:776 (January 2, 1897): 12.

"Flotsam and Jetsam." *The Bauble* 1:1 (July 1895): 7.

"Gossip of the Rialto." *New York Times*, September 14, 1924, 170.

"In Vanity Fair." *Munsey's Magazine* 17:1 (April 1897): 154.

"Latest Fads." *Munsey's Magazine* 16 (1896–1897): 252.

"Notes." *Miss Blue Stocking* 1:5 (March 1, 1896): n.p.

"Notes." *The Chap-Book* 2 (1894–1895): 446.

"The Aesthetic Magazine." *Leslie's Weekly* 81 (October 17, 1895): 246.

"The Decadent's Progress." *The Chap-Book* 6 (March 15, 1897): 370.

"The Extensions of Literary Activity." *The Dial; a Semi-monthly Journal of Literary Criticism, Discussion, and Information* XXI:247 (1896): 000–002, 001.

"Those Jesting Paragraphers Whose Lively Pens." *Vogue* 1:2 (December 24, 1892): 17.

"Weird Costumes at Cubist Ball." *New York Times*, April 14, 1914, 11.

"What Middletown Read," http://www.bsu.edu/libraries/wmr/index.php (July 4, 2013).

Aching, Gerard. *The Politics of Spanish American Modernismo.* New York: Cambridge University Press, 1997.

Agha, M. F. "Surrealism, or the Purple Cow." *Vogue* 88:9 (November 1, 1936): 60–61, 129–131, 146.

Albright, Ann Cooper. *Traces of Light: Absence and Presence in the Work of Loïe Fuller.* Middletown, CT: Wesleyan University Press, 2007.

Anesko, Michael. *"Friction with the Market": Henry James and the Profession of Authorship.* New York: Oxford University Press, 1986.

Ardis, Ann, and Patrick Collier. *Transatlantic Print Culture, 1880–1940: Emerging Media, Emerging Modernisms.* New York: Palgrave Macmillan, 2008.

Armstrong, Paul. *The Phenomenology of Henry James.* Chapel Hill: University of North Carolina Press, 1983.

Auriol, George. *Le Chat Noir Guide.* Paris, 1887.

Bagocius, Benjamin. "Queer Entomology: Virginia Woolf's Butterflies." *Modernism/Modernity* 24:4 (November 2017): 723–750.

Barabási, Albert-László. *Linked: How Everything Is Connected to Everything Else and What It Means for Business, Science, and Everyday Life.* New York: Plume, 2002.

——. "Scale-Free Networks: A Decade and Beyond." *Science* 325 (2009): 412–413.

Barthes, Roland. *The Pleasure of the Text,* translated by Richard Miller. New York: Hill and Wang, 1975.

Bartlett, Rosamund. *Chekhov: Scenes from a Life.* London: Free Press, 2004.

Baudelaire, Charles. "The Painter of Modern Life." In *The Painter of Modern Life and Other Essays*, translated and edited by Jonathan Mayne, 1–41. London: Phaidon Press, 1964.

——. *Le Spleen de Paris.* 1869.

Baumbach, Jonathan. "Who Do They Think They Are?: A Personal History of the Fiction Collective." In *The Little Magazine in America: A Modern Documentary History*, edited by Elliott Anderson and Mary Kinzie, 625–647. Yonkers, NY: Pushcart Press, 1978.

Beam, Dorri. *Style, Gender, and Fantasy in Nineteenth-Century American Women's Writing.* New York: Cambridge University Press, 2010.

Bederman, Gail. *Manliness and Civilization: A Cultural History of Gender and Race in the United States, 1880–1917.* Chicago: University of Chicago Press, 1996.

Beer, Thomas. *The Mauve Decade: American Life at the End of the Nineteenth Century.* 1926; New York: Caroll and Graf, 1997.

Benfey, Christopher. "The Library of America interviews Christopher Benfey about Stephen Crane." Interview with the Library of America, April 2011, http://www.loa.org/images/pdf/LOA_Benfey_on_Crane.pdf.

Bennett, Paula Bernat. *Poets in the Public Sphere: The Emancipatory Project of American Women's Poetry, 1800–1900.* Princeton: Princeton University Press, 2003.

Bergel, Giles. "The Chap-Book." In *The Oxford Critical and Cultural History of Modernist Magazines*, vol. 2, edited by Peter Brooker and Andrew Thacker, 154–175. New York: Oxford University Press, 2012.

Berlant, Lauren. *Cruel Optimism.* Durham, NC: Duke University Press, 2011.

Berryman, John. *Stephen Crane.* New York: William Sloane Associates, 1950.

Bersani, Leo. *The Freudian Body: Psychoanalysis and Art.* New York: Columbia University Press, 1986.

Best, Stephen, and Sharon Marcus. "Surface Reading: An Introduction." *Representations* 108 (Fall 2009): 1–21.

Bhattacharya, Abhijit. *A guide to the Hitesranjan Sanyal Memorial Collection: an archival collection of old Bangla periodicals; documents relating to the social history of Bengal and the Communist parties of India and Great Britain in microfilm rolls; colour transparencies of 19th and early 20th century paintings, lithographs and photographs; reports of the Indian Census, 1872–1951, and occasional papers of the CSSSC on microfiche cards at Centre for Studies in Social Sciences.* Calcutta: Centre for Studies in Social Sciences, 1998.

Bishop, Claire. "Antagonism and Relational Aesthetics." *October* 110 (Fall 2004): 51–79.

Bizzotto, Elisa. "Re-crediting Arthur Symons, Decadent-Modernist Literary Ghost." In *Reconnecting Aestheticism and Modernism: Continuities, Revisions, Speculations*, edited by Bénédicte Coste, Catherine Delyfer, and Christine Reynier, 31–44. New York: Routledge, 2017.

Blair, John. "The Posture of a Bohemian in the Poetry of Stephen Crane." *American Literature* 61:2 (May 1989): 215–229.

Blake, Laurel. "Censorship, Puffing, 'Piracy,' Reprinting: Decadence and Transatlantic Re-Mediations of Walter Pater, 1893–1910." *Modernism/Modernity* 19:3 (2012): 419–435.

Boas, Franz. "The Occurrence of Similar Inventions in Areas Widely Apart." *Science* 20 (1887): 485–486.

Bourdieu, Pierre. "The Social Conditions of the International Circulation of Ideas." In *Bourdieu: A Critical Reader*, edited by Richard Shusterman, 220–228. New York: Blackwell Publishers, 1999.

Bourriaud, Nicolas. *Relational Aesthetics.* Translated by Simon Pleasance and Fronza Woods. Paris: Les Presses du Réel, 2002.

Bragdon, Claude Fayette. *Merely Players.* New York: Alfred A. Knopf, 1929.

Brigstocke, Julian. "Defiant Laughter: Humour and the Aesthetics of Place in Late 19th Century Montmartre." *Cultural Geographies*, October 6, 2011, http://journals.sagepub.com/doi/abs/10.1177/1474474011414637.

———. *The Life of the City: Space, Humour, and the Experience of Truth in Fin-de-siècle Montmartre.* Farnham, Surrey: Ashgate, 2014.

Broadhead, Richard. *Cultures of Letters: Scenes of Reading and Writing in Nineteenth-Century America.* Chicago: University of Chicago Press, 1995.

Brooks, Peter. *Henry James Goes to Paris.* Princeton, NJ: Princeton University Press, 2007.

Brown, Bill. "Now Advertising: Late James." *Henry James Review* 30:1 (2009): 10–21.

———. *The Material Unconscious: American Amusement, Stephen Crane, and the Economics of Play.* Boston: Harvard University Press, 1997.

Bucher, Christina. "Perversely Reading Kate Chopin's 'Fedora.'" *Mississippi Quarterly* 56:3 (2003): 373–388.

Bull, Jerome Case. "The Modern Swordsman." *Munsey's Magazine* 17:4 (July 1897): 491–496.

Bulson, Eric. *Little Magazine, World Form.* New York: Columbia University Press, 2016.

Burgess Papers. The Bancroft Library. University of California, Berkeley.

Burgess, Gelett. *Goops and How to Be Them.* New York: Frederick A. Stokes and Company, 1900.

——. "Correspondence: A Protest from Mr. Gelett Burgess." *The Chap-Book* 8:8 (March 1, 1898): 315.

——. "Feminine Modernity." *Sunset* 15 (October 1905): 580–581.

——. "H. R. H., the Princess Perilla." *The Lark* 19 (November 1896): n.p.

——. "Our Clubbing List." *Le Petit Journal des Refusées* (July 1896): n.p.

——. "The Lark His Matin Peal Has Sung." *The Epi-Lark* (May 1897): n.p.

——. "Memoir." *The Epi-Lark* (May 1, 1897): n.p.

——. "The Romance Association." *The Chap-Book* 8:6 (February 1, 1898): 250.

——. "The Wild Men of Paris." *Architectural Record* 27 (May 1910): 400–414.

——. *Bayside Bohemia: Fin de Siècle San Francisco & Its Little Magazines*, edited by James D. Hart. San Francisco: The Book Club of California.

——. *The Burgess Nonsense Book.* New York: Frederick Stokes Company, 1901.

——. *The Maxims of Noah, Derived from his Experience with Women both Before and After the Flood.* New York: Frederick A. Stokes Company, 1913.

——. *The Romance of the Commonplace.* San Francisco: Paul Elder and Morgan Shepard, 1902.

——. *Why Men Hate Women.* New York: Payson and Clarke, 1927.

Burt, Ronald S. *Structural Holes: The Social Structure of Competition.* Cambridge, MA: Harvard University Press, 1992.

——. "Structural Holes and Good Ideas." *American Journal of Sociology* 110:2 (September 2004): 349–399.

Cady, Edwin H. *The Light of Common Day: Realism in American Fiction.* Bloomington: Indiana University Press, 1971.

——. Introduction to *Pebbles, Monochromes, and Other Modern Poems, 1891–1916*, by William Dean Howells. Athens: Ohio University Press, 2000.

——. *Stephen Crane.* Boston: Twayne Publishers, 1980.

Cameron, Sharon. *Thinking in Henry James.* Chicago: University of Chicago Press, 1989.

Casanova, Pascale. *The World Republic of Letters.* Cambridge, MA: Harvard University Press, 2004.

Cate, Phillip Dennis, and Mary Shaw, eds. *The Spirit of Montmartre: Cabarets, Humor, and the Avant-Garde, 1875–1905.* New Brunswick, NJ: Jane Voorheis Zimmerli Art Museum, 1996.

——. "The Spirit of Montmartre." In *The Spirit of Montmartre: Cabarets, Humor, and the Avant-Garde, 1875–1905*, edited by Dennis Phillip Cate and Mary Shaw, 1–94. New Brunswick, NJ: Jane Voorheis Zimmerli Art Museum, 1996.

Cavitch, Max. "Stephen Crane's Refrain." *ESQ: A Journal of the American Renaissance* 54:1–4 (2004): 33–54.

Cazemajou, Jean. *Stephen Crane: Écrivain Journaliste.* Paris: Librairie Didie, 1969.

Chapman, Mary. *Becoming Sui Sin Far: Early Fiction, Journalism and Travel Writing by Edith Maude Eaton.* Montreal: McGill-Queen's University Press, 2016.

Cheek, Donald Grady. "Stephen Crane and *The Philistine*: A Major American Naturalist and the Exercise of His Craft in an Avant-Garde Magazine." PhD diss., North Carolina State University, 1995.

Chekhov, Mikhail. *Anton Chekhov: A Brother's Memoir.* New York: Palgrave, 2010.

Chintz, David. *T. S. Eliot and the Cultural Divide.* Chicago: University of Chicago Press, 2003.

Chopin, Kate, trans. "A Divorce Case" by Guy de Maupassant. In *The Kate Chopin Companion*, edited by Thomas Bonner, Jr., 179–183. New York: Greenwood Press, 1988.

Chopin, Kate. *Complete Novels and Stories.* New York: Library of America, 2002.

——. *Impressions: Kate Chopin's 1894 Diary.* In *Kate Chopin's Private Papers,* edited by Emily Toth and Per Seyersted, 176–194. Bloomington: Indiana University Press, 1998.

——. *Kate Chopin's Private Papers*, edited by Emily Toth and Per Seyersted. Bloomington: Indiana University Press, 1998.

Churchwell, Sarah. "'Lost Among the Ads': *Gentlemen Prefer Blondes* and the Politics of Imitation." In *Middlebrow Moderns: Popular American Women Writers of the 1920s*, edited by Lisa Botshon and Meredith Goldsmith, 135–26. Boston: Northeastern University Press, 2003.

Cleto, Fabio. *Camp: Queer Aesthetics and the Performing Subject—A Reader.* Edinburgh: Edinburgh University Press, 1999.

Colvert, James B. "Fred Holland Day, Louise Imogen Guiney, and the Text of Stephen Crane's *The Black Riders.*" *American Literary Realism* 28:2 (Winter 1996): 18–24.

Corn, Wanda. *The Great American Thing: Modern Art and National Identity, 1915–1935.* Berkeley: University of California Press, 1999.

Coste, Bénédicte, Catherine Delyfer, and Christine Reynier, eds. *Reconnecting Aestheticism and Modernism: Continuities, Revisions, Speculations.* New York: Routledge, 2016.

Cram, Ralph Adams. "The Quest." *Knight Errant* 1:1 (April 1892): 1.

Crane, Diana. *Invisible Colleges: Diffusion of Knowledge in Scientific Communities.* Chicago: University of Chicago Press, 1972.

Crane, Stephen. *The Correspondence of Stephen Crane*, 2 vols., edited by Stanley Wertheim and Paul Sorrentino. New York: Columbia University Press, 1988.

Crary, Jonathan. *Suspensions of Perception: Attention, Spectacle, and Modern Culture.* Boston: Massachusetts Institute of Technology, 1999.

Damrosch, David. *What Is World Literature.* Princeton, NJ: Princeton University Press, 2003.

Davis, Linda H. *Badge of Courage: The Life of Stephen Crane.* New York: Houghton Mifflin Company, 1998.

Delap, Lucy. "The Freewoman, Periodical Communities, and the Feminist Reading Public." *The Princeton University Library Chronicle* 61:2 (Winter 2000): 233-276.

———. "Individualism and Introspection." In *Feminist Media History: Suffrage, Periodicals, and the Public Sphere*, edited by Maria DiCenzo, Lucy Delap, and Leila Ryan, 159-193. New York: Palgrave MacMillan, 2011.

Delap, Lucy, and Maria DiCenzo. "Transatlantic Print Culture: The Anglo-American Feminist Press and Emerging 'Modernities.'" In *Transatlantic Print Culture, 1880-1940: Emerging Media, Emerging Modernisms*, edited by Ann Ardis and Patrick Collier, 48-65. New York: Palgrave Macmillan, 2008.

Deleuze, Gilles, and Felix Guattari. *A Thousand Plateaus: Capitalism and Schizophrenia*, translated by Brian Massumi. Minneapolis: University of Minnesota Press, 1987.

Dewey, John. "Americanism and Localism." *The Dial* 68 (1920): 684-688.

Dickason, David H. "Stephen Crane and The Philistine." *American Literature* 15:3 (1943): 279-287.

Diebel, Anne. "'The Dreary Duty': Henry James, *The Yellow Book*, and Literary Personality." *Henry James Review* 32 (2011): 45-59.

Drucker, Johanna. "Bohemian by Design: Gelett Burgess and *Le Petit Journal des Refusées*." *Le Petit Journal des Refusées*, by Frank Gelett Burgess, 29-40. Houston: Rice University Press, 2009.

———. "*Le Petit Journal des Refusées*: A Graphical Reading." *Victorian Poetry* 48:1 (Spring 2010): 137-169.

———. Afterword to *Le Petit Journal des Refusées* by Gelett Burgess, 29-42. Houston: Rice University Press, 2009.

Durkin, Andrew R. "Chekhov and the Journals of His Time." In *Literary Journals in Imperial Russia*, edited by Deborah A. Martinsen, 228-245. Cambridge, UK: Cambridge University Press, 1997.

Earle, David. "Pulp Magazines and the Popular Press." In *The Oxford Critical and Cultural History of Modernist Magazines*, vol. 2: *North America 1894-1960*, edited by Peter Brooker and Andrew Thacker, 197-216. Oxford: Oxford University Press, 2012.

Edel, Leo, ed. *Henry James: Selected Letters.* Cambridge, MA: Harvard University Press, 1987.

Eldred, Janet Carey. *Literate Zeal: Gender and the Making of a New Yorker Ethos.* Pittsburgh: University of Pittsburgh Press, 2012.

Elias, Amy J. "The Dialogical Avant-Garde: Relational Aesthetics and Time Ecologies in Only Revolutions and TOC." *Contemporary Literature* 53:4 (2012): 738-778.

Eliot, T. S. "The Perfect Critic." In *The Sacred Wood: Essays on Poetry and Criticism*, by T. S. Eliot, 1-15. New York: Alfred A. Knopf, 1921.

Evans, Brad. "'Ephemeral Bibelots' in the 1890s." In *The Oxford Critical and Cultural History of Modernist Magazines*, vol. 2: *North America 1894-1960*, edited by Peter Brooker and Andrew Thacker, 132-153. Oxford: Oxford University Press, 2012.

———. "Howellsian Chic: The Local Color of Cosmopolitanism." *ELH* 71 (2004): 775-812.

———. "Introduction to *Le Petit Journal des Refusées*." The Modernist Journals Project, http://library.brown.edu/cds/mjp/pdf/PJRintro.pdf.

———. "Relating in Henry James (The Artwork of Networks)." *Henry James Review* 36:1 (Winter 2015): 1-23. Also in *Henry James Today*, edited by John Carlos Rowe. Newcastle Upon Tyne: Cambridge Scholars Publishing, 2014.

———. "Review Essay: Johanna Drucker, ed., *Le Petit Journal des Refusées*." *Journal of Modern Periodical Studies* 1:2 (2010): 229-241.

———. "The Original Pussyhat?" *Politics and Letters* (Online Journal), http://politics slashletters.org/the-original-pussyhat/.

———. "What Travels? The Movement of Movements; or, Ephemeral Bibelots from Paris to Lansing, with Love." In *Print Culture Histories beyond the Metropolis*, edited by James J. Connolly, Patrick Collier, Frank Felsenstein, Kenneth R. Hall, and Robert G. Hall. Toronto: University of Toronto Press, 2016.

———. "Where Was Boas during the Renaissance in Harlem?: Race, Diffusion, and the Culture Paradigm in the History of Anthropology." In *Central Sites, Peripheral Visions: Cultural and Institutional Crossings in the History of Anthropology*, History of Anthropology Series, vol. 11, edited by Richard Handler, 69-98. Madison: University of Wisconsin Press, 2006.

———. *Before Cultures: The Ethnographic Imagination in American Literature, 1865-1920.* Chicago: University of Chicago Press, 2005.

Faxon, Frederick Winthrop. *Ephemeral Bibelots: A Bibliography of the Modern Chap-Books and Their Imitators.* Boston: Boston Book Company, 1903.

Felski, Rita. "Context Stinks!" *New Literary History* 42:4 (2011): 573-591.

———. *The Gender of Modernity.* Cambridge, MA: Harvard University Press, 1995.

Ferguson, Frances. "Planetary Literary History: The Place of the Text." *New Literary History* 39:3 (2008): 657-684.

Fields, Armond. *George Auriol.* Utah: Gibbs M. Smith, Inc., 1985.

———. *Le Chat Noir: A Montmartre Cabaret and Its Artists in Turn-of-the-Century Paris.* Santa Barbara Museum of Art, 1993.

Fine, Gary Alan. *Tiny Publics: A Theory of Group Action and Culture.* New York: Russell Sage Foundation, 2012.

Fineberg, Jonathan. *The Innocent Eye: Children's Art and the Modern Artist* (Princeton, NJ: Princeton University Press, 1997).

Fleissner, Jennifer. *Women, Compulsion, Modernity: The Moment of American Naturalism.* Chicago: University of Chicago Press, 2004.

Franco, Adela Pineda. *Geopoliticas de la cultura finisecular en Buenos Aires, Paris y México: las revistas literarias y el Modernismo.* Pittsburgh: University of Pittsburgh, 2006.

Freedman, Jonathan. *Professions of Taste: Henry James, British Aestheticism, and Commodity Culture.* Stanford, CA: Stanford University Press, 1990.

Fried, Michael. *Realism, Writing, Disfiguration: On Thomas Eakins and Stephen Crane.* Chicago: University of Chicago Press, 1987.

Garland, Hamlin. *Crumbling Idols.* Chicago: Stone and Kimball, 1894.

Gladwell, Malcolm. *The Tipping Point: How Little Things Can Make a Big Difference.* Boston: Little, Brown and Company, 2000.

Glazener, Nancy. *Reading for Realism: The History of a U.S. Literary Institution, 1850–1910.* Durham, NC: Duke University Press, 1997.

Goudeau, Emile. *Dix Ans de Bohème.* Paris: A La Librairie Illustrée, 1888.

Gourmont, Remy de. *Les Petites Revues: Essai de Bibliographie.* Paris: Librairie du Mercure France, 1900.

Graham, D. B. "Studio Art in *The Octopus.*" *American Literature* 44:4 (1973): 657–666.

Granovetter, Mark S. "The Strength of Weak Ties." *American Journal of Sociology* 78:6 (1977): 1360–1380.

Gray, Piers. 1982. *T. S. Eliot's Intellectual and Poetic Development, 1909–1922.* Atlantic Highlands, NJ: Humanities Press.

Griffin, Susan. *The Historical Eye.* Boston: Northeastern University Press, 1991.

Grimstad, Paul. *Experience and Experimental Writing: Literary Pragmatism from Emerson to the Jameses.* New York: Oxford University Press, 2013.

Grojnowski, Daniel. "Hydropathes and Company." In *The Spirit of Montmartre: Cabarets, Humor, and the Avant-Garde, 1875–1905*, edited by Dennis Phillip Cate and Mary Shaw, 111–158. New Brunswick, NJ: Jane Voorheis Zimmerli Art Museum, 1996.

———. *Aux commencements du rire moderne. L'esprit fumiste.* Paris: José Corti, 1997.

Gullans, Charles, and John Espey. "More Addenda to Kramer's 'Stone & Kimball.'" *The Papers of the Bibliographical Society of America* 82 (January 1, 1988): 347–367, 360–362.

Habib, Rafey. *The Early T. S. Eliot and Western Philosophy.* Cambridge, UK: Cambridge University Press, 1999.

Hakutani, Yoshinobu. "Yone Noguchi's Influence on Ezra Pound's Imagism." *Chiba Review* 13 (1991): 25–35.

Halverson, Cathryn. "'Typical Tokio Smile': Bad American Books and Bewitching Japanese Girls." *Arizona Quarterly* 63:1 (2007): 49–80.

Hammill, Faye, and Karen Leick. "Modernism and the Quality Magazines." In *The Oxford Critical and Cultural History of Modernist Magazines*, vol. 2: *North America 1894–1960*, edited by Peter Brooker and Andrew Thacker, 176–196. Oxford: Oxford University Press, 2012.

Hanneken, Jaimie. "Going Mundial: What It Really Means to Desire Paris." *Modern Language Quarterly* 71:2 (June 2010): 129–152.

Hart, James D. Introduction to *Bayside Bohemia: Fin de Siècle San Francisco and Its Little Magazines*, by Gelett Burgess, v–x. San Francisco: The Book Club of California, 1954.

Harris, Donal. *On Company Time: American Modernism in the Big Magazines.* New York: Columbia University Press, 2016.

Harte, Walter Blackburn. "Bubble and Squeak." *The Fly Leaf* 1:1 (December 1895): 28.

——. "The Stir in Literature." *The Fly Leaf* 1:1 (December 1895): 4.

——. "Comment." *Lotus* 1:5 (February 1, 1896): 135.

Hext, Kate. "Henry James's Impressionistic Satire of the Decadent Movement in the *Yellow Book.*" *Henry James Review* 38:1 (2017): 37–52.

Hocks, Richard. *Henry James and Pragmatistic Thought.* Chapel Hill: University of North Carolina Press, 1974.

——. *"The Ambassadors": Consciousness, Culture, Poetry.* London: Twayne Publishers, 1997.

Hoffman, Daniel G. "Many red devils upon the page: The Poetry of Stephen Crane." *Sewanee Review* 102:4 (1994).

——. *The Poetry of Stephen Crane.* New York: Columbia University Press, 1956.

Hoffman, Frederick J., Charles Allen, and Carolyn F. Ulrich. *The Little Magazine: A History and Bibliography.* Princeton, NJ: Princeton University Press, 1947.

Honey, Maureen, ed. *Breaking the Ties that Bind: Popular Stories of the New Woman, 1915–1930.* Norman: Oklahoma University Press, 1992.

Howells, William Dean. "Editor's Study." *Harper's Monthly* 76 (December 1887): 153–156.

——. *Editor's Study*, edited by James W. Simpson. Troy, NY: The Whitston Publishing Company, 1983.

Hubbard, Elbert. *Elbert Hubbard: An American Original.* Directed by Paul Lamont. Arlington, VA: PBS, 2009.

Hughes, Rupert. "James Huneker." *The Criterion* n.s. 3:2 (May 1902): 38–49.

Huneker, James G. "The Dream of a Decadent." *M'lle New York* 1:3 (September 1895): n.p.

——. "The Ghost of a Turtle." *M'lle New York* 1:7 (November 1895): n.p.

——. *Steeplejack.* New York: Charles Scribner's Sons, 1922.

Hutton, Laurence. "Literary Notes." *Harper's Monthly* 94:561 (February 1897): 1.

James, Henry. "The Lesson of Balzac." In *Literary Criticism*, vol. 2: *French Writers, Other European Writers, The Prefaces to the New York Editions*, 115–139. New York: Library of America, 1984.

——. *Roderick Hudson.* In *The Novels and Tales of Henry James*, vol. 1. New York: Charles Scribner's Sons, 1907.

——. *The Ambassadors.* In *The Novels and Tales of Henry James*, vol. 21. New York: Charles Scribner's Sons, 1907–1909.

——. *The Ambassadors.* In *The Novels and Tales of Henry James*, vols. 21–22. New York: Charles Scribner's Sons, 1909.

——. *What Maisie Knew.* In *The Novels and Tales of Henry James*, vol. 11. New York: Charles Scribner's Sons, 1908.

James, William. "Does Consciousness Exist?" In *Writings 1902–1910*, by William James, 1141–1158. New York: Library of America, 1987.

———. *Essays in Radical Empiricism.* New York: Dover, 2003.

———. *Psychology: Briefer Course.* In *Writings 1878–1899*, by William James, 1–443. New York: Library of America, 1992.

———. *Writings, 1878–1899.* New York: Library of America, 1992.

Jan, Alfred. *A Gelett Burgess Sampler: Ethics and Aesthetics* (n.p.: Surinam Turtle Press, 2012).

Jehlen, Myra. "On How, to Become Knowledge, Cognition Needs Beauty, no. 2: On How Philosophers Tend Not to Recognize This Condition." *Raritan* 30:4 (Spring 2011): 47–65.

Johnson, Charles S. "The Rise of the Negro Magazine." *Journal of Negro History* 13 (January 1928): 7–21.

Kamiya, Gary. "Anarchic Bon Vivants Thrived at S.F.'s Original Hipster Cafe." *San Francisco Chronicle*. November 12, 2016.

Kaplan, Amy. *The Social Construction of American Realism.* Chicago: University of Chicago Press, 1988.

Keet, Alfred Ernest. "Stephen Crane: New York Poet." *Bruno's Weekly* 3:12 (September 2, 1916): 951–953.

Kessler, M. "Bibliographic Coupling between Scientific Papers." *American Documentation* 14 (1963): 10–25.

Keyser, Catherine. *Playing Smart: New York Women Writers and Modern Magazine Culture.* New Brunswick, NJ: Rutgers University Press, 2010.

Knights, Pamela. Introduction to *The Awakening and Other Stories*, by Kate Chopin, ix–xlviii. New York: Oxford University Press, 2000.

La Rose, Pierre. "The Yellow Book." *The Chap-Book* 1 (August 15, 1894): 161–165.

Latour, Bruno. *An Inquiry into the Modes of Existence: An Anthropology of the Moderns.* Cambridge, MA: Harvard University Press, 2013.

———. *Pandora's Hope: Essays on the Reality of Science Studies.* Cambridge, MA: Harvard University Press, 1999.

———. *Reassembling the Social: An Introduction to Actor-Network Theory.* New York: Oxford University Press, 2005.

Lears, T. J. Jackson. *No Place of Grace: Antimodernism and the Transformation of American Culture, 1880–1920.* Chicago: University of Chicago Press, 1981.

Levin, Jonathan. *The Poetics of Transition: Emerson, Pragmatism, and American Literary Modernism.* Durham, NC: Duke University Press, 1999.

Liu, Alan. *The Laws of Cool: Knowledge Work and the Culture of Information.* Chicago: University of Chicago Press, 1994.

Lloyd, Rosemary. *Mallarmé: The Poet and His Circle.* Ithaca, NY: Cornell University Press, 2005.

Longworth, Deborah. "The Avant-Garde in the Village: *Rogue* (1915)." In *The Oxford*

Critical and Cultural History of Modernist Magazines, vol. 2: *North America 1894-1960*, edited by Peter Brooker and Andrew Thacker, 465-482. Oxford: Oxford University Press, 2012.

Looby, Chris. Introduction to *"The Man Who Thought Himself a Woman" and other Queer Nineteenth-Century Short Stories*, edited by Chris Looby, vii-xxiv. Philadelphia: University of Pennsylvania Press, 2017.

Loos, Anita. "The Biography of a Book." In *Gentlemen Prefer Blondes and but Gentlemen Marry Brunettes*, by Anita Loos, xxxvii-xlii. New York, Penguin Classics, 1998.

Lord, Isabel Garland. *A Summer to Be: A Memoir by the Daughter of Hamlin Garland.* Lincoln: University of Nebraska Press, 2010.

Love, Heather. "Close but Not Deep: Literary Ethics and the Descriptive Turn." *New Literary History* 41:2 (Spring 2010): 371-391.

Lowell, Amy. Introduction to *The Black Riders and Other Lines*, The Work of Stephen Crane, vol. 6, x-xxix. New York: Russell and Russell, 1926.

MacLeod, Kirsten. "The Fine Art of Cheap Print: Turn-of-the-Century American Little Magazines." In *Transatlantic Print Culture, 1880-1940: Emerging Media, Emerging Modernisms*, edited by Ann Ardis and Patrick Collier, 182-198. New York: Palgrave Macmillan, 2008.

———. *American Little Magazines of the 1890s: A Revolution in Print.* Sunderland, UK: Bibelot Press, 2013.

———. *American Little Magazines of the Fin de Siècle: Art, Protest, and Cultural Transformation.* Toronto: University of Toronto Press, 2018.

Maddrey, Joseph. *The Making of T. S. Eliot: A Study of the Literary Influences.* Jefferson, NC: McFarland, 2009.

Mahoney, Kristin. *Literature and the Politics of Post-Victorian Decadence.* New York: Cambridge University Press, 2015.

Makela, Maria Martha. *The Munich Secession: Art and Artists in Turn-of-the-Century Munich.* Princeton, NJ: Princeton University Press, 1990.

Mallarmé, Stéphane. "Arthur Rimbaud." *The Chap-Book* 5:1 (May 1896): 8-17.

———. *Collected Poems and Other Verse,* translated by E. H. and A. M. Blackmore. New York: Oxford World's Classics, 2006.

———. *Divagations.* Paris: Bibliothèque-Charpentier, 1897.

———. "Les loisirs de la poste." *The Chap-Book* 2:2 (December 1894): 111-115.

Mao, Douglas. "The Naughtiness of the Avant-Garde: Donald Evans, Claire Marie, and *Tender Buttons*," forthcoming.

Maupassant, Guy. "A Divorce Case," translated by Kate Chopin. In *The Kate Chopin Companion*, edited by Thomas Bonner, Jr., 179-183. New York: Greenwood Press, 1988.

McElarath, Joseph R., Jr., and Jesse S. Crisler. *Frank Norris: A Life.* Urbana: University of Illinois Press, 2006.

McGann, Jerome. "Pseudodoxia Academica." *New Literary History* 39:3 (2008): 645-656.

McHenry, Elizabeth. *Forgotten Readers: Recovering the Lost History of African American Literary Societies.* Durham, NC: Duke University Press, 2002.

McKenna, Paul. *A History and Bibliography of the Roycroft Printing Shop.* New York: Tona Graphics, 1986.

McLean, Paul. *Culture in Networks.* Malden, MA: Polity Press, 2017.

McWhirter, David. "Bersani's James." *Henry James Review* 32:3 (2011): 211-217.

Mencken, H. L. *Prejudices: First Series.* In *Prejudices: First, Second, and Third Series*, 3-152. New York: Library of America, 2010.

——. *Prejudices: Third Series.* In *Prejudices: First, Second, and Third Series*, 301-489. New York: Library of America, 2010.

——. *Newspaper Days 1899-1906.* In *The Days Trilogy, Expanded Edition*, edited by Marion Elizabeth Rogers, 205-406. New York: Library of America, 2014.

Merrill, Stuart. "Oscar Wilde." *La Plume* 5:94 (March 15, 1893): 116-118.

Michaels, Walter Benn. *Our America: Nativism, Modernism, and Pluralism.* Durham, NC: Duke University Press, 1995.

Miller, J. Hillis. "What Is a Kiss?" *Critical Inquiry* 31:3 (Spring 2005): 722-746.

Miller, Nina. *Making Love Modern: The Intimate Public Worlds of New York's Literary Women.* New York: Oxford University Press, 1999.

Monroe, Harriet. "Stephen Crane." *Poetry* 14 (June 1919): 148-152.

Monteiro, George. *Stephen Crane's Blue Badge of Courage.* Baton Rouge: Louisiana State University Press, 2000.

Moon, Michael. "Solitude, Singularity, Seriality: Whitman vis-a-vis Fourier." *ELH* 73:2 (Summer 2006): 303-323.

Moore, Sarah J. "*M'lle New York* and James Gibbons Huneker: Awaiting the Apparatus of Civilization." *Arts Magazine* 60:3 (November 1985): 62-65.

Moretti, Franco. *Graphs, Maps and Trees: Abstract Models for Literary History.* New York: Verso, 2005.

Morrissette, Bruce A. "Vance Thompson's Plagiarism of Teodor de Wyzewa's Articles on Mallarmé." *Modern Language Notes* 67:3 (March 1952): 175-178.

Morrison, Mark S. *The Public Face of Modernism: Little Magazines, Audiences, and Reception: 1905-1920.* Madison: University of Wisconsin Press, 2001.

Mosher, Thomas B., ed. *The Bibelot, A Reprint of Poetry and Prose for Book Lovers, chosen in part from scarce editions and sources not generally known*, vol. 1: Testimonial Edition. Portland, Maine: Wm. Wise & Co., 1904.

Mott, Frank Luther. *A History of American Magazines*, vol. 4: *1885-1905.* Cambridge, MA: Harvard University Press, 1957.

Murray, James Augustus Henry. *A New English Dictionary on Historical Principles: Founded Mainly on the Materials Collected by the Philological Society.* Oxford: Clarendon Press, 1887.

Ngai, Sianne. "The Cuteness of the Avant-Garde." *Critical Inquiry* 31 (2005): 811-847.

——. "Network Aesthetics: Juliana Spahr's *The Transformation* and Bruno Latour's *Reassembling the Social*." In *American Literature's Aesthetic Dimensions*, edited by Cindy Weinsten and Christopher Looby, 367-392. New York: Columbia University Press, 2012.

——. *Our Aesthetic Categories: Zany, Cute, Interesting.* Cambridge, MA: Harvard University Press, 2012.

Nietzsche, Friedrich Wilhelm. *Thus Spake Zarathustra,* translated by Alexander Tille. New York: The Macmillan Co., 1896.

Noonan, Mark J. *Reading the Century Illustrated Monthly Magazine: American Literature and Culture, 1870-1893.* Kent, OH: Kent State University Press, 2010.

Norman, Otis. "Gelett Burgess Talks Gravely of Literature as He Observes It." *New York Times*, January 26, 1907, 22.

——. "The Confessions of Carolyn Wells." *New York Times*, January 12, 1907, 22.

Norris, Frank. "A Plea for Romantic Fiction." *Boston Evening Transcript* (December 18, 1901): 14.

——. "An Opening for Novelists." In *Novels and Essays*, by Frank Norris, 1112-1114. New York: Library of America, 1986.

——. *The Octopus: A Story of California.* 1901; New York: Penguin, 1986.

North, Michael. *The Dialect of Modernism: Race, Language and Twentieth-Century Literature.* New York: Oxford University Press, 1994.

Ohmann, Richard. "History and Literary History: The Case of Mass Culture." *Poetics Today* 9:2 (1988): 357-375.

——. *Selling Culture: Magazines, Markets and Class at the Turn of the Century.* New York: Verso, 1996.

Pendergast, Tom. *Creating the Modern Man: American Magazines and Consumer Culture, 1900-1950.* Columbia: University of Missouri Press, 2000.

Penn, Jonathan. "A Humorous Study of Crane." *Lotus* 2 (October 1896): 208-211.

Phillips, Adam. *On Flirtation: Psychoanalytic Essays on the Uncommitted Life.* Cambridge, MA: Harvard University Press, 1994.

Pippin, Robert. *Henry James and Modern Moral Life.* New York: Cambridge University Press, 1999.

Pollard, Percival. "As You Like It." *The Criterion* 16:410 (December 1897): 8-9.

——. "The Criterion Independent Theater." *The Criterion* 16:406 (October 30, 1897): 3-4.

——. *Their Day in Court.* 1909; New York: Johnson Reprint Corporation, 1969.

Porter, Bruce. "My Dear Frank Burgess." *The Lark* 25 (May 1, 1897): n.p.

Potolsky, Matthew. *The Decadent Republic of Letters: Taste, Politics, and Cosmopolitan Community from Baudelaire to Beardsley.* Philadelphia: University of Pennsylvania Press, 2012.

Poulet, Georges. *Les Métamorphoses du Cercle.* Paris: Librairie Plon, 1961.

Pound, Ezra. *ABC of Reading.* 1934; New York: New Directions Books, 1987.

Prendergast, Christopher. "The World Republic of Letters." In *Debating World Literature*, edited by Christopher Prendergast, 1-25. London: Verso, 2004.

Radice, William. Introduction to *Selected Short Stories*, by Rabindranath Tagore, 1-28. New York: Penguin, 1991.

Richardson, Joan. *A Natural History of Pragmatism.* New York: Cambridge University Press, 2007.

Rogers, Stephen. "Bruno's Bohemia." In *The Oxford Critical and Cultural History of Modernist Magazines*, vol. 2: *North America 1894-1960*, edited by Peter Brooker and Andrew Thacker, 445-464. New York: Oxford University Press, 2012.

Rogue, Dame [pseud.]. "Philosophic Fashions." *Rogue* 2:3 (October 1915): 13.

Rowe, John Carlos. *The Theoretical Dimensions of Henry James.* Madison: University of Wisconsin Press, 1984.

Ruskin, John. *The Elements of Drawing.* In *The Works of John Ruskin*, vol. 15, edited by E. T. Cook and Alexander Wedderburn. New York: Longman's, Green, and Co., 1903-1912.

Schiau-Botea, Diana. "Performing Writing." In *The Oxford Critical and Cultural History of Modernist Magazines,* vol. 3: *Europe 1880-1940,* edited by Peter Brooker, Sascha Bru, Andrew Thacker, and Christian Weikop, 38-59. New York: Oxford University Press, 2013.

Schlereth, Wendy Clauson. *The Chap-Book: A Journal of American Intellectual Life in the 1890s.* Ann Arbor: UMI Research Press, 1980.

Schmidgall, Gary. *Containing Multitudes: Walt Whitman and the British Library Tradition.* New York: Oxford University Press, 2014.

Schneirov, Matthew. *The Dream of a New Social Order: Popular Magazines in America, 1893-1914.* New York: Columbia University Press, 1994.

Schwab, Arnold T. *James Gibbons Huneker: Critic of the Seven Arts.* Stanford, CA: Stanford University Press, 1963.

Sedgwick, Eve. "The Beast in the Closet." In *Sex, Politics, and Science in the Nineteenth-Century Novel*, Selected Papers from the English Institute, 1983-84, edited by Ruth Bernard Yeazell, 148-186. Baltimore: Johns Hopkins University Press, 1986.

——. *Epistemology of the Closet.* Berkeley: University of California Press, 1990.

Shaw, Mary. "All or Nothing?: The Literature of Montmartre." In *The Spirit of Montmartre: Cabarets, Humor, and the Avant-Garde, 1875-1905*, edited by Dennis Phillip Cate and Mary Shaw, 111-158. New Brunswick, NJ: Jane Voorheis Zimmerli Art Museum, 1996.

Shedel, James. *Art and Society: The New Art Movement in Vienna, 1897-1914.* Palo Alto, CA: Society for the Promotion of Science and Scholarship, 1981.

Sherry, Vincent. *Modernism and the Reinvention of Decadence.* Cambridge, UK: Cambridge University Press, 2014.

Shusterman, Richard, ed. *Bourdieu: A Critical Reader.* New York: Blackwell Publishers, 1999.

Simmel, Georg. *On Women, Sexuality and Love*, translated Guy Oakes. New Haven: Yale University Press, 1984.

Sloan, John. *American Art Nouveau, The Poster Period of John Sloan.* Lock Haven, PA: Hammermill Paper Co., 1967.

So, Richard Jean, and Hoyt Long. "Network Analysis and the Sociology of Modernism." *Boundary 2* 40:2 (2013): 147–182.

Solla Price, Derek J. de. "Networks of Scientific Papers." *Science* 149 (1965): 510–515.

Sorrentino, Paul. *Stephen Crane: A Life of Fire*. Cambridge: The Belknap Press of Harvard University Press, 2014.

Sorrentino, Paul, ed. *Stephen Crane Remembered.* Tuscaloosa: University of Alabama Press, 2006.

Stallman, Robert Wooster. *Stephen Crane: A Biography*. New York: G. Braziller, 1968.

———. *Stephen Crane: A Critical Bibliography.* Ames: Iowa State University Press, 1972.

Stallman, Robert Wooster, and Lillian Gilkes, eds. *Stephen Crane: Letters.* New York: New York University Press, 1960.

Stein, Sadie. "Disgusting Lives." *Paris Review* (March 11, 2014), https://www.theparisreview.org/blog/2014/03/11/disgusting-lives/.

Stewart, Susan. *Nonsense: Aspects of Intertextuality in Folklore and Literature.* Baltimore: The Johns Hopkins University Press, 1978.

Stone, Wilbur Macey. "The Poster and the Cat." *Lotus* 2 (1896): 53–54.

Storey, Robert F. *Pierrot: A Critical History of a Mask.* Princeton, NJ: Princeton University Press, 1978.

Symons, Arthur. "Stella Maris." *The Yellow Book* 1 (April 1894): 129–131.

Taupin, René. *L'Influence du symbolisme français sur la poésie Americaine.* 1929; Geneva: Slatkine Reprints, 1975.

Thompson, Vance. *Woman.* New York: E. P. Dutton & Co., 1917.

Tiffany, Daniel. *Infidel Poetics: Riddles, Nightlife, Substance.* Chicago: University of Chicago Press, 2009.

Tomkins, Calvin. *Duchamp: A Biography.* 1996; New York: MOMA, 2014.

Tompkins, Juliet Wilbor. "A Butterfly Lover." *Munsey's Magazine* 17:3 (June 1897): 400–408.

Toth, Emily. *Kate Chopin: A Life of the Author of "The Awakening."* New York: William Morrow and Company, Inc., 1990.

———. *Unveiling Kate Chopin.* Jackson: University Press of Mississippi, 1999.

Toth, Emily, and Per Seyersted, eds. *Kate Chopin's Private Papers.* Bloomington: Indiana University Press, 1998.

Underwood, John Curtis. "Review." *Bookman*, July 1899. Rpt. in *Stephen Crane: The Critical Heritage*, edited by Richard Weatherford, 235–237. Boston: Routledge and Kegan Paul, 1973.

Vanouse, Donald. "Hobby-Horses, Horseplay, and Stephen Crane's 'Black Riders.'" *Courier* 13:3 and 13:4 (1976): 29–31.

Velter, André. *Les Poètes du Chat Noir.* Editions Gallimard, 1996.

Warburg, A. "Amerikanische Chap-Books." *Pan* 2:4 (October 1896): 345–348, http://digi.ub.uni-heidelberg.de/diglit/pan1896_97_2/0206.

Warner, Michael. "Publics and Counterpublics." *Public Culture* 14:1 (2002): 49–90.

———. *Publics and Counterpublics.* New York: Zone Books, 2002.

Watts, Duncan J. "A Simple Model of Global Cascades on Random Networks." *Proceedings of the National Academy of Sciences of the United States of America* 99:9 (2002): 5766–5771.

———. "The 'New' Science of Networks." *Annual Review of Sociology* 30 (2004): 243–70.

Watts, Duncan J., and Steven H. Strogatz. "Collective Dynamics of 'Small-World' Networks." *Nature* 393 (1998): 440–442.

Weatherford, Richard, ed. *Stephen Crane: The Critical Heritage.* Boston: Routledge and Kegan Paul, 1973.

Weir, David. *Decadent Culture in the United States: Art and Literature against the American Grain, 1890–1926.* Albany: State University of New York Press, 2008.

Weisberg, Gabriel P., ed. *Montmartre and the Making of Mass Culture.* New Brunswick, NJ: Rutgers University Press, 2001.

Wells, Carolyn, ed. *A Nonsense Anthology.* New York: Charles Scribner's Sons, 1902.

———. *The Rest of My Life.* Philadelphia: J. B. Lippincott Company, 1937.

White, Edmund. *Hotel de Dream.* New York: Harper Perennial, 2007.

White, Eric. "In the American Grain: *Contact* (1920–3, 1932): and *Pagany: A Native Quarterly* (1930–3)." In *The Oxford Critical and Cultural History of Modernist Magazines*, vol. 2: *North America 1894–1960*, edited by Peter Brooker and Andrew Thacker, 249–270. Oxford: Oxford University Press, 2012.

———. *Transatlantic Avant-Gardes: Little Magazines and Localist Modernism.* Edinburgh: Edinburgh University Press, 2013.

Wilde, Oscar. *The Complete Letters of Oscar Wilde*, edited by Merlin Holland and Rupert Hart-Davis. New York: Henry Holt, 2000.

Williams, Carolyn. *Gilbert and Sullivan: Gender, Genre, Parody.* New York: Columbia University Press, 2011.

Wyatt, Edith. "Stephen Crane." *New Republic* 4 (September 11, 1915): 148–150.

Ziff, Larzer. *The American 1890s: Life and Times of a Lost Generation.* New York: Viking Press, 1966.

Index

Page numbers in *italics* refer to illustrations.